.UILDINGS OF IRELAND

E SMALLER BUILDINGS OF TOWN & COUNTRYSIDE

SEAN ROTHERY

LILLIPUT

First published in 1997 by
THE LILLIPUT PRESS LTD
4 Rosemount Terrace, Arbour Hill,
Dublin 7, Ireland.

A CIP record for this title
is available from
The British Library

ISBN 1 874675 86 4(HBK)
ISBN 1 874675 81 3(PBK)

Design by Jarlath Hayes
Set in 10.5 on 12 Adobe Garamond by
Susan Waine
and printed in Dublin by
βetaprint Limited of Clonshaugh

FOR HANNAH AND CIARA

CONTENTS

IX
List of Illustrations

XV
Foreword by Maurice Craig

1
Introduction

3
Acknowledgments

5
Churches, Early Christian to Mediæval

17
Friaries, Priories and Abbeys

23
Churches from the Seventeenth to the Twentieth Century

49
Castles and Fortifications

69
Houses

103
Buildings of Town and Village

165
Buildings of the Estate

193
Buildings of Industry and Transport

215
Buildings of the Coast

229
Location Maps

235
Selected Book List

239
Glossary of Architectural Terms

247
Index

LIST OF ILLUSTRATIONS

EARLY CHRISTIAN TO MEDIAEVAL CHURCHES

1 Gallarus Oratory, Co. Kerry
2 Teampull Benin, Co. Galway
3 St Mc Dara's Island, Co. Galway
4 St Cronan's Church, Co. Tipperary
5 Clonfert Cathedral, Co. Galway
6 Jerpoint Abbey, Co. Kilkenny
7 Ardfert Cathedral, Co. Kerry
8 Kilcooley Abbey, Co. Kilkenny
9 Cistercian cell, Co. Mayo
10 Taghmon Church, Co. Westmeath

FRIARIES, PRIORIES AND ABBEYS

11 Dunbrody Abbey, Co. Wexford
12 Athassel Priory, Co. Tipperary
13 Adare Franciscan Friary, Co. Limerick
14 Sligo Abbey, Co. Sligo

CHURCHES FROM THE SEVENTEENTH TO THE TWENTIETH CENTURY

15 St John's Church, Co. Donegal
16 Methodist church and manse, Co. Mayo
17 St James Church, Co. Louth
18 Cratloe Catholic church, Co. Clare
19 Eadestown Catholic church, Co. Kildare
20 Coolbanagher Church, Co. Laois
21 Massmount Church, Co. Donegal
22 Rockcorry Catholic church, Co. Monaghan
23 Kilternan Church of Ireland, Co. Wicklow
24 St Colmcille's Church, Co. Offaly
25 Wesley chapel, Co. Sligo
26 Pro-Cathedral, Co. Cork
27 Church of Ireland, Co. Carlow
28 Gorey Catholic church, Co. Wexford
29 St Kevin's Church, Co. Wicklow
30 Warrenpoint Presbyterian church, Co. Down
31 Cootehill Methodist church, Co. Cavan
32 Cootehill Presbyterian church, Co. Cavan
33 Quaker meeting house, Co. Offaly
34 Rathdaire Church of Ireland, Co. Laois

35 O'Growney tomb, Co. Kildare
36 Spiddal Catholic church, Co. Galway
37 Church of Christ the King, Co. Galway
38 St Michael's Church, Co. Donegal

CASTLES AND FORTIFICATIONS

39 Roscommon Castle, Co. Roscommon
40 St Laurence's Gate, Co. Louth
41 Clara Castle, Co. Kilkenny
42 Doe Castle, Co. Donegal
43 Drumharsna Castle, Co. Galway
44 Coolhull Castle, Co. Wexford
45 Enniskillen Castle, Co. Fermanagh
46 Monea Castle, Co. Fermanagh
47 Leamaneh Castle, Co. Clare
48 Portumna Castle, Co. Galway
49 Charles Fort, Co. Cork
50 Gateway, Charles Fort, Co. Cork
51 Military barracks, Co. Wicklow
52 Fortified barracks, Co. Galway
53 Martello tower, Co. Dublin
54 Signal tower, Co. Sligo
55 Police barracks, Co. Waterford

HOUSES

56 Vernacular house, Co. Donegal
57, **58** Vernacular house, Co. Wexford
59 Vernacular house, Co. Leitrim
60 Post office, Co. Meath
61 Vernacular house, Co. Meath
62 Vernacular house/shop/pub Co. Cavan
63 Rothe House, Co. Kilkenny
64 Beaulieu, Co. Louth
65, **66** Almshouses, Co. Cork
67 Shannon Grove, Co. Limerick
68 Westport House, Co. Mayo
69 Bellinteer, Co. Meath
70 Port Hall, Co. Donegal
71 Summer Grove, Co. Laois
72 Gothic castle, Co. Sligo
73 Town house, Co. Offaly
74 Rectory, Co. Westmeath
75 Rectory, Co. Laois
76 Rectory, Co. Wexford
77 R.C. presbytery, Co. Cork
78 Sexton's house, Co. Carlow

79 House, Co. Louth
80 House, Co. Laois
81 House, Co. Wexford
82 County Council cottages, Co. Dublin
83 Lambay Castle, Co. Dublin
84 Suburban house, Co. Dublin
85 Modern house, Co. Limerick

BUILDINGS OF TOWN AND VILLAGE
86 Deserted village, Co. Wicklow
87 Blacksmith's house, Co. Wicklow
88 Forge, Co. Wicklow
89, 90 Morovian village, Co. Antrim
91 Quarry manager's house, Co. Wicklow
92 Stone barn, Co. Wicklow
93 Town gate, Co. Tipperary
94 Town hall, Co. Derry
95 Town hall, Co. Cavan
96 Town street, Co. Galway
97 Town street, Co. Cork
98 Printer's shop, Co. Tyrone
99 Shop and house, Co. Antrim
100 Bootmaker's shop, Co. Kilkenny
101 Shop row, Co. Cavan
102 Shop row, Co. Kerry
103 Jeweller's shop, Co. Offaly
104 Chemist and shop, Co. Cork
105 Draper's shop, Co. Tyrone
106 Tiled shopfront, Co. Louth
107 Shop and house, Co. Limerick
108 Shop and house, Co. Limerick
109 Bank of Ireland, Co. Armagh
110 Belfast Bank, Co. Tyrone
112 National Bank, Co. Longford
113 Royal Bank, Co. Tyrone
114 Provincial Bank, Co. Cavan
115 Hibernian Bank, Co. Donegal
116 Munster and Leinster Bank, Co. Cork
117 Post office, Co. Mayo
118 Charter school, Co. Kildare
119 Mastergeehey National School, Co. Kerry
120 Ballinasloe National School, Co. Galway
121 Bush National School, Co. Louth
122 Mountshannon National School, Co. Clare
123 Vicarstown School, Co. Laois

124 Clonsilla School, Co. Dublin
125 St Mary's National School, Co. Dublin
126 Ballyduff Library, Co. Waterford
127 Carnegie Library, Co. Armagh
128 Carnegie Library, Co. Kilkenny
129 Kinsale Court House, Co. Cork
130 Ballyjamesduff Market House, Co. Cavan
131 Newtownbutler Market House, Co. Fermanagh
132 Athy Market Hall, Co. Kildare
133 Dundalk Courthouse, Co. Louth
134 Skibbereen Courthouse, Co. Cork
135 Dundrum Courthouse, Co. Dublin
136 Dunfanaghy Workhouse, Co. Donegal
137 Letterkenny Workhouse, Co. Donegal
138 Cork City Gaol, Co. Cork
139 Newport Gaol, Co. Tipperary
140 Bridewell Gaol, Co. Kerry
141 Observatory, Co. Armagh
142 Observatory, Co. Armagh (rear elevation)

ESTATE BUILDINGS

143 Gateway, Clongowes Wood College, Co. Kildare
144 Bryansford Gate, Co. Down
145 Shankill Castle, Co. Kilkenny
146 Gatelodge, Co. Meath
147 Gatelodge and gates, Co. Cork
148 Gate and gatelodge, Co. Antrim
149 Gatelodge, Co. Dublin
150 Tullow Gatelodge, Co. Carlow
151 Estate cottage, Co. Longford
152 Powerscourt Estate cottage, Co. Wicklow
153 Estate house, Co. Cavan
154 Gamekeeper's lodge, Co. Derry
155 Farm steward's house, Co. Wicklow
156 Estate farm, Co. Down
157, 158 Farm buildings, Co. Wicklow
159 Courtyard farm, Co. Down
160 Dovecote, Co. Down
161 Barn, Co. Donegal
162 Pebble house, Co. Down
163 Gazebo, Co. Kildare
164 Folly, Co. Galway
165 Gothic cottage, Co. Galway
166 Triumphal arch, Co. Galway

BUILDINGS OF INDUSTRY AND TRANSPORT
167 Mill and waterwheel, Co. Wexford
168 Castellated mill, Co. Kilkenny
169 Distillery, Co. Kilkenny
170 Engine house, Co. Cork
171 Lock-keeper's house, Grand Canal
172 Lock-keeper's house, Co. Kilkenny
173 Canal warehouse, Co. Kildare
174 Grand Canal hotel, Co. Kildare
175 Ballinasloe Railway Station, Co. Galway
176 Portarlington Station, Co. Laois
177 Railway housing, Co. Louth
178 Carlow Station, Co. Carlow
179 Water tank, Co. Louth
180 Bridge operator's cottage, Co. Galway
181 Draw-off tower, Co. Wicklow
182 Water works, Co. Down
183 Water commissioner's gatelodge, Co. Down

BUILDINGS OF THE COAST
184 Hook Head Lighthouse, Co. Wexford
185 Wicklow Head Lighthouse, Co. Wicklow
186 Youghal Lighthouse, Co. Cork
187 Lighthouse and keeper's cottage, Co. Louth
188 Automatic light, Co. Clare
189 Lighthouse and keeper's cottage, Co. Mayo
190 Coastguard station, Co. Donegal
191 Lifeboat house, Co. Cork
192 Maritime house, Co. Wexford
193 Port warehouse, Co. Donegal
194 Yacht Club, Co. Cork

COUNTY AND PROVINCIAL MAPS
Ulster
Munster
Leinster
Connacht

FOREWORD

ORDINARY BUILDINGS – everyday buildings – have for far too long passed unnoticed in Ireland. Plenty of attention has been given to the grander of the big houses, to the Early Christian churches, to the mediæval monasteries and friaries, and to castles of all epochs. Vernacular and thatched cottages have been appreciated: more admired, it must be said, than studied or conserved, though some people, and some counties, have a creditable record in this respect. But the buildings in between have been neglected. Neglected because not seen: not seen because not *looked at.* That which is familiar is for practical purposes invisible. How otherwise to account for the horrible things which people have done to inoffensive buildings in our towns and countryside?

Sean Rothery has been among the foremost of those who have helped to change this state of affairs, in a little pamphlet called *Everyday Buildings in Ireland* as long ago as 1975 (which he is too modest to mention in his bibliography but which is now a collector's item), three years later in *The Shops of Ireland*, and all the time by keeping ordinary buildings in our sights by every means in his power.

The best way to do this is by a combination of succinct and clear descriptions with illustration. Photographs are all very well, and indeed indispensable. But the best way of all is by drawings, for only in a drawing can a building be shown as its designers and builders intended it to be seen. By his sensitivity of line and texture he has brought out latent qualities invisible to the casual eye.

Some of the buildings in this book are by known architects, but most are the work of anonymous builders and craftsmen who, thinking first of the practical uses the building was to serve, were none the less imbued with a grammar of design that extends both backwards and forwards in time. This book, like those of Patrick and Maura Shaffrey in 1983 and 1985, has appeared none too soon. We learn, in Sean Rothery's Introduction, with sorrow but without surprise, that 'most of the buildings illustrated still existed up to about 1993', which means that a good few of them have, since then, been demolished, mutilated or allowed to fall into irrecoverable decay. The fabric of our towns and villages is so vulnerable that we cannot afford to let this continue.

But there are welcome signs of a change of heart. The old imperative – demolish first and think afterwards – is yielding to those of retain, reuse, adapt, revitalize. Private individuals, businesses, political parties and the organs of government are coming round to this way of thinking.

Most of these buildings went up when Ireland was less immediately open to external influences than it is now. Though pattern-books were the heralds of stylistic change, and components were occasionally imported (cast-iron from Glasgow, ceramics from Staffordshire), they were used in a locally idiosyncratic way, with a flavour all too easily destroyed by that faceless 'multinational' uniformity which now threatens us. The educated eye is the all-important thing and is our best defence. This is what Sean Rothery so persuasively provides.

MAURICE CRAIG
Dublin, 17 March 1997

INTRODUCTION

THIS GUIDE attempts to identify the various types of buildings encountered in the towns, villages and countryside of Ireland. Its aim is to try to answer the questions "what is that building?" and "what was it for?" Buildings are identified by type and, where appropriate, sub-types are given. The groupings are general: for example, churches, castles, houses; buildings of the village and town; buildings of the great estate; buildings of industry and transport and, finally, the buildings of the coast.

A Field Guide to the Buildings of Ireland is largely concerned with the wealth of small "everyday" buildings of Ireland, the structures of ordinary folk-dwellings, workplaces, churches, schools and the other local symbols of administration and institution. The great works of architecture have generally been omitted (except where the historical development of churches, castles, houses etc. is described), the large country house and the monumental architecture of the city; all of these are well celebrated in specialist works listed at the end of the book. Each type of building is illustrated and its identifying features noted; its function is outlined and its place in the political, economic or social history of the times suggested. Architectural styles are described and terms explained in the glossary and, where appropriate, in the context of the drawing. Simple vernacular structures are included, alongside buildings designed by architects. A small number of architects whose work is especially significant are singled out and other examples of their work are mentioned. Regional locations, where some of the best examples of the various building types can be found, are also given.

Most of the buildings illustrated still existed up to about 1993. A smaller number were visited and still existed about fifteen years ago. Ordinary buildings, as many of these are, have little protection and can be demolished quickly for various reasons; redundancy, poor repair, valuable sites etc. Fortunately old buildings, no longer in use, tend to be left to die slowly in Ireland rather than suffer the quick death of demolition. Small communities are increasingly recognizing the potential value of retaining these relics of the past and finding new uses for them. Shops tend to have the shortest life and although there has been a revival in restoring and even replicating traditional shopfronts, individual examples can vanish overnight. The older castles and churches, particularly the National Monuments, are more assured of preservation but other everyday buildings of past generations need to be appreciated for their history and particularly for the wealth of beautiful stonework which is one of the great joys of historic Irish architecture.

The best maps for exploration are to be found in the new 1:50,000 series. The whole of Northern Ireland is covered by the "Discovery Series" and this overlaps with the border counties. The Republic of Ireland is to be totally mapped in this way and, up to the end of 1996, approximately forty-seven new 1:50,000 maps have been published, detailing the coasts, the mountains and scenic areas. A further twenty-four maps will complete the coverage of the whole island of Ireland at the rate of nine new maps each year.

Although the scale of these excellent new maps is rather large for car touring, the detail and tracing of the myriad small roads and laneways make them essential for the determined explorer of the Irish countryside. The antiquities – the buildings of pre-history – are marked on the maps, as are the early churches, monasteries and castles. Many of these are classed as National Monuments and are signposted from main roads. The churches, dating from post-mediæval times, are one of the most ubiquituous and interesting building types in Ireland and are marked with a black cross on the "Discovery Series". The Northern Ireland maps differentiate between churches with towers, churches with spires and churches without either, offering interesting speculations about particular denominations.

These large-scale maps manage to show most individual buildings, at least outside the towns and villages, but different types of buildings are not noted. The older maps, at half an inch to the mile, while not totally accurate for all of the minor roads, nevertheless mark the antiquities, churches, castles and even country schoolhouses. The older maps also mark the locations of the larger estates.

The majority of the prehistoric sites, monasteries and castles are accessible to the public but in some cases the permission of the landowner must be sought before entering on the land. Many of the other buildings illustrated are privately owned but almost all can be viewed from a public roadway, particularly those in towns and villages. Many of the great estates are now in State ownership and have become forest or country parks, and the small estate buildings, follies, planned farms and gatelodges are often still there to be discovered and appreciated. Some houses are open to the public and the information on opening times etc. can be obtained from the local tourist office.

This is a book for the enthusiastic explorer, to be added to the diverse natural history field guides and to enlarge the potential, and enjoyment, of discovery in the long-inhabited land of Ireland.

ACKNOWLEDGMENTS

I express my special thanks to the School of Irish Studies Foundation for a generous grant towards the research for this book.

Many people helped in one way or another towards the completion of the work. Scholarly information was supplied, puzzles solved, doors were opened and encouragement and support freely given.

My thanks to: Liam Boyce and John Clancy and Iarnród Éireann, Maurice Craig, Robert Fowler, David Griffin and the Irish Architectural Archive, Brendan Grimes, Dr Paul Larmour, Dr Edward McParland, Sean McQuaid and Bank of Ireland, Joseph Masterson, Adrian Rouiller, Niall Kerrigan and AIB, Sean and Rosemarie Mulcahy, Kevin B. Nowlan, Frederick O'Dwyer, Professor Roger Stalley, Jeremy Williams, Alex White.

I acknowledge also the scholarship of many writers in the field of Irish architectural studies, some of whose works are named in the reading list.

Finally, eternal gratitude to Nuala, with appreciation of her unique support.

CHURCHES
EARLY CHRISTIAN TO MEDIAEVAL

IRELAND, at the dawn of Christianity, was a land covered in forests and it seems likely that the first church structures were made of wood. No trace of any of these remain today but the first church buildings in stone probably date from at least the seventh century. The Early Christian Style, as it is known, is interesting in that it evolved in Ireland without any influence from the powerful tradition of Roman architecture, which prevailed in the rest of Western Europe. This style developed rather from the prehistoric forts and megaliths, and its small-scale, simple forms are unique.

Romanesque architecture in Ireland can be recognized by the arrival of the round-headed, Roman arch as distinct from the flat lintel used in the Early Christian phase. As the style developed, simple decorations, strongly carved in stone, embellished the arch and the jambs at the sides of the doorways. The later phases of the Romanesque saw an outburst of lavish carvings on rings of arches and on columns, caps and bases. The inward sloping sides of the door openings, known as a "batter" and already introduced in the Early Christian period, became more pronounced and helped to create a distinctive Irish identity for the Romanesque. The favoured ornament of the style in Europe was the chevron or zig-zag and this device, along with a deeply cut saw-tooth carving, became common for Irish church decoration. The most bizarre details, however, were the stone human heads and animal figures which enlivened many of the late stages of Irish Romanesque.

The Gothic style began in the Île de France about 1130 and reached its full flowering in the great cathedrals with their high soaring piers, intricate stone vaults and a skeleton of structure framing huge windows. Gothic in Ireland was a much more modest affair. Building to the heavens was not an ambition and later Irish mediæval churches remained relatively small, with little structural innovation. The round arch became pointed and the last phases of the style saw the appearance of a modestly elaborate stone tracery. The evolution from Romanesque was often gradual, with round-headed and pointed arches happily combined in the same building, forming something of a transitional style.

The Cistercian order is credited with the introduction of Gothic to Ireland and from about the end of the twelfth century to the dissolution of the monasteries in the mid-sixteenth century the Irish version of the style flourished. The picturesque ruins of the monastic foundations are plentiful and are as much part of the landscape in the peaceful Irish countryside today as the hills, lakes and rivers.

I

Early Christian
GALLARUS ORATORY DINGLE
CO. KERRY *c.*800 AD

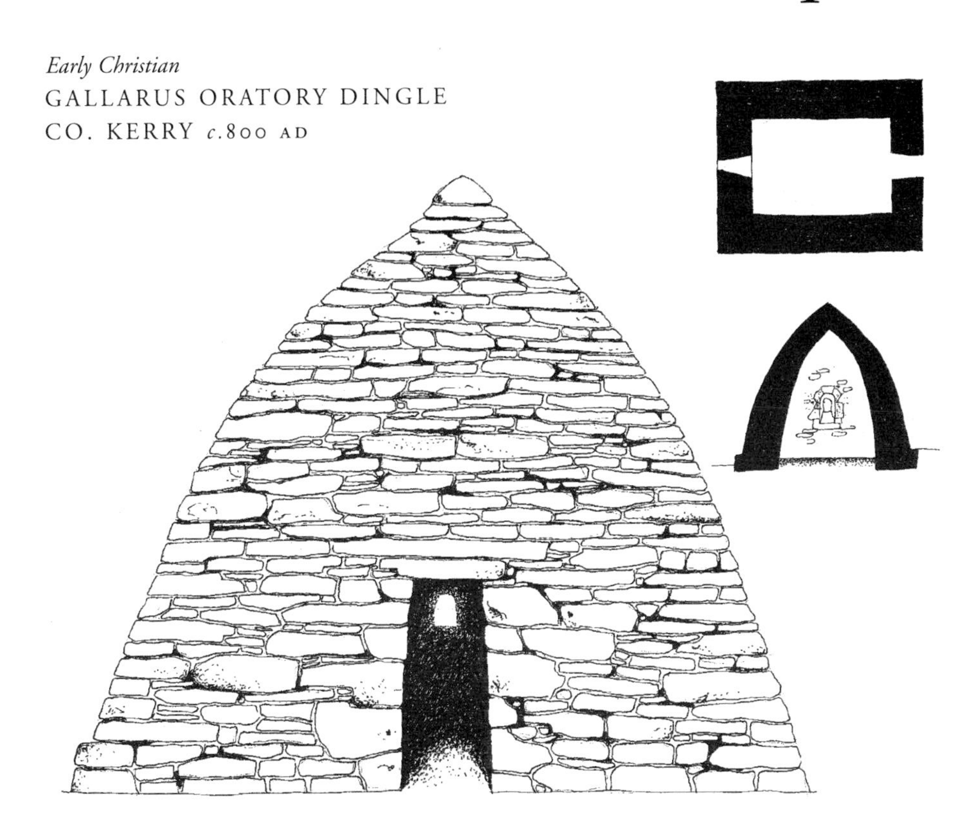

THIS LITTLE oratory is one of the oldest surviving buildings of the Early Christian period, standing for over 1200 years. The structural method is to fit relatively small stones closely and carefully together without mortar, to form what is known as corbel construction. This technique, already known in Ireland for several thousand years and used in the great pre-historic burial chambers, involves placing each successive layer of stones to project slightly inwards until the last stones on each side meet at the top. Thus walls and roof are one. The most perfect use of the corbel technique was in the construction of the stone beehive cells of the early monasteries. The most spectacular of these is on the great 200-metre-high rock called Sceilg Mhicíl which stands out in the wild Atlantic, south-east of Valentia Island, Co. Kerry. The plan shape of the Gallarus oratory is rectangular but corbel construction is more stable when it takes a circular form. The built-in instability of the rectangular form has led to the collapse of most of the ancient oratories of Ireland. Gallarus is about six kilometres north-west of the town of Dingle. A semi-collapsed oratory of similar date can be found nearby, at Kilmalkedar.

2

Stone-roofed churches

TEAMPULL BENIN INISHMORE
ARAN ISLANDS CO. GALWAY *c.*10th c.

THE VERY early churches of Ireland are tiny structures with simple rectangular plans and steep stone roofs. Teampull Benin on the island of Inishmore, Aran, is only just over three metres long and two metres wide. Most of these little buildings date from the ninth to the tenth centuries. A favoured place for the building of an Early Christian church was a remote island even though this gave little protection from the Viking raiders. A lonely island gave the promise of peace and the means to live a life of austerity. Most of the islands all around the coast of Ireland and many islands in inland lakes have the remains of an early stone church or monastery. An intriguing feature of these little edifices was the use of huge stones for the walling, as can be seen in the side wall of Teampull Benin. This was hardly for reasons of economy since the hewing and placing of large blocks was more arduous than bonding many smaller stones. The ancient masons could be said to have been proud to demonstrate their skill and to delight in the unexpected, even the contradiction, of a giant block in a dwarf building.

3

ST MC DARA'S ISLAND
CARNA CO. GALWAY *c.*10th.

THE STONE roof of this early church has been recently restored, using the original stones found on the site. The projections on the gable ends are known as antae and are a feature of many of these early churches, which form a distinct sub-group. The use of antae has been attributed to a memory of earlier timber construction and possibly mirrors the early corner posts of the long-vanished churches in wood. A unique feature of St Mc Dara's and a handful of others is the continuity of the antae up to the apex of the roof. This again is attributed to earlier timber construction – the "cruck" or bent-tree-pole method – where the poles or antae crossed over to form a finial. The stone finials were often carved and decorated. One of the finials survived at St Mc Dara's and both have now been restored. St Mc Dara's island is just off Carna, on the south Connemara coast. There are many early churches on the Aran islands and the best intact stone-roofed buildings are St Kevin's, Glendalough, Co. Wicklow; St Flannan's Oratory, Killaloe, Co. Clare, and St Columb's House, Kells, Co. Meath. Some of the best-known Early Christian sites are at Glendalough, where there are many early churches and a magnificent round tower, at Clonmacnoise, Co. Offaly, Inishmurray, Co. Sligo, and Devenish, Co. Fermanagh.

4

Irish Romanesque

ST CRONAN'S CHURCH
ROSCREA
CO. TIPPERARY 12th c.

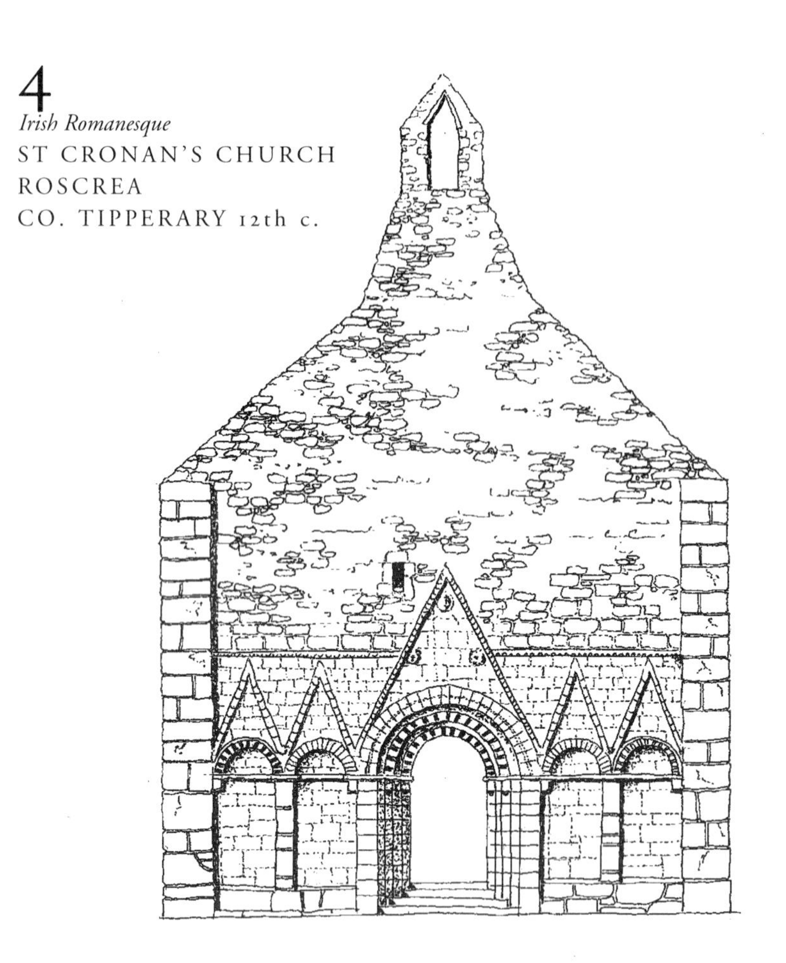

ONLY THE west gable façade survives of the church of St Cronan's monastery at Roscrea, incongruously fronting a modern road. The church is twelfth century but retains a few features of the earlier style. Strong antae frame the façade and the original gable roof pitch was steeper, in the early Irish manner. The elevation is a carefully ordered one with a central Romanesque doorway and blind or blank arcades on each side. A powerful vertical effect was created by the steep gables over the arcades and the porch. Much of the ornament has been eroded away but this design had an effect on later Irish architecture, as will be seen subsequently. The most splendid and complete example of Irish Romanesque is Cormac's Chapel in Cashel, Co. Tipperary – a building of quality which can rank equally with many Western European exercises in the style. This little masterpiece is stunningly situated, high up on the Rock of Cashel, although dwarfed by the later mediæval cathedral. The last phase of Irish Romanesque is well illustrated in St Saviour's Priory at Glendalough, Co. Wicklow, and in the Nuns' Church at Clonmacnoise. Splendid doorways are to be seen at Rahan, Co. Offaly, Killeshin, Co. Laois, and Kilmore, Co. Cavan.

5

CLONFERT CATHEDRAL
CO. GALWAY *c.*1160

THE MOST spectacular Irish Romanesque doorway is at Clonfert, situated on the west bank of the river Shannon and about eight kilometres north-west of Banagher, Co. Offaly. It is the tallest of all of the types in the country and without doubt it is the most stunningly beautiful. Every surface of the doorway and the steeply pitched pediment is covered in decoration, chevrons, interlacing and foliage. A bizarre and even barbaric effect is created by the profusion of stone human heads, set in deep sharp triangles in the pediment and lurking menacingly in the arcades over the arch. The little columns of the door jambs have a pronounced batter and the surfaces are pocked and chiselled to a rich texture of patterns.

6

Transitional
JERPOINT ABBEY
CO. KILKENNY *c.*1160

THE RUINED monastery at Jerpoint, just south-west of Thomastown, Co. Kilkenny, is the most famous and in many ways the most beautiful of all of the Cistercian sites in Ireland. Architecturally the nave of the church building could be said to demonstrate that the knowledge of the value of the pointed arch for its superior load-carrying capability did not result in a complete change to the Gothic style. The clere-storey windows are still round-headed while the stumpy columns are Romanesque in character. Jerpoint was a daughter house of the Cistercian monastery of Baltinglass, Co. Wicklow, where there was the same arrangement of clere-storey windows over the columns and between the arches. Structurally this would not have been done in a true Gothic design where the piers would have soared high up to carry stone vaults. Since vaulting was only seldom used in these churches, the alternative spacing of window and arch was an acceptable and lively device. Building continued at Jerpoint for at least another 240 years and the great glory there is the sculptured arcade of the cloister built about 1390. The late mediæval carving here is a sumptuous and riotous array of saints, bishops, ladies, knights, animals and grotesque beasts. In this delicious mixture of the sacred and the profane it is easy to believe that the mediæval masons were enjoying themselves and perhaps poking fun at all things grave and dull.

7

Gothic
ARDFERT CATHEDRAL
CO. KERRY *c.*1253

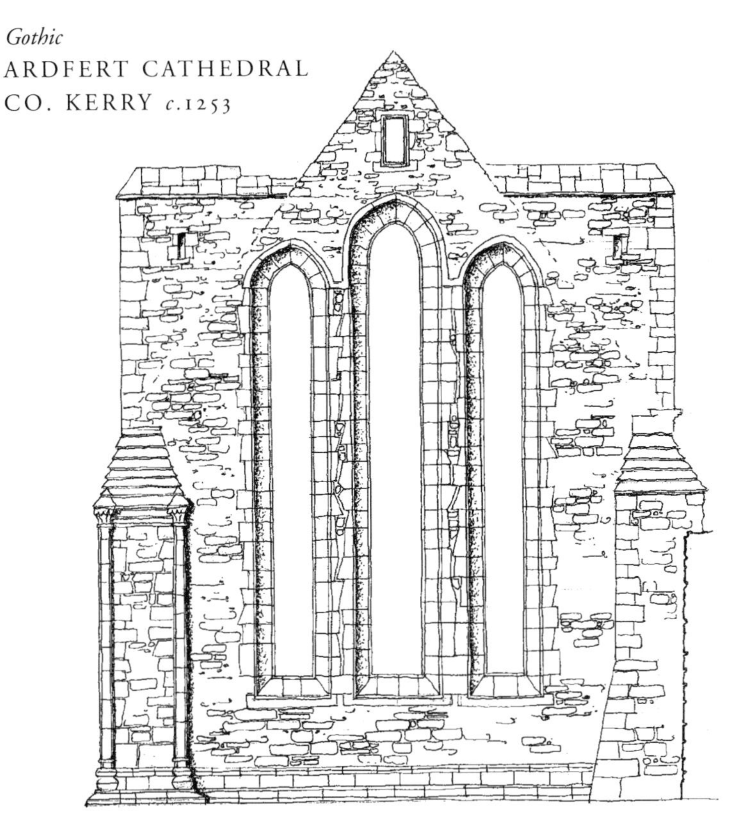

THE GOTHIC style became well established before the middle of the thirteenth century having been introduced by the Cistercians at Grey Abbey on the Ards peninsula, Co. Down, in 1193. The earliest parts of Ardfert Cathedral, eight kilometres north-west of Tralee, are of twelfth-century origin but the main church took shape in the middle of the thirteenth century. The tall triple-lancet window is pure Gothic and the churches are now becoming larger and taller in the spirit of the style. Unlike the Romanesque when the mass of stone walls predominated, here the window openings, particularly with the wide splays inside, seem to take up most of the gable wall. Increased daylight and the possibility of large areas of stained glass were enticing prospects for the mediæval builders. At Grey Abbey the early triple lancets are shorter than at Ardfert, with a second smaller row over the lower group. Five light lancet windows were used in the east wall of the Franciscan friary, also at Ardfert and no less than nine in the south wall of the aisle. A more daring development took place later when the piers between the lancets were whittled away to reduce them to extraordinarily thin stone mullions. A good example of this is the east window of the Franciscan friary at Ennis, Co. Clare.

Late Gothic

KILCOOLEY ABBEY
URLINGFORD
CO. KILKENNY

MID-15th c.

THE DEVELOPMENT of Gothic architecture in Ireland may be clearly seen in the evolution of the design of windows over the 200 years or so of the style. Wider windows needed a network of mullions or tracery to support the iron bars which in turn took the weight of the pieces of stained glass. The sheer ingenuity and skill of the stone masons of the Later Gothic in Western Europe created dazzling displays of thin stone tracery, emulating flowing foliage. This progression became known as the Flamboyant and windows in the style began to appear in Ireland in the fifteenth century. The east window of the chancel of Kilcooley Abbey, near Urlingford, Co. Kilkenny, illustrates the art of the Flamboyant in a monastic foundation which had a chequered and sometimes violent history. The Cistercian community was founded in 1184, burnt in 1418 and again burnt and almost totally destroyed in 1445 in an armed attack.

The restored Cistercian abbey at Holycross, Co. Tipperary, has several examples of Flamboyant windows but the most marvellous use of the style is in the tomb in the friary at Strade, south of Foxford, Co. Mayo. As well as the screen of delicate, foliated tracery there is, at the base, a lovely panel of carved figures.

9

Residential church

CISTERCIAN CELL CLARE ISLAND CO. MAYO *c.*1500

IT WAS not unusual in Early Christian times to have living quarters located over the vaults of some of the little churches or oratories. By the fifteenth century the practice became more common and the Cistercian cell on Clare Island is a good example of the deliberate integration of a residence into the design of a church. This was a simple nave building with a two-storied chancel. The room for the monks was on the upper level, over a simple barrel vault, and a narrow staircase was provided within the thickness of the walls. An interesting feature of the church is the mediæval frescoes, rare in Ireland, which can be seen on the chancel walls. These consist of paintings of human and animal forms but are difficult to see in the dark interior. False ribs were painted on to the underside of the vault, presumably to give an impression of more structural sophistication to the rudimentary barrel shape. The monastic community on this island must have been very isolated since Clare Island is well out in an often stormy ocean. The earliest settlement is said to have been banished by pirates but, unusually, despite the dissolution of the monasteries, monks may have continued to live here until well into the seventeenth century.

10

Fortified church

TAGHMON CHURCH

CO. WESTMEATH 15th c.

FORTIFIED CHURCHES, as distinct from those which included residential accommodation, are a less frequent type but a few still exist. The late mediæval church of St Munna at Taghmon, about twelve kilometres north of Mullingar and east of the road to Castlepollard, is a product of the turbulent times in the fifteenth century. The tower contained the living quarters and was built shortly after the church was completed. It is identical to the tower-houses which were the favoured residences for landowners and chieftains desiring the security of living on the upper floors of a defensible building. The roof of the Taghmon church is a stone vault and the Irish-type battlements, combined with the marked batter or slope of the walls of both the church and the tower, create a strong impression of a fortress. The church was attacked and plundered by Farrell Macgeoghan in 1452 and was in ruins by 1622. The building was restored in the mid nineteenth century as a Protestant parish church and is now disused and cared for by the State as a National Monument. Another dramatic, castle-like, fortified church survives in what was once the town of Clonmines, Co. Wexford, now a series of ruins.

FRIARIES, PRIORIES AND ABBEYS

ST PATRICK is reputed to have brought Christianity to Ireland, although there were some Christians here before the patron saint arrived in the middle of the fifth century. In the sixth and seventh centuries monasteries spread and grew rapidly, and today there is hardly a county in Ireland without the remains of at least one Early Christian foundation. The first settlements were built of wood and all have long since vanished. The earliest surviving monasteries consist of small groups of scattered buildings of stone and their layout conforms to no particular pattern or design. Some regions, like the remote and stony landscape of Clare, are particularly richly endowed with ancient sites, but evidence of early monasteries is widespread in almost every county.

The Anglo-Norman invasion of 1169 changed more than the military and political fate of Ireland; its architecture was also to be powerfully and dramatically altered. The great new religious orders of Western Europe – already beginning to reach out to this most westerly part of the continent – flooded into Ireland in advance of the secular invaders in the twelfth century. The Cistercians, the Augustinians, the Franciscans and the Dominicans were the most dominant of these monastic foundations and with incredible rapidity, beautiful and orderly edifices, of a scale far greater than ever seen before in Ireland, spread throughout the land. These new building types are remarkable for their planning where the central organizing feature was the square or rectangular cloister with open arcades. The church, refectory, kitchen and living quarters were then arranged around the four sides to form a great enclosed complex.

For more than 300 years these monasteries multiplied, were altered and added to, reflecting the march of architectural fashions in the mediæval era from Romanesque to the late flowering of the Gothic style. The beginning of the end was in the reign of King Henry VIII when the slow and painful dissolution of the monasteries started, but it was not until the military juggernaut of Cromwell stormed through the island in the seventeenth century, burning the buildings and smashing the sculpture, that the end finally came. Today the great mediæval friaries and abbeys survive as splendid ruins; a few are in towns, but most of them stand near lakes or rivers, or in peaceful water meadows, romantic and silent.

The Cistercians were the most prolific builders, and of their thirty-three foundations some twenty-one survive in various stages of ruin. Most of the monastic remains are now National Monuments and there are about twenty each of Franciscan and Augustinian, and at least fourteen Dominican, priories and friaries still to be seen. Other Orders have far fewer remains; the Carmelites are represented by priories at Loughrea, Co. Galway, and a fine site at Rathmullan, Co. Donegal. The Benedictines left a magnificent abbey at Fore, Co. Westmeath, and at Shanagolden, Co. Limerick, there is the curiously named Manisternagalliaghduff Abbey – a rare example of a mediæval nunnery.

11

Cistercian monastery

DUNBRODY ABBEY CO. WEXFORD 12th c.

THIS IS one of the most impressive monastic ruins in the country. The dominant view is of the great church seen across the fields and overlooking the confluence of the rivers Barrow and Suir. In mediæval times Waterford harbour and the lower reaches of the two rivers were an important waterway. The abbey was founded by the Cistercian Order towards the end of the twelfth century and the church is a good example of early Gothic. The monastery was dissolved by Henry VIII in 1545 and given to Sir Osborne Itchingham. Incongruously, a Tudor manor house was built over the south transept (seen in the drawing on the left of the main church).

One of the most beautiful Cistercian monasteries is Jerpoint (illus. 6) and highly interesting remains are at Baltinglass, Co. Wicklow, Boyle, Co. Roscommon, and at Mellifont, Co. Louth, which was the first Cistercian abbey, founded in 1142. The abbey of Holycross, Co. Tipperary, has been recently restored and some of the finest examples of Late Gothic architecture can be seen here. The chancel of the church is fifteenth century and there is a superb east window and other windows with flamboyant tracery. The glory of Holycross is the ribbed vaulting, particularly over the crossing, which is the most splendid in Ireland.

12

Augustinian monastery

ATHASSEL PRIORY CO. TIPPERARY LATE 12th c.

ATHASSEL PRIORY, situated near the village of Golden, south-west of Cashel, was founded by the Augustinians at the end of the twelfth century. It is one of the largest monastic ruins in Ireland, covering an area of about four acres. It was surrounded by a wall, much of which survives, and outside the wall there was once a mediæval town. All traces of the town have vanished but the great monastery is a fine sight on the banks of the river Suir. The church has a sturdy square tower over the junction of the choir and nave. The west doorway of the church, consisting of simple, receding pointed arches, finely cut, is one of the best Gothic doorways in Ireland. As well as being defended by the enclosing wall there was a moat across the meadows, which is now dry, with a stone bridge connecting to a defended gatehouse.

One of the earliest Augustinian priories in Ireland is Ballintubber, Co. Mayo. This was founded in 1216 and suffered the same fate as many of the mediæval monasteries at the destructive hands of the forces of Cromwell in 1653. The church was restored in 1963. The Augustinian convent of Killone, Co. Clare, founded as early as 1190, is notable as one of a handful of ancient convents for nuns in Ireland.

13

Franciscan friary
ADARE CO. LIMERICK 1464

MEDIÆVAL ARCHITECTURE, both secular and religious, is well represented in and around the pleasant village of Adare. The silent, roofless ruins of the Franciscan friary are in many ways the most impressive in this quiet countryside. The friary was founded in 1464 and took two years to build. The tower, tall, slender and noticeably tapering, is characteristic of Franciscan monasteries, compared to the often squat and powerful towers built by the Cistercian Order. Other mediæval buildings nearby are the Augustinian friary of 1325, now the Church of Ireland parish church; the White or "Trinitarian" Monastery of 1275, now the Roman Catholic parish church; the thirteenth-century St Nicholas Church and the thirteenth-century walled castle.

The distinctive towers of the Franciscan friaries are often a prominent feature of the Irish landscape and many of the monasteries still have their towers mostly intact. Good examples of these beautiful towers can be seen at Claregalway and Kilconnell, Co. Galway; Moyne and Rosserk, Co. Mayo; Kilcrea and Timoleague, Co. Cork, and Aherlow, Co. Tipperary. The early fifteenth-century Franciscan friary at Quin, between Ennis and Kilmurray, Co. Clare, is one of the most interesting in the country. The monastery was built on top of a large castle of the late thirteenth century and three of the huge round bastions and parts of the curtain wall were incorporated into the fabric of the friary. Unusually, the monastery survived both the dissolution and Cromwell and continued into the nineteenth century.

14

Dominican friary
SLIGO ABBEY 15TH C.

THE DOMINICAN friary in Sligo town was founded in 1253, accidentally burned in 1414 and rebuilt shortly afterwards. The ruined friary today is largely an excellent example of fifteenth-century Gothic architecture. The oldest part of the church is the choir, dating from the thirteenth century. There is a beautiful east window, a finely sculptured altar and a fifteenth-century rood screen which divided the choir from the nave. The illustration shows the splendid cloister arcade dating from the fifteenth century where the slim columns are decorated with delicate carving. The reader's desk was projected out on to a curving stone corbel. The carved tombs in the church are notable pieces of sculpture. There is a late historic tomb in the church – the O'Conor Sligo monument of 1624 which is Renaissance in style. The friary survived the dissolution in the mid sixteenth century but was finally burned in 1641.

The Dominican friary at Kilmallock, Co. Limerick, has two of the best mediæval windows in the country and, in addition, superb examples of stone carving. The friary in Roscommon is notable for a fifteenth-century tomb which has the carved figures of eight gallowglasses or mercenary soldiers. There are Dominican foundations in the towns of Kilkenny, Youghal and Cashel, and other friaries at Athenry, Co. Galway; Ballindoon, Co. Sligo; Burrishoole and Rathfran, Co. Mayo; Castlelyons, Co. Cork; Lorrha, Co. Tipperary, and Portumna, Co. Galway.

CHURCHES FROM THE SEVENTEENTH TO THE TWENTIETH CENTURY

IN THE turbulent years of the reign of the Tudors there was little or no new church building in Ireland. The dissolution of the monasteries began about 1536 on the orders of Henry VIII but, after the initial period when many of the abbeys and friaries were closed, some of the foundations in more remote parts of the land continued to function, albeit in reduced circumstances, until the end of the sixteenth century. After the Reformation the mediæval churches in the towns were gradually taken into use by Protestants. Catholics struggled to continue their worship in isolated areas into the seventeenth century but after the destructive Cromwellian campaign of 1649 most of the Catholic clergy either fled or were driven out. The end of old Gaelic Ireland followed the defeat of the forces of James II by William of Orange in 1691. There were few churches built in the seventeenth century and fewer still which remain relatively unaltered. Derry Cathedral was completed in 1633 but had several later additions. One of the rare, early rural churches which is largely intact is the Church of Ireland Middle Church at Ballinderry, Co. Antrim, of 1664.

The Penal Laws were enacted to totally suppress the Catholic Church in Ireland at the end of the seventeenth century and except for a few Mass Houses there were no Catholic churches built until later in the eighteenth century when the Penal Laws were somewhat relaxed. This resulted in the building of a number of modest churches which were simple and vernacular in form. The Presbyterians suffered the same fate as the Catholics during some of this period and their churches in the eighteenth century were quite similar to the Catholic buildings, particularly in the rural areas.

The eighteenth century brought in a new era of church building. Nearly all of the churches which were designed by architects in the Georgian period were Protestant and the classical style now predominated. St Werburgh's in Dublin was built by Thomas Burgh in 1715 and is one of the earliest classical churches in Ireland. Later in the century there were many beautiful classical parish churches built in towns and in the country.

With Catholic Emancipation in 1829 a flood of new and often large Catholic churches spread throughout the country, and Catholic church building was to be the dominant architectural activity until well into the twentieth century. The revival of Gothic was a notable feature of church design in the middle of the century, particularly with the influence of Augustus Welby Pugin and his followers, although classical still persisted. In the later part of the century the Celtic Revival style saw a return to Romanesque forms for churches and this lasted into the early twentieth century.

Modernism in the design of churches in Ireland was late to arrive, although there were flickers of innovation as in the designs of W. A. Scott at the turn of the century. Most of the churches in the first half of the twentieth century were traditional classical, Gothic or in a safe economical Italianate style. In the 1960s the Council of the Catholic Church, Vatican II, brought an end to traditionalism and a rich variety of modern styles enlivened the churches built for the second half of the century.

15

Classical
ST JOHN'S CHURCH
BALLYMORE
CO. DONEGAL
1752

St John's church at Ballymore near Port na Blagh is a fine, rural Church of Ireland designed in the classical style which was common in the eighteenth century. The building is a very simple rectangular box with a plain belfry. The windows are round-headed on the long elevations and the gable has a large, beautifully proportioned Venetian window. This type of window has three lights with the centre opening round-headed. The surrounds to the windows, projecting stone blocks, are known as Gibbs surrounds after the classical architect James Gibbs. The interior is generally intact, with wood pews and a gallery. The walls are also panelled to form a two-metre-high wainscot. Since economy was obviously important, cut stone was reserved for the window surrounds and the quoins – the corners – of the building. These are in the form known as rusticated, that is, with cut bevelled edges which give a image of massive strength to the little building. This device is common in Irish architecture of the period. The architect may have been Michael Priestley who designed several buildings in Co. Donegal, including the Lifford Courthouse of 1746.

Two fine classical churches were built in Co. Down in the first half of the eighteenth century, at Moira in 1725 and at Newtownbreda in 1747, built by Richard Cassels, architect of many great houses. The famous St Ann's Church, Shandon, Cork, with its tall graceful steeple, was built in 1722.

16

Vernacular churches

METHODIST CHURCH AND MANSE CASTLEBAR CO. MAYO *c.*1800

THE MEDIÆVAL tradition of including living accommodation with a church building under one roof continued into the early nineteenth century. For instance, the example of the fifteenth-century Taghmon church (see illus. 9) was followed when the Catholic church was built nearby in 1844. The Methodist church and manse, beautifully sited on one edge of the open green park in the centre of Castlebar, continues the type where the roof line flows unbroken over the two-storeyed house.

The Moravian church at Ballinderry Lower, Co. Antrim, and the Presbyterian church at Inch, Inishowen, Co. Donegal, are very similar. These plain structures clearly demonstrate that the communities which did not conform with the Established Church built modestly and did not approve of the need to advertise their presence with towers, spires or elaborate styles. The plain rectangular plan was common for the early Presbyterian churches and one of the most splendid of these is the tiny church at Dunmurry, Co. Antrim, of 1779. There is a similar Presbyterian church near Edgeworthstown, Co. Longford, but without the decorative stone surrounds of Dunmurry. This is Corboy Church, which dates from the mid-eighteenth century.

17

ST JAMES CATHOLIC CHURCH GRANGE CO. LOUTH 1762

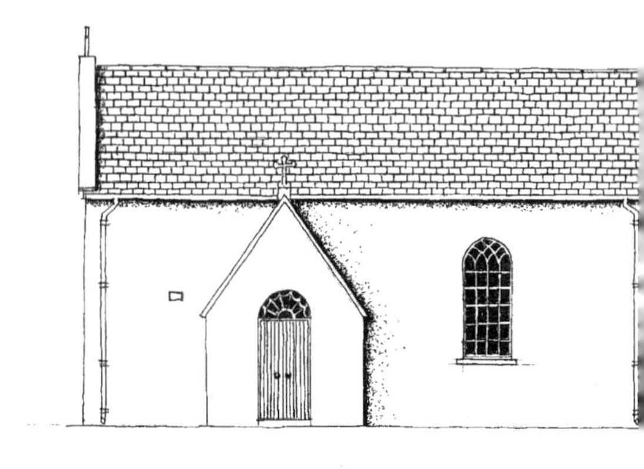

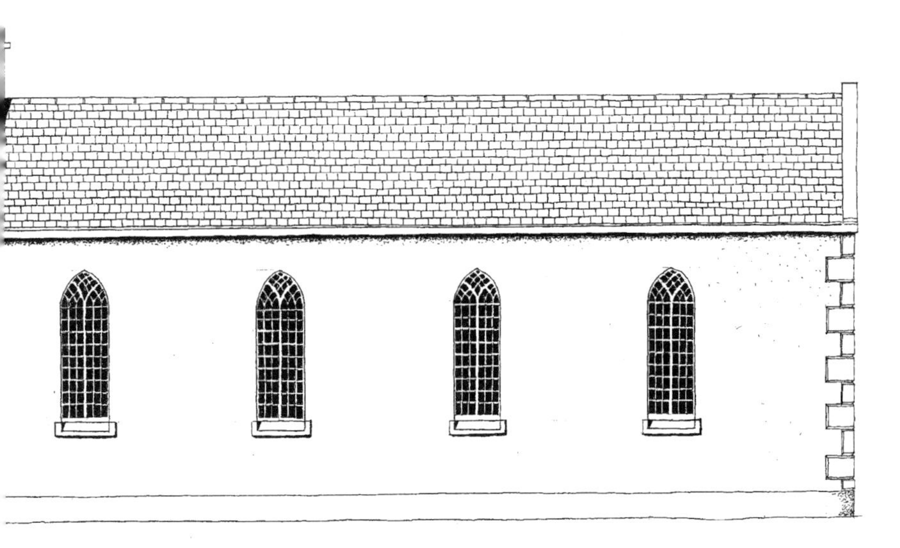

THE CHURCH of St James on the Cooley peninsula, near Carlingford, is one of the earliest surviving vernacular Catholic churches of the period before Emancipation. Vernacular churches can be best described as being simple structures, usually designed by a local builder or mason. They are one of the most interesting type of buildings in the country and form a special group which rewards seeking out and study. Most have no named architect or builder but the church at Grange is attributed to Thaddeus Gallagher, a local builder. The present plan-form of St James is the T-plan which is the most common form for Catholic churches of the period. It is likely, however, that the original church was a simple long rectangle with an extension at a later date making it into a conventional nave and transepts arrangement. There are galleries constructed of timber at the ends of each leg, a common feature as it economically increased the capacity of the building. The two sets of doors were common to Catholic and Presbyterian churches of the time and separated the sexes into different areas inside. The porches and the belfry tower were a later addition and date from the mid-nineteenth century.

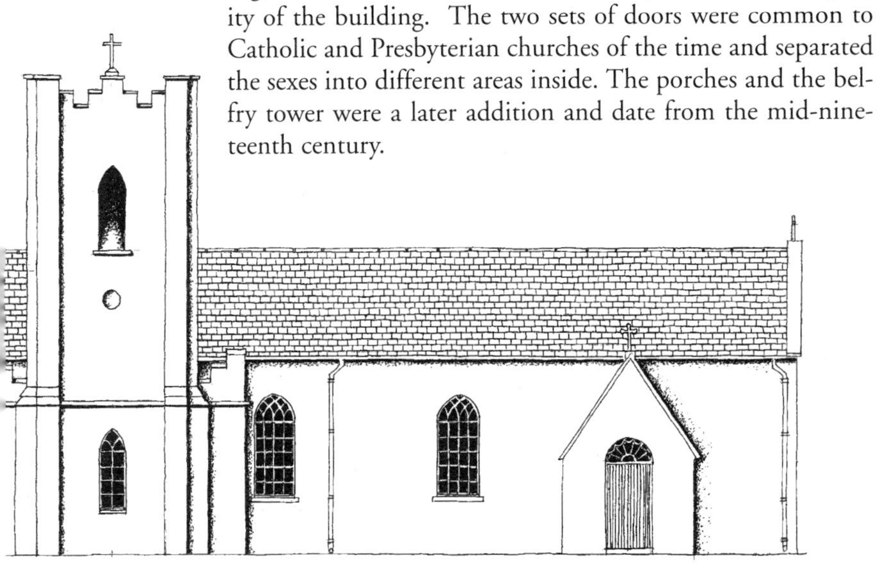

18

CRATLOE
CATHOLIC CHURCH
CO. CLARE *c.*1800

CRATLOE CATHOLIC church, situated just above the main road between Limerick and Shannon, is one of the most beautiful of these pre-Emancipation structures. Cratloe is also a T-plan building with long low roofs and the interior spaces are narrow for the purpose of enabling light and economical timbers to roof the span. The poor rural congregations who built these places of worship could not afford a cut-stone, classically correct design much less a high and wide nave with traceried windows. Cratloe has the usual two doors but one of these, shown on the right of the drawing, appears mediæval. The church probably dates from about 1806, which is marked on a stone, but there is another date stone giving 1781. The simple bell cote is typical and appears on many Catholic rural churches well into the nineteenth century. As in the church at Grange it is likely that Cratloe began as a simple rectangle and the T-shape evolved to cater for increasing congregations. Despite the austerity of the exteriors some of these early churches added a quite decorative Gothic or classical reredos.

19

CATHOLIC
CHURCH
EADESTOWN
CO. KILDARE
EARLY 19TH C.

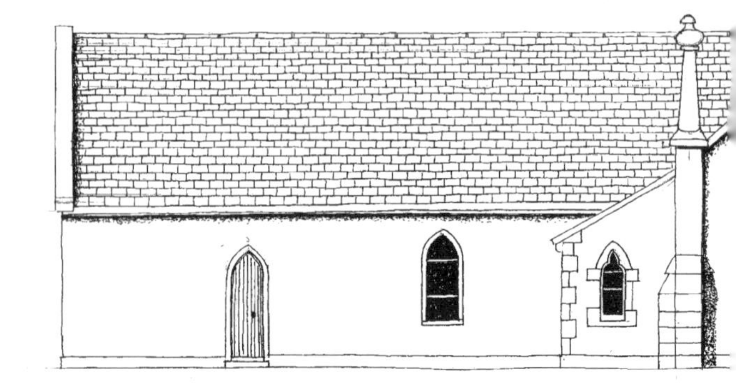

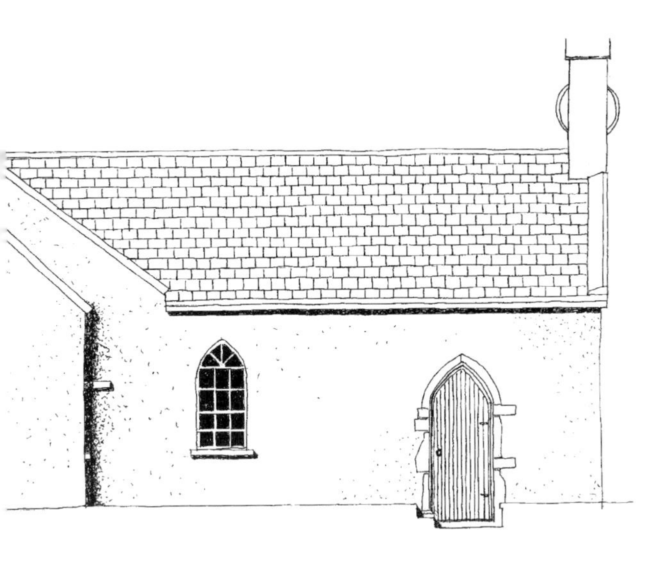

THE VERNACULAR church at Eadestown can be found on the road between Naas and the village of Blessington in Co. Wicklow. In this building the T-plan has been extended to form a sanctuary which, in contrast to the austere exteriors of the wings and nave, is embellished with cut-stone inserts, decorative pinnacles, a delightful little belfry and a simple three-light Gothic window. There are cut stone quoins and miniature buttresses which serve no function in such a small low building. All of these indulgences lead to the conclusion that this was the work of the stonecutters of the nearby village of Ballyknockan, Co. Wicklow. Not far away in Co. Wicklow there is another more elaborate vernacular Catholic church in the village of Valleymount where the stone carvings are similar to Eadestown. The names of the first parish priests are often carved in the churches but very occasionally the name of the architect builder is recorded. The original roof slating on the Eadestown church has only recently been replaced with a uniform artificial material and unfortunately this has removed one of the features which give these early churches a special character. The original slating was natural stone, which has an interesting texture, and the size of slates was also graduated from the eaves to the apex of the roof, a device which gave a subtle scale to such a small building.

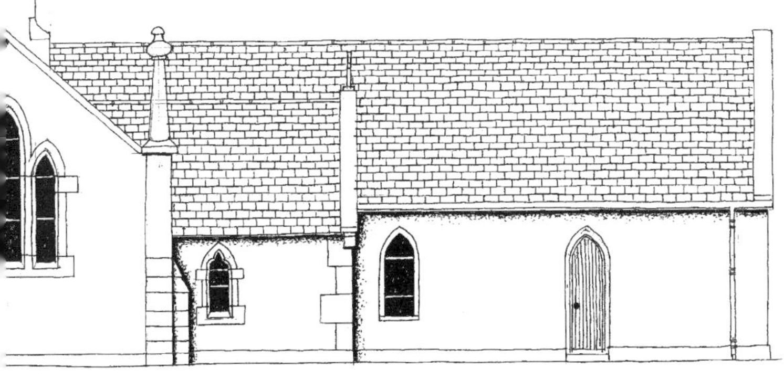

20

James Gandon (1743–1843)
COOLBANAGHER CHURCH
CO. LAOIS 1786

THE CHURCH of Ireland at Coolbanagher, near Emo, Co. Laois, was designed by the famous late eighteenth-century architect, James Gandon. Trained in London with Sir William Chambers, Gandon came to Dublin to build the Custom House in 1781. This elegant riverside building, one of the most beautiful in Ireland, is complemented upstream by the Four Courts and together with the portico of the former House of Lords in D'Olier Street (now the Bank of Ireland) ensures Gandon's reputation as Dublin's greatest architect of the eighteenth century. The slim, elegantly proportioned, Coolbanagher Church was built for his patron, Lord Portarlington, for whom he also designed the splendid classical style house, Emo Court, nearby.

21

MASSMOUNT CHURCH
ROSNAKILL CO. DONEGAL *c.*1800

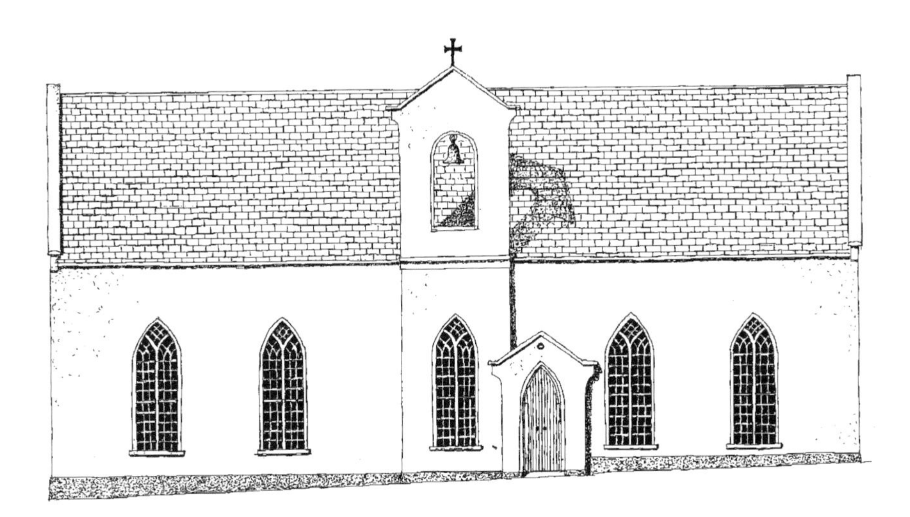

THE SMALL Catholic church at Rosnakill is one of the most remote of these unpretentious pre-Emancipation buildings. It is on the west side of the Fanad peninsula in the north of Co. Donegal. Unusually, since many of the Catholic churches of the late Penal days were almost hidden away, this one is sited prominently on a hillock overlooking Mulroy bay. The plan shape is a simple rectangle, a proper "barn" church instead of the larger T-shaped building, although many of these must have begun as simple rectangles and expanded later. The altar is in the middle of one wall, which interestingly is also the arrangement which is favoured in many of the plain Presbyterian churches of the time. In some parts of Co. Donegal, in particular, there seems to be little difference in outward appearance between Catholic and Presbyterian buildings.

There were some 250 vernacular Catholic churches in Ireland still standing up to about 1980. Before this many had been destroyed or abandoned to remain as ruins, in favour of new nineteenth- or twentieth-century structures. A substantial number remain, however, to be found by exploration of the smaller country roads and villages. Those remaining examples of a building form which grew out of the history of hard times for ordinary people comprise a unique architectural type, which deserves to be cherished.

22

CATHOLIC CHURCH
ROCKCORRY
CO. MONAGHAN 1841

THE TINY rural Catholic barn church near the village of Rockcorry in Co. Monaghan is post-Emancipation but represents clearly the frugal concerns of a small farming community immediately before the Great Famine. Although the building could hardly be more modest, careful effort was made to create an image of a religious building. The pointed arch and flowing glazing bars in the fanlight over the entrance door, along with the slim lancet windows and their minimal, pointed hoods, recognize the Gothic Revival then in full flow in the greater towns. In the north of the country, as mentioned, many of the vernacular Presbyterian churches are almost identical, the Catholic ones identified merely by the roof cross. An intriguing feature of the church at Rockcorry is at the apex of the gable under the cross, where the roof barges cross over to form antae as in the Early Christian stone-roofed churches. Another feature of Rockcorrig is the painting on of the quoins, door surrounds and the plinth. A poor community could not afford real stone for the dressings but the image of these features is still considered important. The contrast provided by painting the quoins, surrounds and plinth in a dark colour and whitewashing the main walls was both architecturally satisfying and helped to identify the building in the dark winter countryside.

23

John Semple (*d*.1880)
CHURCH OF IRELAND
KILTERNAN CO. DUBLIN 1826

JOHN SEMPLE was one of the most original architects working in the first half of the nineteenth century. His output consisted almost entirely of churches, and he designed and built about seventeen as architect for the Board of First Fruits, the official body which was in charge of building for the Established Church. John Semple was appointed as architect for Dublin diocese and all of his churches are either in the county and city or in south Leinster. At Kilternan, in south Co. Dublin, the closely spaced buttresses give a strong rhythm to the nave and the pinnacles, while string courses and plinths are all robustly delineated by smoothly dressed and weathered details. In contrast the spire is quite delicate and the sharp pinnacles on the four corners give a pronounced vertical emphasis to this lovely little building. The stone used is the local granite and in the nineteenth century there were quarries all around, particularly at Glencullen and Barnacullia in the hills above the church. The local stone has a high content of mica which sparkles in the sunlight and can be seen in buildings and walls in the area.

Semple's most innovatory design is the so-called Black Church, off Dorset Street in north Dublin, where he used a parabolic-shaped arch to roof the building. His most splendid design is the church at Monkstown, Co. Dublin, all battlements, pinnacles in the shape of chessmen, with immensely tall thin windows and glorious swirling ogee arches over the doors.

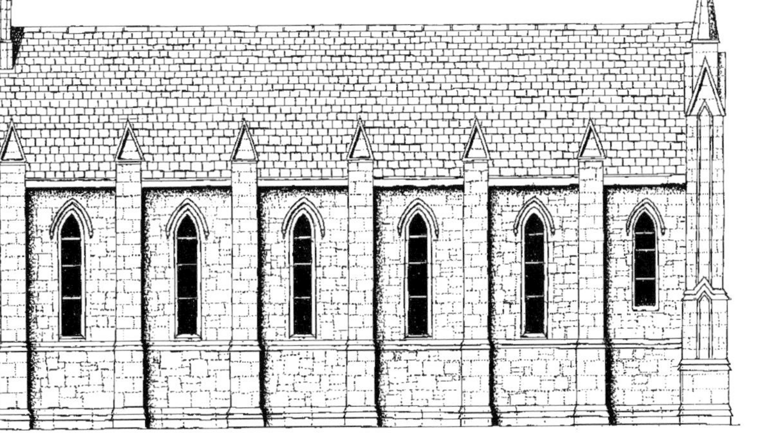

24

Gothic Revival

ST COLMCILLE'S CHURCH DURROW CO. OFFALY 1831

St colmcille's Catholic church at Durrow, on a side road just north of Tullamore, is in fact a barn church, not much larger than the simple vernacular structures of the Penal days. Catholic Emancipation came in 1829 and the little church in Durrow can now safely be assertive. The sides of the building have simple pointed windows but the entrance façade is a full exercise in Gothic. The tall tower is embellished with battlements of the peculiar "Irish" variety where the embrasures are stepped. The most endearing feature of the church is the way the little corner pinnacles, embellished with crockets or knobs, are daringly corbelled out in a somewhat precarious manner. An odd feature of the façade is the mismatch of the rusticated stone quoins of the left-hand sides of nave and tower with the right-hand sides. Since building in stone is a relatively slow process this could hardly be a mistake and must be deliberate but it appears to give an unbalanced feel to the design – almost a Post-Modern contradiction! The church has a splendid Gothic interior with delicate plaster vaulting on the ceiling and ogee arches on the reredos. Nearby is the site of the ancient Durrow Abbey, source of the famous Book of Durrow now in Trinity College, Dublin.

25

Methodist
WESLEY CHAPEL
WINE STREET
SLIGO 1830

EARLY METHODIST churches, like those of the Presbyterians and Catholics of the late eighteenth centuries, were simple structures reflecting their congregations' lower status in terms of the Establishment. The Wesley Chapel in Sligo town is an altogether different design. The building is still a simple hall but the two-storied entrance façade is now a careful exercise in full classical style. Moreover the façade is entirely in stone and instead of the more usual economical rubble masonry for the main walling, this is in ashlar – rectangular blocks of stone with the faces finely dressed smooth. The surrounds to the door and windows are only slightly emphasized, unlike the more positive Gibbsian fashion popular in the province of Ulster. This tends to give a flatter, more restrained appearance to the façade which was probably deliberate in view of the more austere nature of the worship. Sligo was a busy port in the nineteenth century and has many interesting and important buildings. It is likely that this influenced giving more architectural importance to the church .

26

Nineteenth-century classical
PRO-CATHEDRAL
SKIBBEREEN
CO. CORK 1826

THE CATHOLIC Pro-Cathedral in the town of Skibbereen, Co. Cork, is a pre-Emancipation church of some size. Although the great increase in the number and architectural importance of Irish Catholic churches began after the Act was passed in 1829, a significant number of substantial churches was built for Catholic congregations from the latter half of the previous century when the Penal Laws were relaxed. The splendid St Patrick's Church in Waterford of 1764 is probably the best of these. The front façade of the Skibbereen Pro-Cathedral is a strongly modelled exercise in classicism. Wide pilasters divide the façade into three parts and the blind niches on the upper level are matched by blank recesses on the ground level, each fitted with stone stoups. The completely stone ashlar front is in huge contrast to the simple vernacular churches of the countryside. The most magnificent of the classical Catholic churches of this early nineteenth century were in the cities. The church of St Francis Xavier, 1829, in Gardiner Street, Dublin, is certainly one of the most beautiful.

27

Church of Ireland
NURNEY CO. CARLOW *c.*1800

THIS TINY church at Nurney, Co. Carlow, conforms to a simple geometrical formula which makes the buildings of the Church of Ireland instantly recognizable in the countryside and villages throughout Ireland. A rectangular box has a vertical tower attached to one gable so the perfect marriage of the vertical and horizontal is achieved. The halls were small, reflecting the relative scale of the congregations, but the high tower advertised the dominance of the Established Church. At Nurney the style is basic Gothic with a sharp stone spire and pointed windows, a favoured style for most of the country churches. Occasionally a variation of the type can be seen, where the windows are round-headed and the tower has battlements rather than a spire.

28

Augustus Welby Northmore Pugin (d. 1852)

CATHOLIC CHURCH
GOREY
CO. WEXFORD 1842

THE ENGLISH architect A.W.N. Pugin had a major influence on Irish Catholic architecture in the short period after Catholic Emancipation. Catholic church-building gained rapid momentum with magnificent new structures erected in most of the major towns. Pugin was a passionate advocate for the "Gothic Revival", believing mediaevalism to be the only correct formula for Catholic religious buildings. His first Irish church was St Peter's College Chapel, Wexford, in 1839 and this was followed by twelve other churches, mostly in the south-east. Unusually, the style followed for the Gorey church was Romanesque, his only Irish exercise in that formula. Pugin's insistence on high-quality stone masonry is evident in the entrance façade with its neat corbels and quoins and the weathering on the twin buttresses. His church at Enniscorthy dominates the town in a spectacular fashion and his main work outside County Wexford is the splendid Killarney Cathedral. Other notable work by Pugin includes Maynooth College and the Loreto Convent, Rathfarnam, Co. Dublin. After his death in 1852 his practice continued with his son E.W. Pugin in partnership with George Ashlin, and further great Gothic Revival churches followed in quick succession.

29

J.J. McCarthy (1817–82)
ST KEVIN'S CHURCH
GLENDALOUGH CO. WICKLOW 1849

JAMES JOSEPH McCarthy has been called the "Irish Pugin", mostly because of his whole-hearted identification with Pugin's enthusiasm for the principles of the Gothic Revival. The church of St Kevin's at Glendalough, Co. Wicklow, is an early design by McCarthy and already demonstrates many of the individual touches of McCarthy as an exponent of the mediæval revival style. The strong buttresses seem to anchor the church to the hill slope but the beautiful, if simply detailed, south porch is pure McCarthy. The nearby church at Rathdrum of 1860, also by McCarthy, has two porches of even more striking character. St Kevin's Church is built of granite with smoothly worked limestone used for the dressings. Unfortunately the main walling has been plastered over, presumably because the granite on such an exposed site in an area of high rainfall let in water. Some of the dressings are still exposed and help to give an early mediæval character to the building. McCarthy built about seventy churches throughout the country over the next forty years and one of his greatest commissions was the completion of the Cathedral of Armagh. McCarthy was a Catholic and nationalist at a time when the Irish Catholic Church was triumphantly re-asserting itself and, since only a few architects were Catholics, McCarthy prospered.

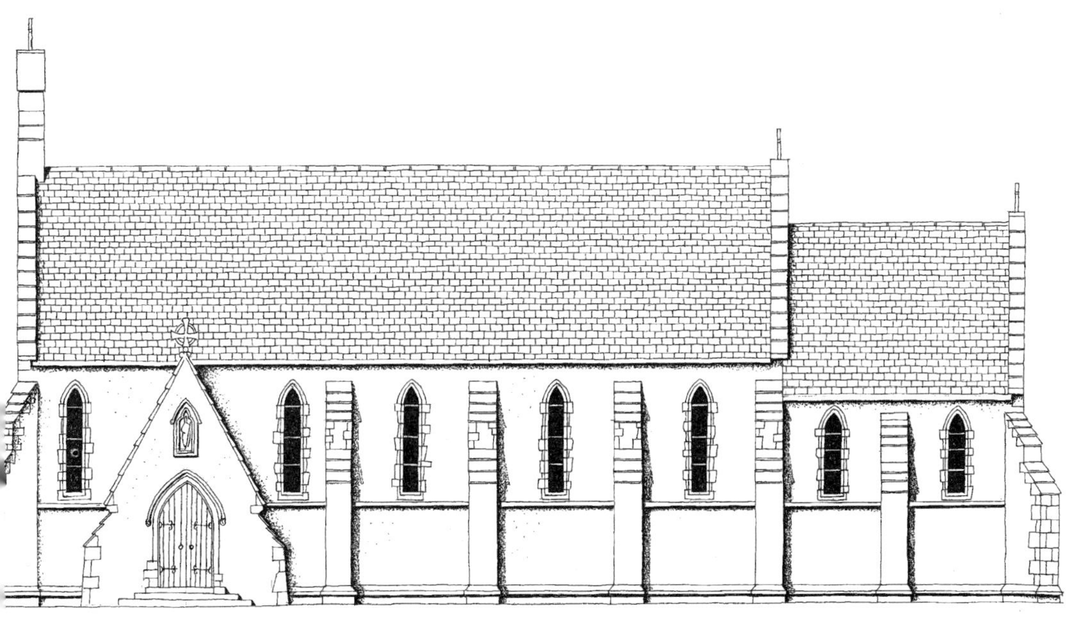

30

Gothic Revival

PRESBYTERIAN CHURCH
WARRENPOINT CO. DOWN LATE 19TH C.

THE GOTHIC Revival was embraced by all of the denominations in Ireland although the Presbyterians, particularly in the north of Ireland, were often building in a full classical style in the first half of the nineteenth century. In the later part of the century Gothic became commonplace for most Christian churches and the Presbyterian church in the sea-side town of Warrenpoint in Co. Down is a lively interpretation of the style. Positioning the bell tower at the side of the church as a separate vertical feature was usually a device to emphasize the soaring Gothic effect, as was the continuation of buttresses above the eaves' line. Here in Warrenpoint the opposite effect seems to have sought by keeping the tower squat and placing the buttresses low down, so that they appear to sink into the ground. Architects often had fun with design by appearing to break the rules, and perhaps this was the case here.

31

Vernacular Gothic
METHODIST CHURCH
COOTEHILL
CO. CAVAN 1860

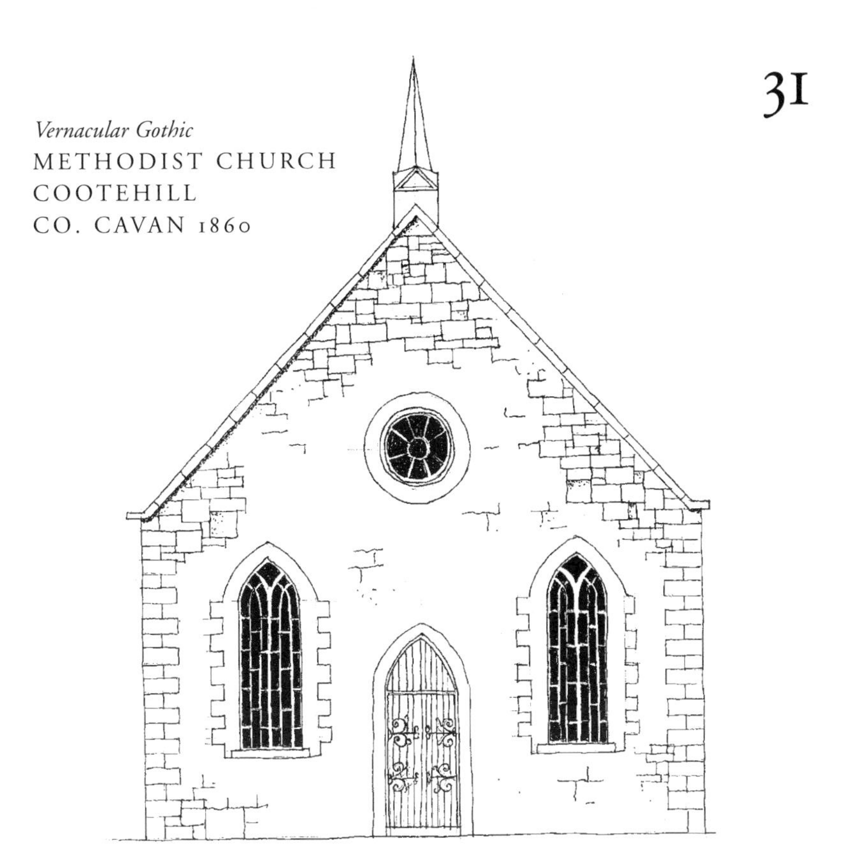

THE METHODIST church was very much a tiny minority, at least in the provinces of Connacht, Munster and Leinster. The larger Methodist churches, often classical in design, tend to be found in Ulster. In the southern part of the country the Methodist churches of the later part of the nineteenth century are invariably small halls, sometimes with a little porch but more often single cells. The tiny church in Cootehill, Co. Cavan, is a perfect architectural set-piece carried out in beautiful stone-work, so typical of that masterly craft which had a long history in Ireland. The building has sandstone dressings to the quoins, windows and door and the main walling is in the form known as squared, snecked rubble in limestone. "Rubble" is the term for the variation of block sizes; "squared" is the description of the blocks cut in rectangular shapes and the "sneck" is the small stone used to make the different-sized stones fit together. The idea was to create an interesting texture, but the possibility of the stone-masons showing off their skills must be a factor in the development of this method of walling. These later Methodist churches were a good deal less austere in their architectural fancies than those of the early century. There is a splendid Methodist church in the southern town of Bantry and the church in Arklow, Co. Wicklow, is a glorious exercise in decorative granite.

32
PRESBYTERIAN CHURCH
COOTEHILL CO. CAVAN 1877

THE PRESBYTERIANS, in common with Methodists and Catholics, had emerged from the period when discretion as well as economic necessity kept their places of worship modest and even starkly simple. Like the Methodist church nearby, the Presbyterian church in the town of Cootehill could now afford to construct a building in beautiful stonework. Again, as in several good buildings in Cootehill, the materials are sandstone and limestone. Unlike the Methodist church, the limestone is in a random rubble (small stones fitted together in no particular pattern). This gives a more natural texture than the method used in the Methodist building and serves to emphasize the dressed stone in the corners and surrounds. The shaped stone corbels under the eaves are an elegant feature which became a favourite device for many buildings towards the end of the nineteenth century. The small five-light window is a gesture to the great mediæval abbeys and cathedrals, and the stone mullions are delicate and made to appear even thinner by the device of cutting the sharp edges to create a bevel or chamfer. The tiny oval window and the round openings cut in the pointed stone fanlight are notable features of this delightful building.

33

Quakers
MEETING HOUSE
CLARA CO. OFFALY MID-19TH C.

THE QUAKER meeting house in the village of Clara, Co. Offaly, looks more like a small country house than a church. Its secular character was in accordance with the democratic and non-conforming beliefs of the Quakers. The building has nevertheless been given a strong and definite architectural character with a beautiful stone façade in fine ashlar or square dressed blocks of stone. The round-headed windows are in the Italian style made fashionable in the mid-nineteenth century by the influential John Ruskin. The architect was J.S. Mulvany, famous for his design of railway stations. The great terminus at Broadstone in Dublin was his most celebrated work but he also designed the midland stations of Athlone and Mullingar. The village of Clara was the home of the Quaker Goodbody family who had a large jute-spinning business here. The family constructed houses for their workers and several houses for themselves in the village. The village of Castletown Geoghegan in Co. Westmeath is close by; this was also a Quaker village and had a milling operation. The well-known village of Ballitore in Co. Kildare was one of the first Quaker settlements in Ireland.

34

Celtic Revival

RATHDAIRE CHURCH OF IRELAND
BALLYBRITTAS CO. LAOIS 1883

THE CHURCH of Ireland at Rathdaire, just east off the main road to Portlaoise at Ballybrittas, Co. Laois, is one of the best examples of the revival of a so-called Hiberno-Romanesque architectural style which began in the second half of the nineteenth century. Drawing from the Irish Romanesque architecture of the churches, high crosses and even earlier Celtic artefacts, the movement was both nationalist and a reaction to eighteenth-century classicism and the later Gothic Revival.

35

O'GROWNEY TOMB
MAYNOOTH COLLEGE CO. KILDARE 1905

THE RATHDAIRE church represents one extreme of the Celtic Revival in architecture, with almost every surface covered in Celtic or Romanesque decoration. The entrance façade is modelled on the Romanesque façade of St Cronan's at Roscrea while the decorations and carvings are from a variety of sources including the early High Crosses. The Honan Chapel in Cork was also modelled on the façade of Roscrea. The architect for Rathdaire was James Fuller who was appointed in 1862 as architect for the Church of Ireland. In Fuller's church at Clane, Co. Kildare, the interior is a riot of Romanesque carving on the arches and column caps.

The minute O'Growney Tomb in the college graveyard at Maynooth, Co. Kildare, is at the other extreme of the Celtic Revival. The architect, W.A. Scott, adopted the stark simple style of the Irish Early Christian stone churches and monastic cells. Scott, however, was a proto-modern architect in a sense and his interpretation of the early style has more than a hint of modern abstraction in the simple geometry and the highly original tiny window and cross.

Timothy Hevey built a fine Hiberno-Romanesque Catholic church in the spectacular setting of Dunlewy, Co. Donegal, under the white quartzite cone of Errigal mountain. Completed in 1877, the church has a reproduction round tower as a belfry and this became a favourite Hiberno device for churches even as late as the 1950s when one appeared on the Catholic church on Merrion Road in Dublin. One of the earliest and possibly the best Celtic Revival churches is St Patrick's at Jordanstown, Co. Antrim, by the masterly W.H. Lynn in 1866. This Church of Ireland building has a fine round tower, high roof and superb round arches.

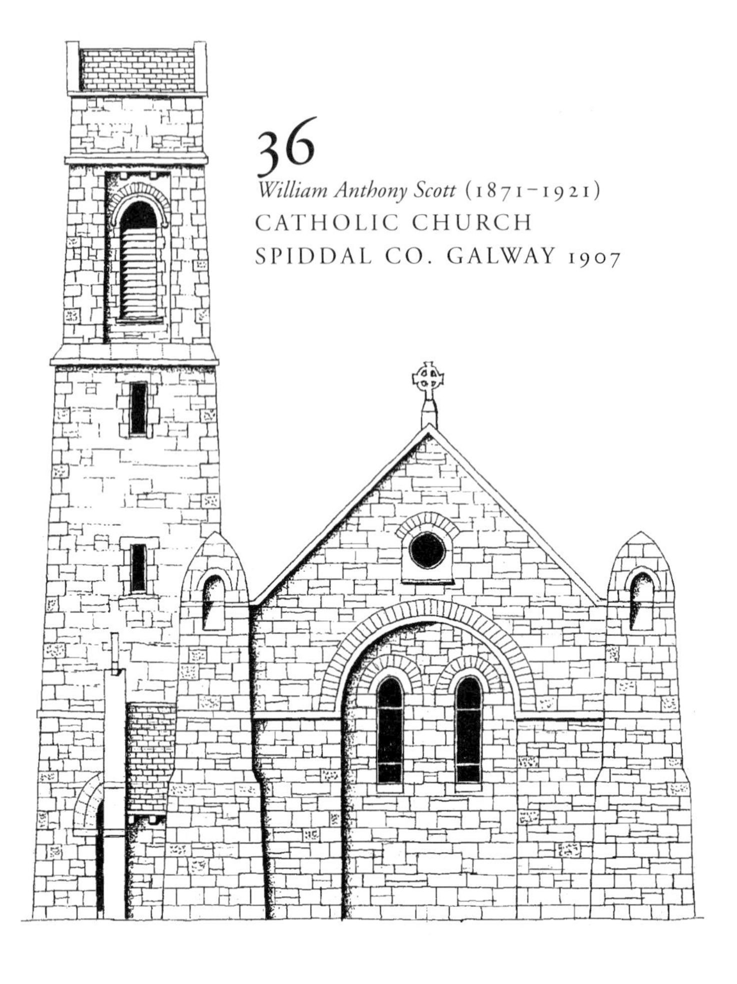

36

William Anthony Scott (1871–1921)
CATHOLIC CHURCH
SPIDDAL CO. GALWAY 1907

W. A. SCOTT was one of the most interesting architects of the early part of the twentieth century. His initial career in the *avant-garde* Fire Brigade branch of London County Council gave his work a contemporary flavour at the turn of the century. His church at Spiddal can be seen as belonging to the spirit of the Celtic Revival although Scott does not slavishly copy the Romanesque, as at Rathdaire, but adapts and abstracts the style in his own unique way, producing a building which can be appreciated as an introduction to the new century. The tower has accentuated a Hiberno-Romanesque batter. The strange piers have undecorated caps, like abstract early stone cells, and the rugged stonework seems highly appropriate to the site at the edge of Galway bay. Scott built a handful of other churches; a simple one at Monea, Co. Fermanagh, and others in Castleblayney, Co. Monaghan; Moore, Co. Roscommon, and at Edenderry, Co. Offaly. He was responsible for interior work at a number of other churches including the cathedral at Loughrea, Co. Galway. On the other side of the road from the Spiddal church Scott built the archway and gatelodge for Spiddal House and also extensions to the existing house. There are delightful, mediæval-style carvings by the sculptor Michael Shortall on the new arcades.

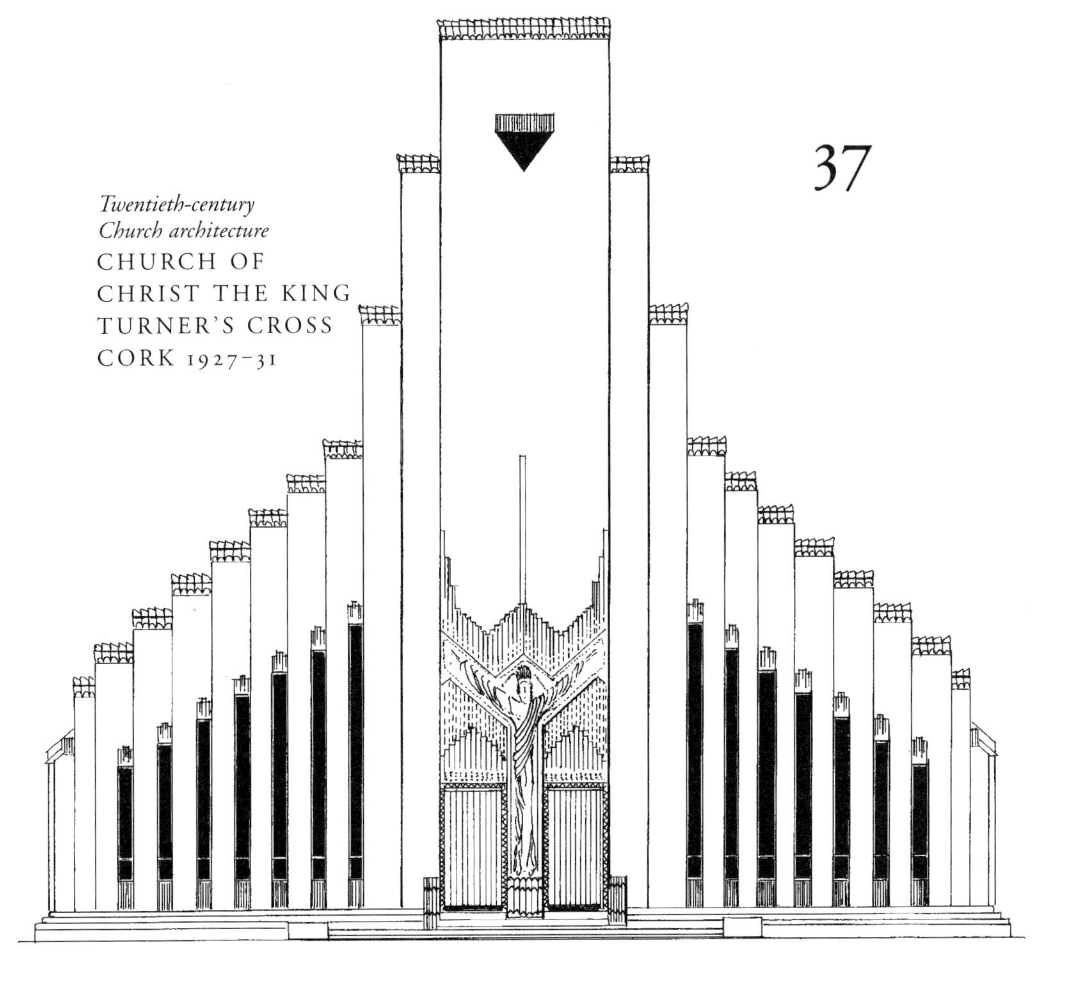

37

Twentieth-century Church architecture

CHURCH OF CHRIST THE KING TURNER'S CROSS CORK 1927–31

FOR THE first sixty years of the twentieth century almost all of the hundreds of new churches commissioned by the Catholic Church were traditional in plan and followed historical styles. The Gothic Revival died out in the early decades and there was a strong return to classical for the new great cathedrals at Cavan and Mullingar. The single, outstanding exception to the traditionalism of Catholic church design was the Church of Christ the King, built in a new suburb of Cork city. The architect was Barry Byrne of Chicago who had worked in the Oak Park studio of Frank Lloyd Wright from 1902 until 1908, a period of dazzlingly creative design which had a profound effect on modern architecture throughout the world. Turner's Cross Church was constructed of concrete and the radical plan produced a wide space without columns. Walls were replaced by closely spaced piers, and slit windows gave long shafts of light in between. Steel roof trusses support a false ceiling which is designed to create a dramatic focus on the altar. The style could be said to be Art Deco but this extraordinary design is better described as Expressionist and can be compared with new churches in that style of the 1920s in Denmark, the Netherlands and Germany. The sculpture around the doorways is also in concrete and is the work of the American John Storrs.

38

ST MICHAEL'S CHURCH
CREESLOUGH CO. DONEGAL 1970

CATHOLIC CHURCH architecture in Ireland began to change dramatically in the early 1960s when modern design was no longer frowned upon by the Catholic Hierarchy. One of the most interesting groups of modern churches in the country comes from the practice of Liam McCormick and his partners, and these are clustered mainly in the north-west. The church at Creeslough in the north of Co. Donegal is seen as a white curved shape, against a mountain backdrop. The main influence is from the famous pilgrimage church of *Notre-Dame-du-Haut* at Ronchamp by the great master of Modernism, Le Corbusier. This work had a powerful influence on modern church building worldwide after it appeared in the early 1950s. The irregular small windows filled with coloured glass, and the gargoyle delivering rainwater down the heavy chain to a water basin, are in the tradition of Le Corbusier.

Another beautiful church by the McCormick office is at Burt, just west of the city of Derry. This design echoes the shape of the ancient stone fort, the Grianán of Ailech, on a hill overlooking the new circular church with its curving copper roof and sharp spire. There are other churches by McCormick and Partners at Glenties, Lifford, Milford and Desertigney, all in Co. Donegal, and at Steelstown in Derry. The church at Garrison, Co. Fermanagh, is by Joe Tracey of the partnership. The interiors of most of these modern churches are worth visiting, not just for the architecture, but for the wealth of modern religious iconography in sculpture, stained glass, metalwork and textiles by a wide variety of contemporary Irish artists.

CASTLES AND FORTIFICATIONS

THE EARLIEST stone forts in Ireland belong to the Iron Age or even earlier but it is possible that these ancient structures, circular dry-stone enclosures, had more to do with prevention of theft of cattle than defence against military attack. The Anglo-Norman invasion of 1169 introduced a new architectural type – the castle as a defensive building and as a symbol of conquest or dominion. The first type of fort to be quickly erected by the invaders is known as a mote and bailey. A large mound of earth, the motte, was thrown up and a timber stockade on top protected the defenders while a larger enclosure below, the bailey, gave protection to the horses and cattle. There are several of these, now grass-covered hillocks, still to be seen in the countryside.

The thirteenth century was notable for the large number of great castles in stone which were erected throughout the country. Many of these had curtain walls with bastions to protect the walls and a inner keep or stronghold if the walls were breached. Some used natural features such as rocky escarpments or hilltops to reinforce the defences, as at Roche Castle in Co. Louth. Castles in towns were also built in this period, as in Dublin, Limerick and Kilkenny. Round bastions, at corners or flanking the gates, were a common feature of these early castles and the type lasted well into the fifteenth century.

Few castles were built in the fourteenth century but from the early part of the fifteenth a new type of small square or rectangular stone tower began to appear in most parts of the country. Today most of these are popularly called "castles" and are so designated on maps, but these structures were in fact fortified dwellings for the minor chieftains or well-to-do landowners. The term best used to describe one of these ubiquitous structures is a tower-house and an extraordinary number survive throughout the country. Only a handful have the original bawn or high wall which once surrounded them and the vast majority are seen today as romantic ivy-covered ruins, although many are in a good state of preservation.

A distinctive style of castle appeared in the north of the country at the beginning of the seventeenth century which became known as a

Plantation castle and this type was built by the settlers from Scotland and England. Tower-houses continued to be built well into the seventeenth century and the invention of firearms and artillery, which utterly changed the design of fortifications in Europe in the sixteenth century, had little effect on the standard Irish tower-house. The old round bastion had the effect of creating blind spots in the defence of the walls of castles and the angled or star-shaped bastion was introduced at the beginning of the seventeenth century, notably at Rathfarnham Castle, Co. Dublin. Square corner bastions, although less effective than the star shape, also became common at this time. There were a few unfortified houses built in the century, mostly in towns, but the dominant type was a semi-fortified one which took the form of a strongly built house with larger windows and corner towers or bastions.

By the latter half of the seventeenth century the danger posed by siege artillery ended the old style of castle with its high vulnerable walls. Forts were now sunk low into the ground with gun embrasures to cover every angle, and an elaborate system of dry moats or ditches, protective slopes known as *glacis*, and sometimes a network of outworks and gun emplacements were provided. Large numbers of these forts and new fortifications to principal towns such as Cork, Waterford, Derry and Limerick were planned or built in that century, a time of wars and massive destruction.

The eighteenth century was a more peaceful time and military activity was confined to barrack building in the early years. Towards the end of the century a new threat of invasion emerged when France went to war against Britain, then engaged in a war with the American colonies. An attempted French invasion at Bantry in 1796, when the force could not land due to unfavourable winds, and a small invasion at Killala in 1798, frightened the authorities so much that a huge new building programme of sophisticated fortifications was set in place. The purpose of these was to defend the coasts and the Shannon waterway, and the work lasted until Napoleon was safely incarcerated in St Helena. These vast military works were ignored by architectural historians until recently but they must offer a fascinating field of study and their very durability must ensure their survival.

After 1815 the main military activity lay in building strong defences and heavy gun emplacements at all of the great British naval anchorages and ports around the coasts. Three of these, Cork, Bere Haven and Lough Swilly, were held by the Royal Navy until 1938.

39

Stone castle

ROSCOMMON CASTLE
CO. ROSCOMMON 1269

THE GREAT thirteenth-century Norman castle at the edge of the town of Roscommon is fairly typical of the stone castles built during this century. It consists of a large quadrangle with round bastions at each corner. The most interesting feature at Roscommon is the twin-towered gate building shown in the illustration. The passage between the towers is long and narrow and easily defended. The cross-shaped narrow openings on either side of the entrance are known as loop-holes and at Roscommon these allowed a bowman to shoot arrows both outwards and downwards at attackers of the gateway. In 1580 there were many alterations, and the original defensive loops in the twin towers were enlarged to provide new stone-mullioned windows to more comfortable living quarters.

The largest castle of the time was at Trim, Co. Meath, where high walls with round bastions enclose a large area and a tall square keep stands in the middle. There is a splendid barbican gate, a typical defensive feature of the time which consists of a small tower built forward of the main gate and connected by an arched bridge to the main wall. Holes in the floor of the bridge allow the defenders to threaten any attackers of the gate from above. A good example of a thirteenth-century castle on a rocky escarpment is Roche Castle, Co. Louth. The most spectacular of the great early castles in Ireland, and one of the first, is Carrickfergus, Co. Antrim.

40

Town gate

ST LAURENCE'S GATE DROGHEDA CO. LOUTH 13TH c.

St laurence's gate in the large town of Drogheda is actually a barbican gate since it was built forward of the main entrance as an extra fortification. It now stands alone, a formidable reminder of the early walled town. Drogheda was walled on both sides of the river and parts of the old wall can be seen on the south side in the grounds of St Mary's Church of Ireland. The battlements on the gate are the stepped Irish variety.

Most of the coastal towns down the east coast of Ireland were enclosed by walls from the thirteenth century and later, including Carlingford, Drogheda, Dublin, Wexford, Waterford, New Ross and Youghal. In the west, Limerick and Galway were walled as were some inland towns such as Kilkenny, Athenry and Fethard, Co. Tipperary. No town has much more than fragments of wall, bastions or a few gates left today. The old walls of Athenry, Co. Galway, are amongst the best remaining examples. Wexford has several short stretches of the old wall to be seen and Reginald's Tower in Waterford was part of the town defences. The only almost complete walled town in Ireland today is the old town of Derry but the walls there are much later, dating from the first decade of the seventeenth century.

41

Tower-house

CLARA CASTLE CO. KILKENNY 15TH C.

CLARA CASTLE is situated about ten kilometres north of Kilkenny and is a perfect example of an Irish tower-house. This is one of the most ubiquitous types of old stone buildings to be found in the Irish countryside and although no comprehensive survey has been done, it is variously estimated that there are perhaps 2000 remaining in various states of ruin. The majority of these are found in the southern half of the country with very large numbers in counties Limerick, Clare, Galway, Tipperary and Kilkenny. Most of the tower-houses date from the fifteenth, sixteenth and the early seventeenth centuries.

The simple square plan of the Irish tower-house was little varied over several centuries and the tall fortified house at Clara is typical and one of the best preserved in the country. The ground floor was dark and defended by a few loops and a "murdering hole" over the lobby just inside the entrance. The main living-room occupies the whole of the top storey and there is a secret chamber, the entrance of which is disguised as a garderobe or lavatory seat! The original oak beams for the floors remain at Clara which is unusual and the walled forecourt, with numerous musket loopholes, is a good example of a feature missing from the majority of surviving tower-houses.

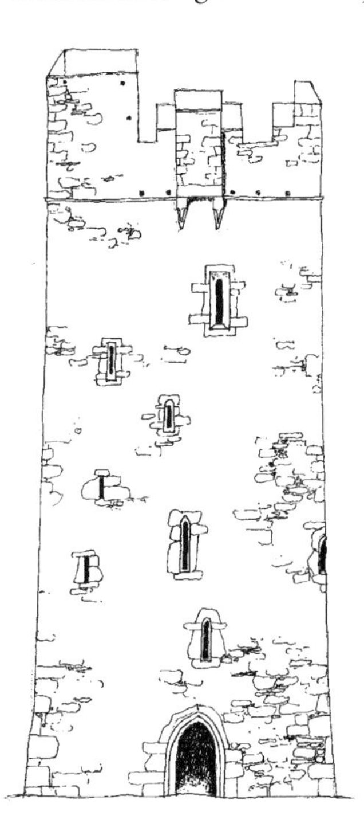

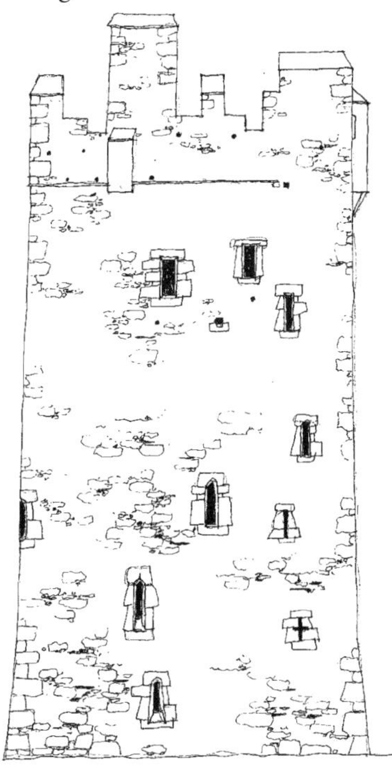

42

Castle

DOE CASTLE CO. DONEGAL 16TH C.

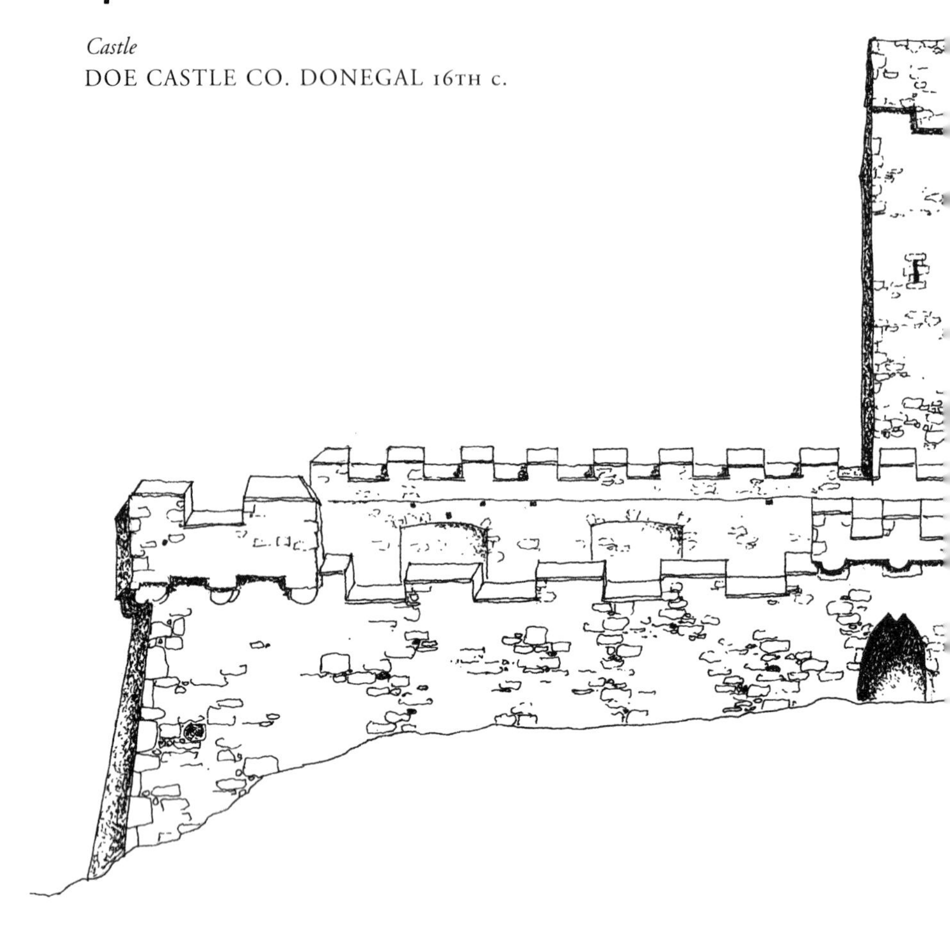

DOE CASTLE, near Creeslough in the north of Co. Donegal, is a perfect example of the romantic ideal of a castle. It is splendidly sited for defence on a little promontory of Sheephaven bay and protected by the sea, a rocky cliff and a ditch cut in the rock. Although quite small, the castle has a central keep, battlemented walls, corner bartizans and a fine round bastion. The keep, or central strong point for last-ditch defence, is four-storeys high and contained living quarters. Bartizans are features to reinforce the defence of the vulnerable parts of castles. Corner bartizans project out over the walls and allow the defenders to drop lethal objects down on attackers attempting to undermine the corners. The beehive-shaped structure is a casement or further strong point. From the middle of the sixteenth century, when the castle was built, this must be one of the most attacked, taken and retaken fortified places in Ireland. It is said that sailors from some of the wrecked ships of the Spanish Armada were given

refuge here in 1588 . The castle was captured by the Cromwellians in 1650 and finally by the Williamites at the end of the century. In the early nineteenth century the abandoned castle was acquired by a Captain Hart who converted it into a private residence. It was deserted again in 1843 and is now restored as a National Monument.

43

Tower-house
DRUMHARSNA CASTLE
ARDRAHAN
CO. GALWAY
16TH C.

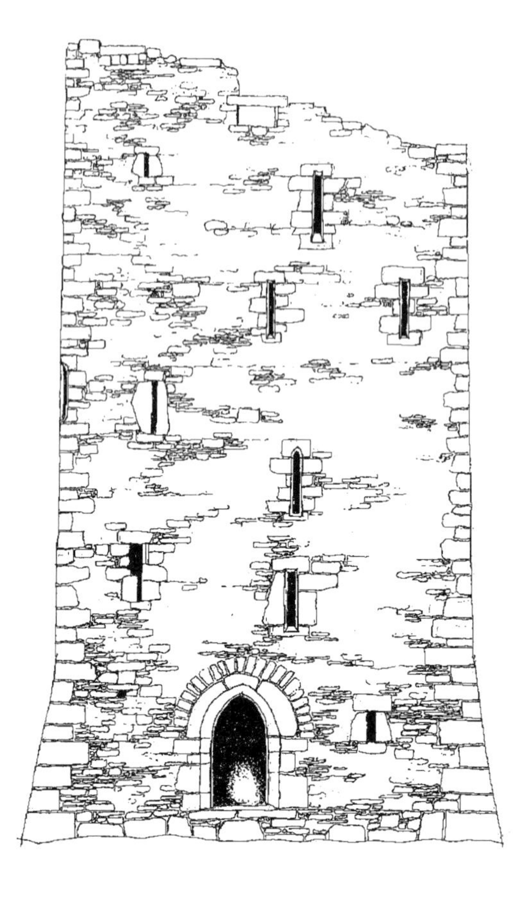

THIS TYPICAL tower-house of the sixteenth century can be found near the little village of Ardrahan on the Galway to Limerick road and about twelve kilometres north of the town of Gort. This is a small area which is thickly clustered with historical ruins, from pre-historic sites to castles, churches and houses. Drumharsna Castle was the home of Shane Ballagh in 1574 and this type of well-fortified dwelling shows how the Irish chieftains and landowners learned from the Anglo-Norman castle-builders the advantage of having a defensible home. This tower-house has five storeys and although the battlements are missing, the fine batter to the walls and the accentuated outward slope at the base make this building a striking feature in the landscape. The purpose of this widening at the base was to strengthen the lower part of the tower by thickening the masonry, thus making a breach of the wall more difficult. It had the added advantage that if stones were dropped from the battlements above they would bounce out with more force on any attacker. Co. Galway has a large number of castles, about 270, but Co. Limerick leads the way with over 400.

44

COOLHULL CASTLE
DUNCORMICK CO. WEXFORD LATE 16TH C.

THE MOST common type of tower-house in Ireland has a simple square or rectangular plan form. There are a few interesting variations of this plan and the splendid little castle of Coolhull in Co. Wexford is one of a type which consists of a high-walled oblong shape. The castle is about four kilometres west of the village of Duncormick which is in the south of the county. The curious slender tower at one corner is a defensive element with gun loops, and the round-headed windows in the main wall are to give daylight to the main living quarters which were on the first floor. Coolhull demonstrates a good example of the peculiarly "Irish" battlements with their stepped profile. The stonework is strong and unsophisticated, but with attractive window surrounds consisting of dressed stones of irregular shapes. Unusually deep bonding stones are used in the quoins or corners. There is a fine angle bartizan on stone brackets built onto one corner. The castle of Rathmachnee is similar in size and shape but has a more complete tower and a round bartizan. This can be found three kilometres north-west of the village of Killinick which is on the main road from Wexford to Rosslare harbour. There are some 130 castles in Co. Wexford. This number includes a few remains of the early motes built by the Anglo-Norman invaders who came ashore at Bannow bay in the south of the county in 1169.

45

THE WATERGATE
ENNISKILLEN CASTLE
CO. FERMANAGH EARLY 17TH C.

THE OLD town of Enniskillen was built on an island between Upper and Lower Lough Erne. The castle was constructed to defend the waterway between the two lakes and began life as an stronghold of the Irish clan of Maguire in the fifteenth century. After the Plantation of Ulster in the early seventeenth century the buildings were extensively modified and rebuilt by the new owner, Sir William Cole. In the late eighteenth century the castle became an artillery barracks. The original Maguire keep was built in the fifteenth century and after the castle was first conquered by Captain John Dowdall in 1594 the keep was reduced in size and converted into living quarters. The most spectacular remaining feature of the old castle is the watergate, beautifully located on the edge of the river. The strongly battered lower walls show the original form of the castle, while the tall round bartizans, with conical stone caps, are a Scottish feature. The method of pushing the bartizans out from the walls is called corbelling and has the effect of enabling the defenders to have a wider field of fire. It is likely that the windows and the bartizans date from the early seventeenth century. The castle is now home to a local museum.

46

Plantation castle

MONEA CASTLE CO. FERMANAGH

EARLY 17TH C.

A NEW TYPE of stronghold emerged in the early seventeenth century in the northern part of Ireland and became known as the Plantation castle. These defensive buildings originated with the settlers from Scotland and England, those who were given the lands confiscated from the native Irish clans after the Tudor conquest of Ireland. The majority of these settlers' castles are in the counties Fermanagh and Tyrone. The architectural feature which marks out the Plantation castle from others in the country is the Scottish turret which is corbelled out from the walls or towers. The Plantation castle of Monea, just north-west of Enniskillen, is one of the most complete and dramatic of the type. Monea is an oblong tower-house which was built in 1618 and was originally surrounded by a bawn or fortified wall, only a fragment of which survives. The circular tower bastions guard the entrance and square turrets are achieved at the top by the device of stone corbels. On the other side of the castle the corners are defended by angle bartizans, also corbelled out. Many of these so-called Plantation castles were little more than bawns or fortified enclosures which were hurriedly built in the early seventeenth century to consolidate the captured lands. The picturesquely sited Benburb Castle, Benburb, Co. Tyrone, is a large bawn and stands on a steep cliff above the Blackwater River, presenting a large number of gun loops to the landward side.

47

Transitional

LEAMANEH CASTLE
COROFIN CO. CLARE 1480–EARLY 17TH C.

THROUGHOUT the centuries of stone castle building in Ireland there were many modifications to the strongholds and fortified dwellings which are widespread throughout the land. Apart from the obvious alterations to details like the defensive loops to cater for the invention of firearms, more peaceful intervals tempted the castle owners to make their stark residences a little more comfortable. The defensive loops at higher levels were widened to let in more daylight and this insertion of real windows gave many of the gaunt stone towers a flavour of domestic normality. The most startling juxtaposition of a fortification combined with an almost normal house is Leamaneh Castle in Co. Clare, on the road between Corofin and Kilfenora. The tower of 1480 had a large mansion built on to it in the early seventeenth century to cater for the desire for more comfort and a fashionable architectural style. Defence was, however, not completely forgotten with the bartizan built out over one corner. This was the castle of Conor O'Brien and his redoubtable wife Máire Ruadh whose names are on the original gate, now removed to nearby Dromoland Castle. A legend concerning Máire tells that after her husband was killed by the Cromwellians she married one of the conquerors to keep her lands. She is said to have subsequently kicked him out of a top-storey window when he insulted her dead husband!

48

Fortified mansion

PORTUMNA CASTLE CO. GALWAY 1618

At the end of the sixteenth century and into the first decades of the seventeenth a number of new large buildings appeared in Ireland which, although still fortified, looked more like large mansions than castles. The characteristic features of this special group usually consist of a rectangular or square central block with large bastions on each corner. Portumna Castle is typical of this group of fortified houses and was built in 1618 for the Earl of Clanricarde. The simple square corner towers signal the concern still with defence and gun loops protect the main entrance. The circular porch seen in the illustration was added in the eighteenth century. The battlements are now little more than decoration and the tiny "Jacobean" gables are adorned with slender pinnacles crowned with balls. The house was accidentally burned in 1826 and is now being restored as a National Monument.

Similar fortified great houses are Kanturk, Co. Cork, of 1609 and Burntcourt, Co. Tipperary, of 1640. Glinsk Castle, Co. Galway, is a smaller version of the fortified house where corners are protected by little bartizans. Two of the most splendid examples of the type, Rathfarnham Castle, Co. Dublin, of 1590 and the Bishop's Palace at Raphoe, Co. Donegal, although designed as mansions, are more like great forts since the corner towers are built as angled bastions, a feature of military architecture.

49

Artillery fort

CHARLES FORT KINSALE CO. CORK 1677

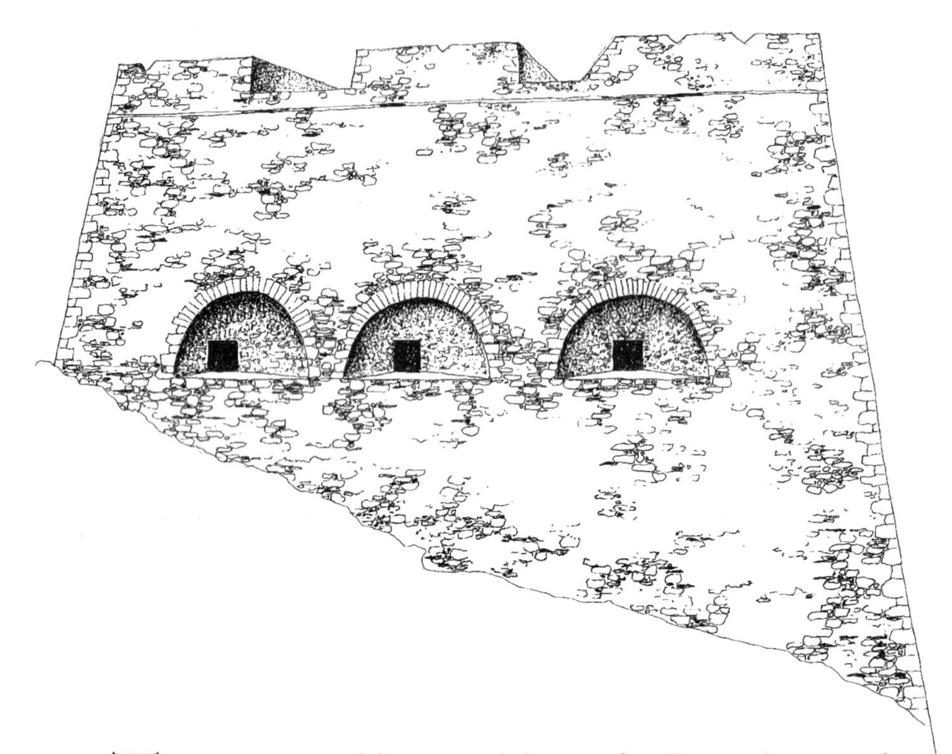

THE INVENTION of firearms and the use of artillery in the sieges of castles forced fundamental changes to the design of fortifications. The high mediæval curtain walls were abandoned in favour of lower and massively thick bastions surrounded by deep ditches. The walls are now steeply battered to deflect cannon shot and the defensive works on plan have a star shape to provide an intricate and interlacing field of defensive fire. Since artillery is also used for defence, the old-fashioned battlements are replaced by casements at lower levels and gun embrasures in the thick parapets.

The huge fort at Kinsale, known as Charles Fort, was begun in 1678 and was designed by the Surveyor-General of Ireland, William Robinson. The fortification was to defend the approaches to the harbour and also to resist a land attack. The grimly military character of Charles Fort is very evident on the landward side but the seaward aspect presents an altogether more dramatic and picturesque prospect. The bastions are sharp cornered and sweep up from the water's edge in steep angles. On one corner, jutting out into the sea, is a little turret which acts as a sentry outlook and is known as a *guérite.*

GATEWAY CHARLES FORT
KINSALE CO. CORK
EARLY 18TH C.

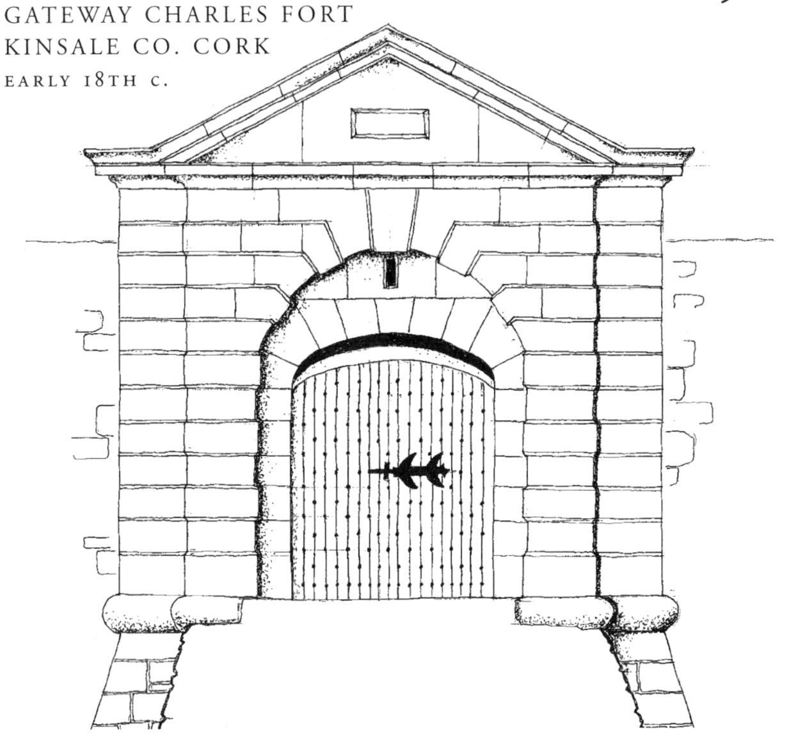

THE ENTRANCE to the fort was approached by a ramp and a drawbridge over the ditch and the robustly detailed classical gateway and arch was added in the early eighteenth century. Inside the ramparts extensive barracks buildings were built and the fort remained as a military installation until 1921. Although Charles Fort was primarily intended to command the approaches to the harbour it would naturally have to resist attack from the landward side. Since there is higher ground here the fort was vulnerable to a land attack, but a proposal to build another fort on the high ground was never carried out. In 1690 during the war between the Jacobites and the Williamites – the forces of King James and the Prince of Orange – the fort at Kinsale, in Jacobite hands, was besieged. The Williamite attack was on the landward bastion and the fort surrendered. It was reported at the time that there were 94 cannon in Charles Fort. During the seventeenth century – a century of wars using great artillery – many towns in Ireland, including Derry, Dundalk, Athlone, Limerick, Clonmel and Thurles, were fortified with bastions and earthworks, and forts were built or expanded to protect Waterford harbour, Cork harbour, Bantry, Valentia and Crookhaven in the south. A significant feature of the fortifications of the seventeenth century was that foreign military engineers, mainly French, were brought in to design and supervize the works.

51

Military barracks

GLENCREE CO. WICKLOW 1803

AFTER THE Treaty of Limerick in 1691 and the defeat of the Gaels there was a hundred years without war in Ireland. The main military activity was the construction of a vast network of barrack buildings to consolidate the conquest of the whole island. These were mainly to resist attacks by rebel or guerrilla groups and were concentrated in towns, passes and river crossings, but the coast was not neglected as the threat from the French was growing in the eighteenth century. Over ninety new barracks for cavalry and infantry were built by the first decade of the century and the ruins of many of these survive today.

The barracks at Glencree in Co. Wicklow was one of a special group built to counter a particular threat. The Irish rebel leader Michael Dwyer continued to hold out in the Wicklow mountains after the end of the Rebellion of 1798 and the authorities determined to invade his stronghold. A plan was drawn up to build a road right through the centre of the mountains from just outside Dublin and to construct a string of military barracks along the route. This became known as the Military Road and barracks were built at Glencree, Laragh, Drumgoff and at the end of the road at Aghavannagh. An outlier barracks was built in the Glen of Imaal at Leitrim. Originally the buildings were defended by outer walls with pointed bastions but most of these no longer exist. The buildings at Glencree and Aghavannagh (now a youth hostel) are mainly intact, and ruins of the others remain.

52

Fortified barracks

SHANNONBRIDGE CO. ROSCOMMON – CO OFFALY 1811

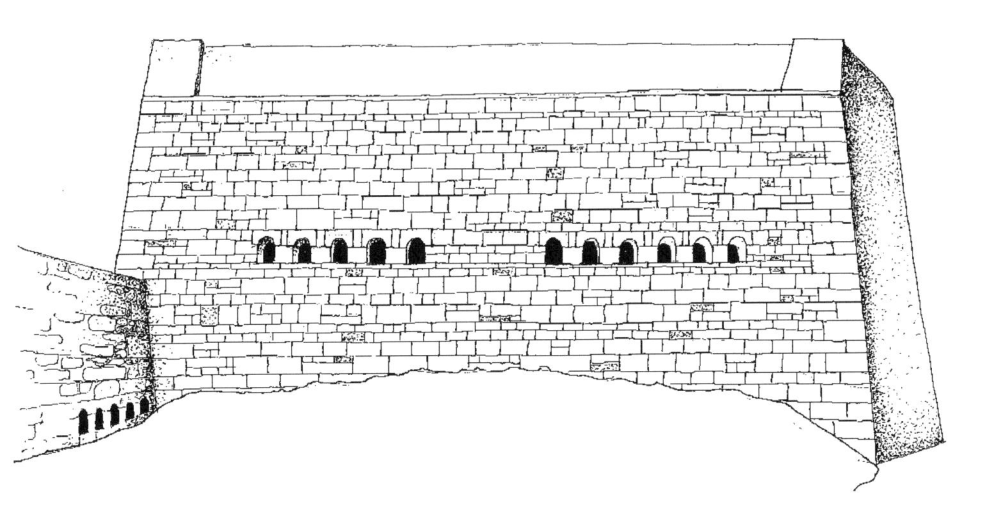

AFTER THE outbreak of war with France in 1793 a new, immense and frantic programme of military fortifications began around the coasts of Ireland and along the river Shannon. This great river effectively divided the country along an east-west line and the threat of a possible French invasion in the west, reinforced by an Irish uprising in support, made it vitally necessary to secure the river crossings. The massive structure on the west bank of the river at Shannonbridge is a combined barracks and a battery and it forms part of a remarkable fortification where the design is based on artillery defence. This military work began in 1804 and is known as a *tête-de-pont* or a bridgehead fortification. The works are in the shape of a triangle with the base on the end of the bridge and the barracks building shown is one of two flanking fortifications on each side. At the point of the triangle is a gun battery known as a redoubt which is surrounded by protective ditches. Just downstream at Keelogue is another battery with a dramatic blockhouse, all in a good state of preservation. Nearby, on Cromwell's Island, there is a Martello tower which housed three guns on a trefoil platform at the top. Around the coasts, extensive defence works were constructed on Lough Swilly, Galway bay, the Shannon estuary, Bantry bay, Cork and Waterford harbours. In all of these locations there are a fascinating collection of early nineteenth-century fortifications of Napoleonic times.

53

Martello tower

SANDYCOVE, CO. DUBLIN 1804

IN 1794 a small tower fortification, with just three guns, on Cap Mortella in Corsica fought off a strong attack by a British navy thirty-two-gun frigate. The powerful opposition which the tower had offered greatly interested military engineers and the Martello tower was born. As a significant part of the response to the Napoleonic threat a large number of these fortifications were built, mainly on the east coasts of Ireland. Most of the towers were circular with massively thick walls of tightly fitted squared blocks of granite and a pronounced battered profile. The thick parapets were sloped to deflect shot and the platforms at the top had revolving traverses for the guns. Braziers were built into the parapets for the purpose of heating red hot shot. This could strike terror into the crews of wooden ships which had canvas sails and decks caulked with pitch. The mediæval style machicolations over the high doorway, which was reached by ladder, was for defence of the entrance if the invaders had succeeded in landing. The Martello towers are thickly clustered on the coast north and south of Dublin, with some sixteen south of the capital and twelve to the north. The Martello towers in Bantry bay and Cork harbour are of a different design and, having only a slight batter, look less formidable than the east coast towers. The most famous Martello tower is at Sandycove, Co. Dublin, and is now the James Joyce Museum.

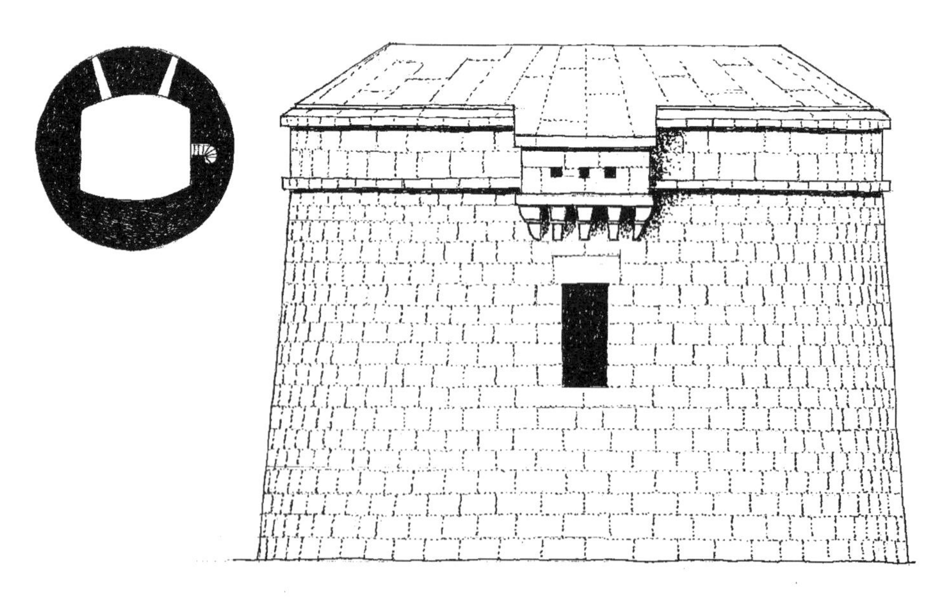

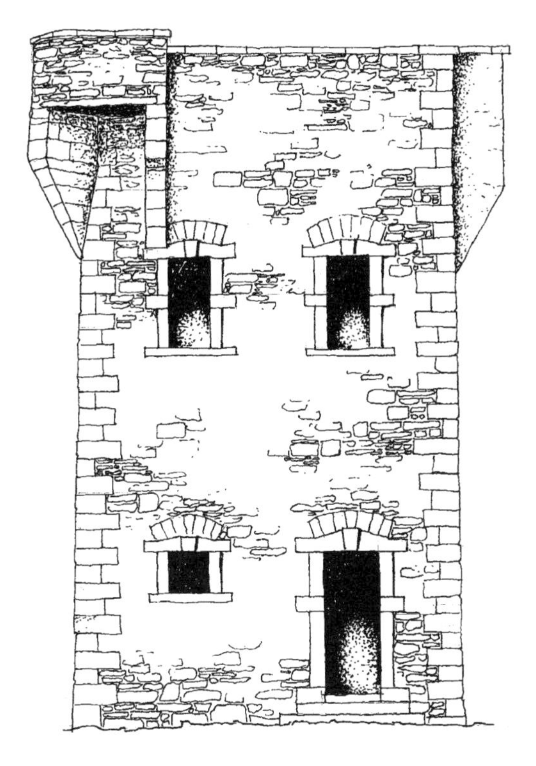

Signal tower
DROMORE WEST
CO. SLIGO 1805

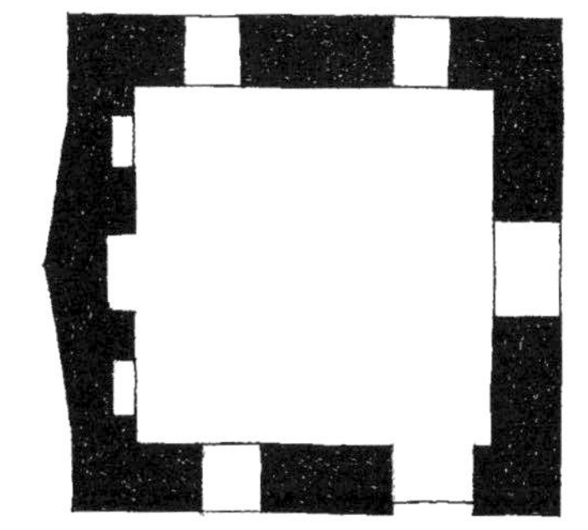

AN ESSENTIAL component of the widespread network of coastal fortifications was an efficient communication system. The French are credited with the invention of a signalling or telegraph method based on the use of poles with moveable arms which could be arranged in certain positions giving coded messages. These signalling positions had to be placed on prominent hills or headlands in sight of each other and where the signals could be seen with telescopes. The method used in the Irish posts was a tall mast on to which balls and flags were hoisted to give the coded signals. A square stone tower, designed to be defensible, was built alongside the masts to house the signallers. These were generally two-storeyed and provided with bartizans to protect the corners, door or windows. It is highly unlikely that these little structures could have provided any significant defence and the almost mediæval features were more likely intended to give a forbidding military character to the works. The tower at Dromore West is just twenty-six kilometres west of Ballysadare. Signal towers were built all around the coasts of Ireland from Dublin to Malin Head in Donegal. In some parts the towers were quite closely spaced, particularly on the south-east coast. Most of these military structures still exist, many picturesquely sited on lonely headlands, reminders of the importance of naval power in the eighteenth and early nineteenth centuries.

55

Police barracks

BALLYDUFF CO. WATERFORD 1869

IN THE LATER nineteenth century, when the large number of soldiers in Ireland was reduced, some of the military barracks built earlier were converted into barracks for the constabulary. Two of the most notable of these were Glencree and Aghavanagh in Co. Wicklow. Most of the ordinary police barracks were undefended but the Fenian uprising of 1867 saw many attacks on the Royal Irish Constabulary and this stirred the authorities to action. The Office of Public Works in Dublin (known at the time as the Board of Works) was ordered to plan a number of specially designed police barracks which could withstand attacks by insurgents who would have been armed mainly with hand weapons. The Jacob brothers, J.H. and E.T., produced a number of designs of barracks with strongly military features. The civil servants, however, were apparently shocked at the probable high cost of these elaborately detailed buildings and only a handful were built. The former RIC barracks at Ballyduff, Co. Waterford, has slim battered bastions, with bartizans, sited on opposite corners. The prominent musket loops are placed to allow for firing downwards at any attacker and the windows have no projecting sills, again to allow direct shooting down to the ground. The former RIC barracks of 1871 in Dungannon, Co. Tyrone, has a magnificent, fortress-like tower with stepped gables which dominates the town centre.

HOUSES

THE EARLIEST houses in Ireland were made of wood and only archæological evidence survives of housing in the Neolithic period. The thousands of raths or ring forts which are still visible in the countryside were inhabited well into the first millennium and the houses inside these protective banks were mostly circular huts of wooden posts and wattle walling. The vernacular cottages and small houses which remain, albeit in dwindling numbers in the countryside, have evolved from the small stone houses of the mediæval period.

The vernacular houses of the north, west and southern regions of Ireland were almost all single storeyed, although in some areas a second storey was added in more prosperous times. Along the east and in the midlands the two-storeyed vernacular house is more common. Even in the villages and towns the single-storeyed cottage often lined whole streets and a few rare examples of these early, traditional, town-houses survive. While most landowners, great and small, lived in fortified tower houses right up to the end of the seventeenth century, the small single-storey house with a thatched roof remained the dwelling of the ordinary family.

Unfortified houses were scarce in the sixteenth and seventeenth centuries, except in the defensible towns, and only a handful survive today. The more peaceful eighteenth century saw the rise of the great country house and the power and influence of the large estates. The classical language introduced by the architects of the country houses had a pronounced influence on the architecture of the smaller dwelling in both town and countryside, and the elegance of the large mansions was reflected in the simple rhythms and proportions of the Irish streetscapes. Two- and three-storeyed houses began to appear in the towns and the planned village was a notable addition to the landscape of the great estate. Architects now were increasingly involved in the smaller dwelling and a variety of designs resulted as the nineteenth century dawned.

The Industrial Revolution spawned a new range of housing. The railway companies built whole rows of small terraced houses for their workers following the example of the earlier canal companies with their houses for the lock-keepers and cottages for the rail crossings. The new middle-class industrialists, millowners, distillers and brewers housed their workers near their enterprises and many of these mass-produced dwellings still exist. Stone was still the main building material but increasingly walls were plastered, principally for the purposes of weatherproofing, but also to allow for economical decorative details and colour washes. The end of the nineteenth century saw the rise of social housing as the state assumed responsibility for the needs of landless people. The earliest examples of these were stone and brick-built cottages in towns and villages; the larger council estates were born later.

The twentieth century saw the emergence of suburbia and an explosion in the number of new houses being built.

56

Vernacular house

GWEEDORE CO. DONEGAL

THE TRADITIONAL HOUSES of the remote north-west of Ireland were moulded by the wild and rugged landscape and the ferocity of the Atlantic gales. All of these houses were rectangular and narrow, just one room deep. The narrow plan was mainly due to the scarcity of timbers for roofing and since only relatively thin poles or timbers salvaged from the ocean were available, the roof spans were inevitably small. These vernacular houses hug the landscape and seem part of it and, in Co. Donegal in particular where the winds were strongest, the thatched roof is held down by ropes tied into stone brackets or pegs built in to the walls. Invariably in the most exposed areas of Co. Donegal and all along the west coast the side walls are taken up as gables which could withstand gale-driven rain more effectively than the hipped roof. The traditional single-storey house tended to expand longitudinally with either extra rooms or animal quarters added on to the ends thus producing the typical "long house". An intriguing feature of the vernacular house in the north-west and west of the country is the bed "outshot", where a small projection in one outer wall could accommodate a bed, thus freeing up the floor space. Rough stone was always used for the walling in these areas and in later years plaster or many layers of whitewash made these simple dwellings stand out in the savage landscape. At one time a broad-coloured band, often blue, was painted around doors and windows but this practice has virtually died out although a few examples may still be found.

57
TAGOAT CO. WEXFORD

A GREAT NUMBER of the surviving thatched traditional houses of Ireland can be found in Co. Wexford. The region known as the Baronies of Bargy and Forth which are in the extreme south-east of the county is of special interest. A distinctive style of traditional building has emerged here from the first settlers in mediæval times after the Anglo-Norman invasion. The houses, outhouses and farm buildings tend to be grouped more formally, sometimes as open courtyards, than the more randomly placed vernacular houses of the west and north-west. The hipped roof is now the commonest feature in an area where wind speeds are far lower and the thatch can be taken down at the sides in a more snug fit. In the case of this little house at Tagoat, near Rosslare, the hip thatching is neatly trimmed in a curve to give a satisfactory façade to the road. The prominent round gate-posts are typical in Co. Wexford and a simple explanation can be offered for their great size and round shape. It is far easier to build a pier to a circular plan when the only material is rough stones of irregular shapes than to form vertical corners for a square pier. The large size means that the weight of the hanging gate can be balanced. The Mourne country in Co. Down is another area where large round gate piers are a characteristic feature of the traditional farm and dwelling.

58

BALLYCANEW, CO. WEXFORD

THIS TYPICAL house of the east coast is one of a group of little cottages forming the tiny village of Ballycanew in north Co. Wexford. This was originally a three-roomed house with the living-room flanked by bedrooms on each side. The simple projecting porch is a common feature of the vernacular houses of the east of the country. The thatch is taken down over the gable walls to form a steep hip, a device which not alone looks well but also insulates the house more efficiently. A wide variety of materials was used for thatching in Ireland but in the east the most common was wheaten or barley straw. Reeds, which are a superior material for roofing are available also in this region of wide rivers and marshes. The thatching, begins at the top of the walls and the bundles of straw are laid overlapping until the ridge is reached. In the eastern counties the ridge is often finished with a roll or twist of dense material and, as here illustrated, the ends are finished with a straw bobbin. Instead of ropes to hold down the thatching the method in the eastern regions allowed the use of flexible hazel rods to pin the thatch to the roof. This is sometimes given a decorative effect along the ridge or at the hips. Many of the villages of Co. Wexford have surviving traditional houses, and good examples may be seen in nearby Blackwater and Screen.

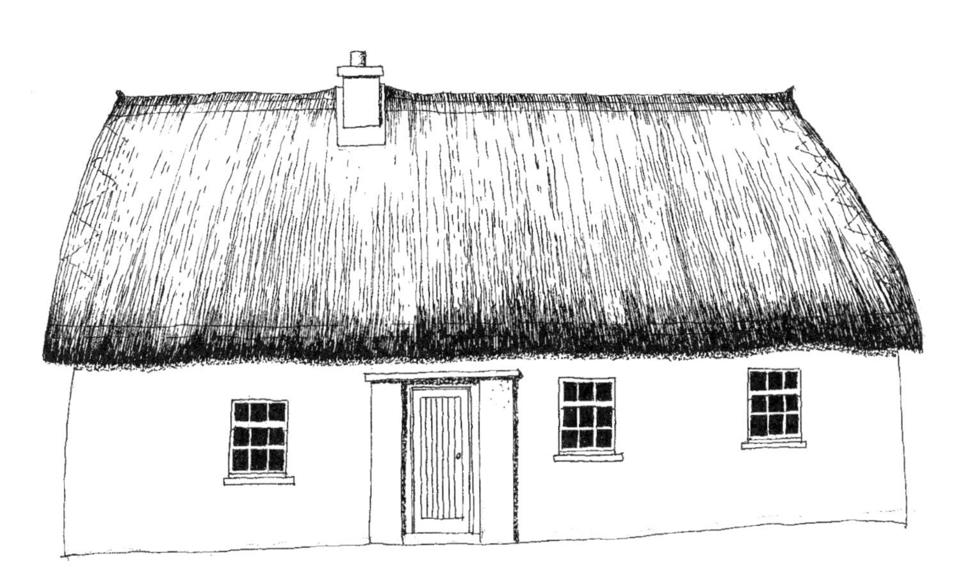

59
MOHILL CO. LEITRIM

MOST OF THE early vernacular houses of Ireland, particularly along the poorer coasts from west Cork to the north-west of Donegal were one-roomed, single-storey dwellings. The two-storeyed version was either a later development of the old house or the home of a more prosperous farmer. The upper rooms were partly contained in the roof space and, in the more sophisticated two-storeyed houses of the south-east, the windows were in the form of attic lights or dormers with the roof thatch neatly trimmed around the openings. The window arrangement in the house in Mohill appears haphazard but was simply a response to the plan of the room behind. The half door had the advantage of allowing more daylight into the living-room and serving the purpose of keeping farm animals or poultry outside. It also allowed conversation with passers-by when the house was in a village street. In the example shown a small byre was housed at one end and the bedroom area was built over this, a device which was common in the western parts of the country. Co. Leitrim is far enough west for the problem of high winds to ensure that gables are used instead of hips. The thatch is firmly held in place with stone and mortar bargeboards finishing the tops of the gables. The windows are plain up-and-down sash types and the original glazing would have consisted entirely of small panes as larger glass sizes were far more expensive and unavailable in rural Ireland until well into the nineteenth century.

60

Post office
TARA CO. MEATH

THE OLD post office at Tara, Co. Meath, was a substantial two-storey house in this most prosperous farming region of Ireland. The midlands as well as the county of Wexford were the areas where the more wealthy smallholders could afford to build these larger houses with their barns and byres built separately, usually around a farmyard. Although stone was the most widespread building material for walls, the use of mud or clay, a method called tempered earth, was common except in the regions of most extreme weather conditions in the west. Mud-walled two-storeyed houses are a feature of Co. Meath and are even more common in Co. Wexford where the earth is well suitable for use. The walling material was prepared in a pit and mixed with water and straw or rushes, trampled down and then the mixture was used to build up the wall in layers. The resultant walls were very thick and in some parts this meant that a distinct batter or slope was given to increase the wall stability. Although these mud-walled buildings can have a long life (some have existed since the seventeenth century), the walls deteriorate quickly when the house is abandoned and the roof caves in. The chamfered corner shown on the right of the drawing is an interesting feature which can be seen on many traditional buildings. It was a protective detail to prevent damage to the corner from the large protruding axle-hubs of wheeled farm carts.

61

Pub

RATHMOLYON CO. MEATH

THIS SMALL public house and shop was typical of the early shops of Ireland. These were not purpose built but were housed in ordinary dwellings with the minimum of advertisement of their special function. A nameboard with painted or projecting plaster letters was considered the only concession to commercial use. In this example, from a quiet Co. Meath village, a further spectacular device was added to the older thatched vernacular house in the nineteenth century by painting on decoration to the quoins and the plinth. This elaboration was an imitation of diamond-pointed rustication, a stone-carving detail, to give a three-dimensional effect in paint. At one time this tradition of paint imitating stone was widespread in Ireland and used mainly on pubs. Whole front façades were sometimes covered in the pattern which was almost a Post-Modernist use of the classical language. In the most restrained use of the technique the only colours used were black and white but more exuberant and exotic combinations of colours and tones were also popular. A few examples of this folk art still exist and can be found mostly in the southern half of the country. The village of Rathmolyon was close to the great mansion of Summerhill, built in the 1730s to the designs of the celebrated architects Sir Edward Lovett Pearce and Richard Castle, and it would seem likely that this classical work would have inspired the humble vernacular artisans. Summerhill was totally destroyed in the 1950s.

62

Shop pub
KINGSCOURT CO. CAVAN

CARTLAN's general store in the village of Kingscourt is a good example of the substantial two-storeyed thatched houses which made up most of the main streets of Irish villages and small towns in the late eighteenth and nineteenth centuries. The more dynamic businesses catered for most needs under the same roof. The bar was on one side of the main shop while on the other side everything from food to farm implements, boots and all items of hardware were stocked. Shopping could be a day's outing for the family and the bar provided the relaxation, for the men at least! The arched opening provided access from the street to the storage yard at the rear and these arches are a characteristic feature of many Irish towns. The rest of the building consisted of the family home and "living over the shop" was commonplace until the late twentieth century. The more orderly arrangement of windows in the façade of Cartlan's, combined with the painted quoins, show the strong influence of the eighteenth-century classicism of the great houses. The builders of the vernacular houses and shops adopted the proportions and details of the formal architecture but often adapted it in delightful ways. The use of colour was quite restrained in the northern counties and one strong hue for the woodwork of doors was often considered sufficient. In the southern regions a more liberal use of several colours was accepted.

63

Town house

ROTHE HOUSE KILKENNY 1594

A FEW examples of unfortified sixteenth-century houses still exist and most of these are in towns which would have been well defended. Rothe House in Parliament Street, Kilkenny, is probably the finest of these. It was built for John Rothe, a wealthy Catholic merchant, and the stone-carved plaque on the front bears the name of the owner and the date of 1594. The centre opening of the arcade leads to a small courtyard and Rothe built another house and a further court in the rear of this elongated site. The steep-pitched roof, shaped chimneys, front gable and small-paned windows are all typical features of the architecture of the sixteenth century. The central window, which is well bracketted out, is called an oriel and lighted the most important room in the house. The two openings to the right in the arcade have had shop windows inserted in modern times, and although Rothe also had a shop on the ground floor it is likely that it would have been set back to give the arcade more prominence and practical use, as in the market houses. The Shee Almhouses, also in Kilkenny, and Lynch's Castle in Galway, are other good examples of houses of the sixteenth century.

64

Country house

BEAULIEU CO. LOUTH LATE 17TH C.–1720

THE GREAT MANSION of Beaulieu, just six kilometres north-east of the town of Drogheda, was traditionally believed to have been built by Sir Henry Tichbourne about 1660. Sir Henry was instrumental in the defeat of the Ulster chieftain Sir Phelim O'Neill in 1642 and was given the lands of the Plunkett family as a reward. The house was extensively altered from 1710 to 1720 by a son of Sir Henry and recent research supports the view that the present house may date from this period. The style of architecture of Beaulieu, however, is very much of the earlier period and such a time-lag was not uncommon in Ireland. The high-pitched roof with the projecting eaves, dormers and elaborate brick chimneys are mainly of Dutch origin and typical of the architecture of the seventeenth century. The illustration shows the west or entrance front and the main wall surfaces are rendered in plaster with light red brick trims to the windows and door surrounds. Brick was a new material in Ireland at this time and its import could be attributed to the Dutch influence. The architect for the later works at Beaulieu was John Curle. Eyrecourt, Co. Galway, now in ruins, was built in the late seventeenth century and was similar in design to Beaulieu. The most splendid surviving, unfortified, house of the late seventeenth century is Richhill Castle, Co. Armagh, built in 1670.

65

Almshouse

SOUTHWELL GIFT HOUSES, KINSALE CO.CORK 1682

THE SOUTHWELL Gift Houses in Kinsale are a group of almshouses built in 1682. In the more enlightened post-mediæval times, ideas of charity and housing the "deserving poor" became fashionable and almshouses of simple construction and accommodation, but in the architectural style of the times, were built in many parts of the country. The earliest almshouses built in Ireland were at Youghal, Co. Cork, and completed in 1634. The Kinsale houses are an interesting little group of buildings arranged around three sides of a rectangular yard. A detached two-storeyed house is the centrepiece of the composition and stands on a higher level, denoting the superior status of the supervisor. The stone walls of this house are plastered and this emphasizes the extraordinarily elaborate design of the brick porch. This is complete with Doric pilasters, a cornice and little pinnacles, all carried out in moulded brickwork, a technique rare in Ireland. A large, deeply recessed plaque is set above the door, containing the Southwell charity coat-of-arms and the date of 1682. The windows, with single mullions, transoms and diamond panes of glass, are typical of eventeenth-century and Jacobean architecture. The quite formal courtyard is entered through a pair of iron gates, set between ornamental piers, and the front of the yard is closed by a simple random rubble wall.

66

SOUTHWELL GIFT HOUSES, KINSALE CO.CORK 1682

THE LOWER LEVEL of the courtyard is flanked by two ranges of single storey houses and these must be amongst of the earliest examples of the semi-detached dwelling type in Ireland. Frugal use of the attic space is made possible by the use of dormer windows and each of these is provided with a neatly curved roof. The elevations of these little houses are carefully designed to make a single composition since the semi-detached housing type always presents a problem of duality. The pairs of central dormers and windows are grouped close together to make a satisfactory resolution of the dilemma. The walls are built of local stone in what is known as the random rubble fashion where stones of unequal shapes and size are used to create an interesting texture. The problem of making precise vertical corners and window and door openings was overcome by the careful selection of thin flat slabs. Skiddy's Almshouses in Cork city were built in 1719 and took the form of two-storeyed arcaded buildings around a courtyard. Small dormer windows were used to light the attic space in the high-pitched roof. The Southwell Charity also built a splendid set of almshouses in Downpatrick, Co. Down, in 1733. These were combined with a school forming a classical composition and may have been the work of the celebrated architect Sir Edward Lovett Pearce, while probably predating him. A large range of almshouses was erected in Mitchelstown, Co. Cork, in the mid-eighteenth century and today form part of a large formal square.

67

Country house

SHANNONGROVE CO. LIMERICK 1709

MUCH OF the Irish landscape was transformed in the eighteenth century by the development of the large estates and the building of the country house. These ranged from the largest mansions, like Castletown in Co. Kildare, to much smaller versions of the type as at Shannongrove in Co. Limerick. This early eighteenth-century house is situated about sixteen kilometres west of Limerick, on the south side of the Shannon estuary. The style is largely of the previous century with the high-pitched roof and above all, the gigantic brick chimneys. The sculptural effect of the diaper-patterned stacks again demonstrate the Dutch influence. The walls are plastered but the doorways, one at the front and another at the rear, have beautifully carved limestone surrounds. The architect of Shannongrove was one of the Rothery family of architects, sculptors and craftsmen who were active in the area. Other houses by the Rotherys are Riddlestown in north Co. Limerick and Doneraile Court in Co. Cork. Damer House in Roscrea, Co. Tipperary, has a staircase which is similar to the one in Shannongrove and may also be a Rothery design. The most beautiful of the Rothery houses, by John and his son Isaac, is Mount Ievers, just north of Limerick at Sixmilebridge in Co. Clare. The accounts of this building survive and show that the house cost £1,478. 7s. 9d., plus a few extras such as "Two horses which I gave Rothery"!

68

WESTPORT HOUSE CO. MAYO 1731

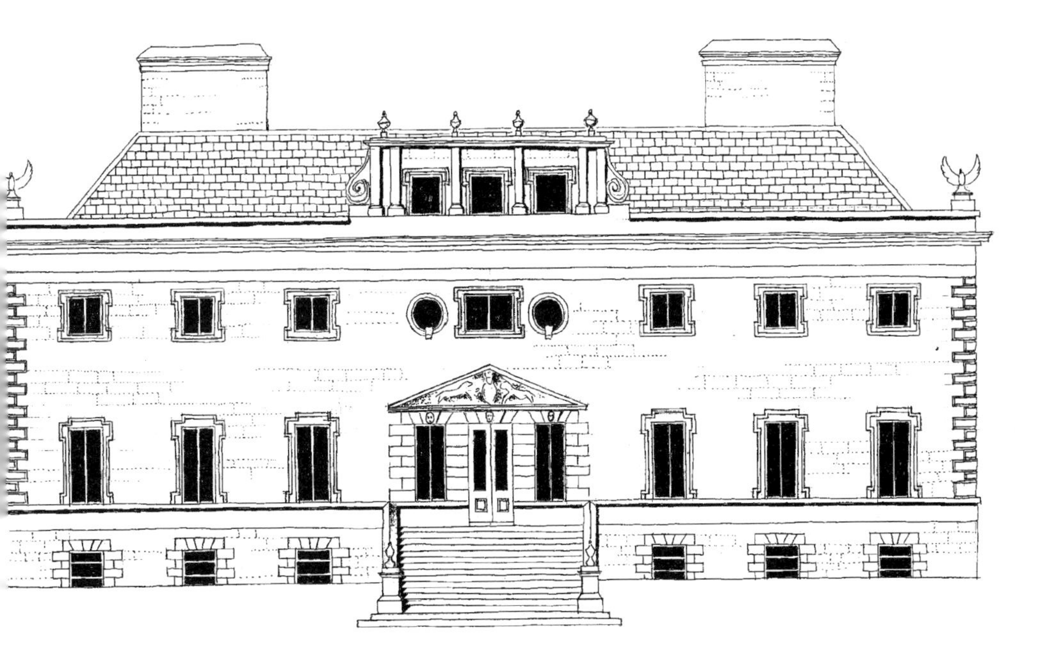

WESTPORT HOUSE stands on high ground in a magnificent parkland setting close to the shores of Clew bay. The drawing shows the entrance front of this large stone house which was designed by Richard Castle and built in 1731, one of Castle's early works. The beautifully proportioned elevation has the main living-rooms taken up above a basement which is half sunk into the ground. This principal floor level is known as the *piano nobile* and was a favourite device of eighteenth-century Irish architecture. It had the advantage of giving wide open views out over the estate and a sense of importance to the arrival point at the main door. The façade is built of finely dressed stone blocks of regular shape, known as ashlar work. The tripartite arrangement of door and window openings in the centre of the façade is used in many of Castle's designs. Below the pediment and over the door there are carved masks of satyrs. Later building resulted in a square block with a court in the middle which was roofed over in the nineteenth century. The interior of the house and some later remodelling are by James Wyatt, who was commissioned for the work in 1781. The landscaping of the house is one of its great attractions. A lake on the garden front was formed by widening the original river and the building is approached along a winding drive with tantalizing glimpses of the house. Westport House and gardens are open to the public.

69

Irish Palladian Richard Castle (1691-1751)

BELLINTER CO. MEATH 1750

IRISH EIGHTEENTH-CENTURY architecture was strongly influenced by the work of Andrea Palladio (1508–80). One of the most notable practitioners of Irish Palladianism was the architect Richard Castle. The architectural style known as Palladianism was characterized by a formal geometrical layout, a restrained use of ornament and a reliance on beautiful proportions. Although Bellinter, just south of Navan, Co. Meath, is actually a relatively small house, it is made to appear quite grand by the flanking pavilions on each side, connected by low arcaded ways. Curved walls hide the yards on each side and, decorated with stone niches, create an imposing approach to the main entrance. The main walling is in rubble work but the quoins, string courses, cornice and openings are in carefully dressed stone. This is the local blue-grey limestone which is hard and dense and allows for sharp-edged carving. The Gibbs surrounds to the door and windows exploit the nature of this material to great effect. In the Irish Palladian house the façade and its proportions have now assumed particular importance. The roof is almost hidden away behind a parapet in the form of a classical cornice so that the rhythm of windows and the relationship of solid to void can be played to the full. Bellinter was restored in recent years and now functions as a conference and retreat centre.

Richard Cassels was born in Germany in 1691 and when he came to Ireland in the 1720s he changed his name to Castle. Castle was one of the most prolific architects of great houses during his relatively short working life in Ireland. He died in 1751. Powerscourt House, near Enniskerry, Co. Wicklow, was the grandest of Castle's country houses and although partly destroyed by fire in the 1960s the façades and flanking buildings still stand and dominate a romantic landscape of Italian gardens and woodlands which can be visited by the public. Castle remodelled this house for his patron Viscount Powerscourt from 1731 to 1740, while for the Earl of Kildare he completed Carton, Maynooth, Co. Kildare. In Dublin he was the architect for Leinster House, now the Dail, and the superb town houses, Tyrone House, Marlborough Street and Number 85 St Stephen's Green, which has been beautifully restored. Russborough, near Blessington, Co. Wicklow, is another good example of Irish Palladianism by Castle and again this house is open to the public.

The most splendid of all the great Irish country houses is Castletown, Celbridge, Co. Kildare. This masterpiece was the prototype of all of the later designs in Ireland which consisted of a central block and flanking, linked pavilions. The architect for the central block, completed about 1720, was the Italian Alessandro Galilei (1691–1737) and the pavilions were the work of Sir Edward Pearce in 1730. Castletown is in State care and is open to the public.

70

PORT HALL
LIFFORD CO. DONEGAL 1746

MOST COUNTRY houses of the eighteenth century were relatively small; many were in effect large farmhouses but designed in the favoured classical style. Port Hall at Lifford, Co. Donegal, is typical of these smaller country houses. It was designed by Michael Priestley and built in 1746 and the style is eminently plain and even austere. The importance of the entrance is emphasized by the simple device of slightly projecting the central bay forward and embellishing it with prominent quoins, matching the main corners. The central bay is then topped with a pediment-type gable and the semi-circular window which enriches this is known as a Diocletian window. The walls are plastered, which strengthens the rugged appearance of the stone Gibbs surrounds to the door and windows. The basement at Port Hall is hidden behind a wall and the principal rooms are located as usual on a *piano nobile,* which in this case is only slightly raised. Almost all of the Irish country houses, even those of the smaller size, were built over a basement. As well as the sense of importance which the raised entrance proclaimed, the basement had the practical value of housing kitchens and servants. The garden front faces the river Foyle and two separate, two-storeyed buildings flank the main house. These were used by the first owner, John Vaughan, as warehouses for his business as a merchant.

71

SUMMER GROVE
MOUNTMELLICK CO. LAOIS *c.*1760

SUMMER GROVE, three kilometres from the town of Mountmellick, was built for a family of Huguenot origin named Sabatier. The largest Huguenot settlement in Ireland was at nearby Portarlington. The house has the older type roof with eaves rather than the more usual parapet of the times. This eaves has a prominent bell-cast, an interesting architectural device to make an overhanging roof appear to sit more comfortably on the walls. Unusually there is no basement although the entrance is on the normal *piano nobile* and at the rear of the house a third floor has been fitted within the same overall height. The projecting front has the characteristic Palladian architectural arrangement of tripartite doorway, Venetian window overhead and a Diocletian window in the pediment. The doorcase is strongly detailed in stone and the windows have flat-arched type lintels and prominent keystones. The keystone over the doorway is huge and greatly exaggerated and appears to hang over the entrance. The walling technique is unique since very small squared stones are used which give the appearance and scale of brickwork and tend to make this quite small house look larger than it actually is. Summer Grove is in private hands and well maintained. There is an excellent view of the house in its setting from the main road.

72

Gothic castle

MARKREE CASTLE COLLOONEY CO. SLIGO 1802

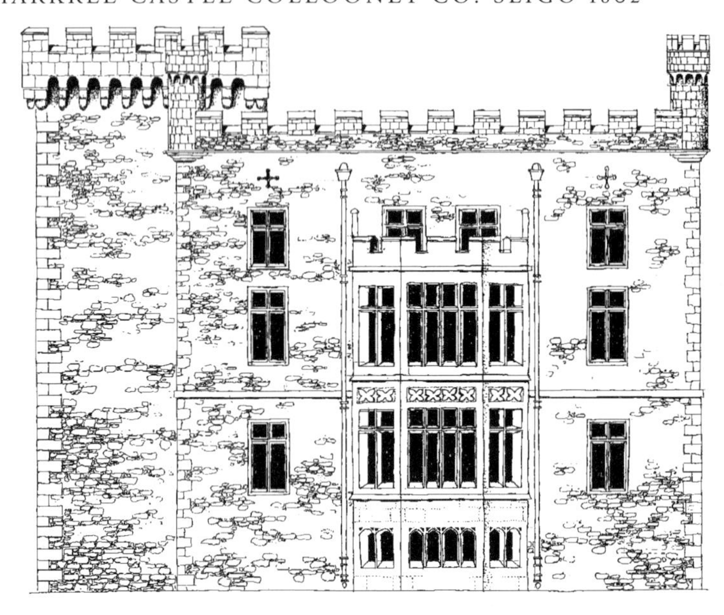

IN THE EARLY years of the nineteenth century there was a fashionable interest in the picturesque which resulted in a growing movement to convert existing classical houses into imitation castles of the mediæval period. The landscape of Ireland was dotted with picturesque ruins of castles and deserted monasteries and the romantic vision of these encouraged country-house owners to gothicize and castellate their strictly formal, classical, buildings into fantasies of the Middle Ages. In 1802 Joshua Cooper commissioned the architect Francis Johnston to enlarge and convert his classical house at Collooney, Co. Sligo, into a Gothic castle. Battlements, machicolated towers, corbelled turrets, arrow loops, Gothic windows, splayed stone mullions and transoms all combined to give the desired flavour of antiquity. The new castle was built in rough random rubble stone but the projecting window bays were in a finely dressed limestone. The building was enlarged and altered again in 1866. The romantic image of the castle was further enhanced by the building of several Gothic entrances to the estate. The castellated entrance from the main Sligo-to-Boyle road is one of the most impressive of these mediæval revival gateways in Ireland. In 1801 Francis Johnston designed one Gothic castle, Charleville Forest, Co Offaly, as a completely new building. The earliest experiment in this revival of Gothic for a great country house was Slane Castle, Co. Meath. This was begun in 1785 to the designs of James Wyatt and completed in the early nineteenth century by Francis Johnston.

73

Town house

BIRR CO. OFFALY EARLY 19TH C.

THE SEVENTEENTH-CENTURY Birr Castle in Co. Offaly was the seat of the Earl of Rosse and under his influence the town of Birr was laid out in the late eighteenth and early nineteenth centuries. From a central square, well-laid-out malls are lined with neatly proportioned terraces and houses in a simple eighteenth-century classical style. The Oxmantown Mall has splendid terraces of three-storey stone houses, each with an elegant fanlight over the entrance door which is flanked by Tuscan columns. There are a number of detached town houses in Birr and the building illustrated demonstrates the strong influence of the architecture of the Classical great house on the dwellings of an emerging middle class. As in many of these smaller houses of the eighteenth and early nineteenth centuries, the grand gesture is reserved for the entrance. This one is particularly resplendent with the solid panelled door set between traceried sidelights and a graceful, elliptical, fanlight overhead. Plaster and sand roll-shaped mouldings are used to frame the doorcase and give importance to the ground-floor windows. The quoins are straight from the classical great house and are in the robust rusticated form. This is the technique of chamfering the joints of the bonded stones to create a frame for the façade of the building. Birr Castle is the home of the famous astronomical telescope built in the 1840s which, until 1917, was the largest in the world.

74

Rectory

MULLINGAR CO. WESTMEATH 1815

In the late eighteenth and early nineteenth centuries the clergy were often provided with purpose-built accommodation close to the church buildings. This rectory was built in 1815 to serve the Church of Ireland, All Saints' Church. The rectory is an excellent example of the language of eighteenth-century architecture being reduced to its barest essential elements to produce a modest dwelling in satisfactory style. The façade is the plainest possible but perfectly proportioned with the *piano nobile* over the half-sunken basement. The composition is serenely balanced with the three-bay arrangement and the closely paired chimney stacks. The architectural display is severely restricted to the doorway and rationed here to a round fanlight, pilasters and curving iron handrails. The delicate tracery of the fanlight is the only frivolity allowed; an entirely acceptable façade for the reverend householder.

The Mullingar Parish Church of All Saints was built in 1813 as a Board of First Fruits Church. It was extensively altered in 1861 by the firm of Welland and Gillespie and again in 1878 by Sir Thomas Drew.

75

WESTPORT CO. MAYO EARLY 19TH C.

THE LITTLE rectory in Westport dates from the early nineteenth century and demonstrates the slackening of the discipline of classical correctness in this period. The fashion of reviving Gothic details is now creeping into simple domestic buildings and can be seen in the pointed arched window openings on the ground floor. It is possible also to surmise that the designer was making a mildly humorous reference to the religious connections! The walls are in local stone built in the economical technique of random rubble but still carefully selected here to provide a surface of lively texture. The formal dressed-stone window and door surrounds point to a building of some importance in the community. The strong architectural character of this small building is typical of Westport, a town planned from the outset. The powerful and dominating presence of Westport House and the Marquesses of Sligo ensured the building of a well-planned town to serve as a satisfactory entry point for the great estate. The planner was possibly James Wyatt, one of the architects of Westport House, and the work dates from 1780. The Carrowbeg River was canalized for a stretch and formal tree-lined malls were laid out on each side with graceful, curved, stone bridges connecting the banks. The buildings all conformed to a simple classical formula which could include shops and houses within a harmonious framework.

76

ERGANAGH MOUNTJOY FOREST CO TYRONE. 1836

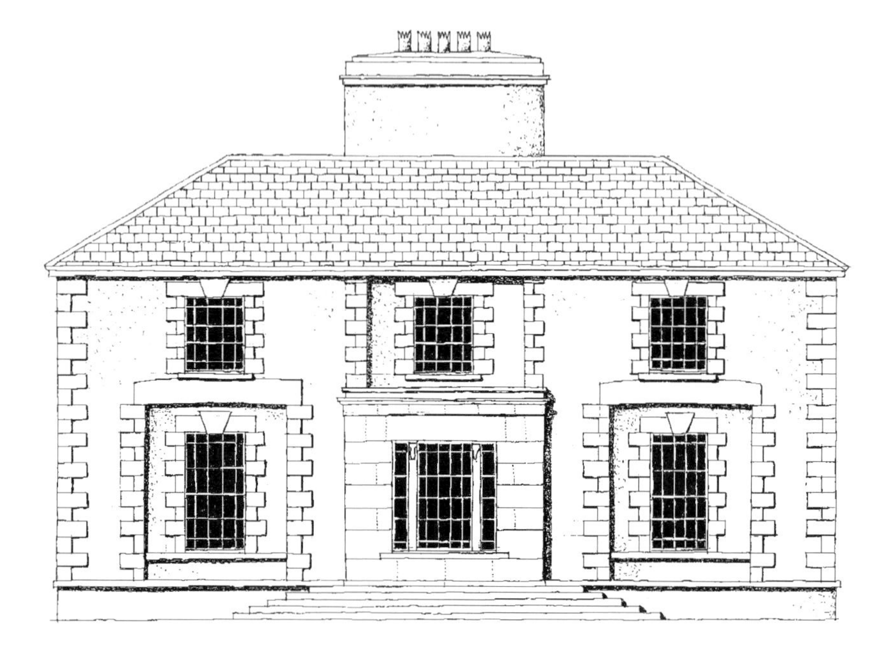

THE RECTORY of Erganagh is situated just north of the substantial town of Omagh in Co. Tyrone. The style of this house is far removed from the usual restrained and plain version of classical which seeks to blend in with the surroundings. Here is a muscular and demonstrative interpretation of the style, almost a Renaissance palazzo! This is still a small building but the gigantic, bombastic, central chimney stack and the heavily rusticated framing to the windows make this a piece of architecture to be noticed. Every feature is heavily overstated, as in the contrived recessed panels to the ground-floor windows and the huge stone lintels in dressed limestone. The architect for the rectory was probably William Farrell, a Dublin architect who had many commissions in the north-west of the country. He designed several rectories in the same massive style as the Erganagh building.

One of the earliest rectories in Ireland is near the interesting old village of Drumquin, some ten kilometres south-west of Mountjoy Forest. This house dates from 1762 and the tiny village has no less than six churches, one ruined, in Drumquin or nearby. The district known as Mountjoy Forest was originally the site of a great forest planted by Luke Gardiner in the late eighteenth century. Only a fragment of this remains today.

77

Roman Catholic presbytery

SKIBBEREEN CO CORK. LATE 19TH C.

AFTER CATHOLIC EMANCIPATION in 1829 the new churches of the majority faith in Ireland spread rapidly throughout the country. The housing of the clergy close to their churches was now common and these ranged from simple buildings in the plain classical style to large parish priests' houses in Victorian brick and stone. The presbytery in Skibbereen in Co. Cork was built to serve the Pro-Cathedral on the other side of the street and the style, a Victorian interpretation of earlier classicism, matched the classical language of the church. The lower windows and the entrance door have segmental roll mouldings and the glass panes are in the fashionably larger size of the later nineteenth century. The twin, narrow, chimney stacks are paired close together and with the hipped roof give this little building a sophisticated and composed look. The façade is neatly ordered and proportioned by the devices of horizontal string course, the plinth at the bottom and the carefully paired timber brackets at the eaves level. The quoins are in the almost mandatory rusticated stone form: a hallmark of Irish eighteenth- and nineteenth-century architecture, whether formal or vernacular, and created in either stone, plaster or paint.

78

Sexton's house

TULLOW CO. CARLOW MID-19TH C.

IT WAS A common practice for the Church of Ireland to construct schools for the parish close to the church building. A house for the schoolmaster was also sometimes added and here in Tullow, Co Carlow, a separate dwelling was included for the sexton. Most of the smaller churches for the Church of Ireland built at this time were in a sober and plain version of Gothic and the ancillary buildings were usually given a few details to match the dominant church. Here at Tullow, instead of the usual Gothic embellishments, the style chosen is the later Elizabethan. This is mainly manifest in the diamond-paned windows with the stone hoods. The unusually large ashlar granite masonry on the front section of the house is a strange contrast to the humble rubble walling for the rest. Its use could hardly have been to impart importance to the sexton. A more likely explanation is that these were stones left over from a larger job and were acquired cheaply.

This Elizabethan Revival style was a favourite of the architect Frederick Darley, who had been appointed architect for the Dublin Archdiocese. His most interesting neo-Elizabethan work is the nearby mansion of Coolbawn, near Enniscorthy, Co. Wexford, now sadly ruined. There are other Tudor Revival buildings in Co. Carlow as several architects of this period played with the style, the house in Tullow known as Ballykealey, now a hotel, being one, Dunleckney another. Carlow Railway Station (illus. 178) is the most spectacular and accomplished of these sixteenth-century revivals.

79

Vernacular house

LOUTH CO. LOUTH MID-19TH C.

ONE ENDURING LEGACY of the classical architecture of the great houses of Ireland in the eighteenth century was the extension of the discipline of classical proportions to the humble dwellings of the ordinary folk. A more entertaining legacy, perhaps, was the borrowing of classical details to embellish the new house for the artisan, farmer or shopkeeper. This sturdy two-storey house in the ancient village of Louth, in Ireland's smallest county, is a simply proportioned block and the classical window relationships have been retained even though the openings have been widened. The box-like mullions contain the weights for the up-and-down sash windows and the narrow sidelights continue the classical proportions. The bullseye window is an amusing copy of an eighteenth-century architectural device, often used to punctuate the centre of a triangular pediment over a main entrance. Here it merely lights the staircase and the deep recess demonstrates the thickness of the wall. The stone boundary in front of the house is a good example of this vernacular craft which is widespread in Ireland and such a distinctive part of the landscape. The stones used for the rubble walling are laid horizontally but for the coping the stones point sharply upwards. This could be to deter trespass but is more likely to be considered an ornamental feature.

80

Town house

DURROW CO. LAOIS LATE 19TH C.

IN THE LATER part of the nineteenth century the restraints of classicism were being shaken off and architects experimented with a wide range of revival styles from past ages. The Gothic, Tudor, Jacobean and Italian pasts were all plundered for new styles and motifs. The sheer austerity of the plain classical country house was to be rejected in favour of lighter, more florid and more frivolous decoration for the ordinary house-owner. Italianate decoration, which up to now was restricted to the interiors of the country house, began to appear on the façades of quite everyday houses and village shops. The ability of cement or lime and sand plasters to achieve nice decorative effects cheaply proved an enormous attraction. There were many craftsmen in the country who could offer their individual designs and the work of the same person can often be observed throughout a particular region. It was in the southern half of the country that the practice of plaster decoration was most common, particularly in the south-west, and many examples can still be seen. The doorway of this house in the village of Durrow is specially fine, with the plaster arch matching the delicate fanlight.

81

BUNCLODY CO. WEXFORD 1911

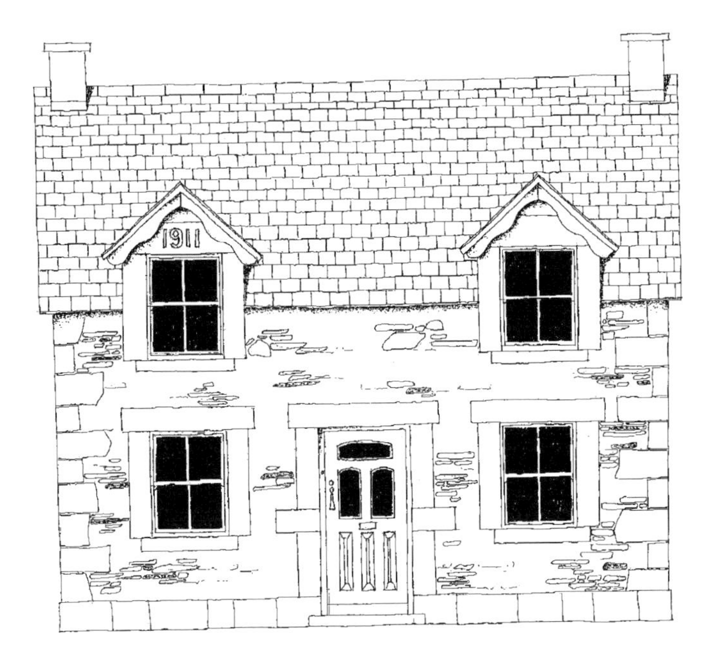

THIS TINY TOWN house in Bunclody, Co. Wexford, demonstrates that by the beginning of the twentieth century it was becoming increasingly desirable to give architectural importance to even the most plebeian of dwellings. Enormous efforts are made here in Bunclody, a little settlement which was formerly called Newtownbarry, to achieve grandeur. The accommodation is minimal, consisting of two rooms upstairs and two downstairs. Economy is served by squeezing the bedrooms into the roof space but the dormer windows are liberal in size and are given decorative bargeboards. The main walling is in the usual random rubble but each opening, window, dormer and door is framed with smoothly dressed stone blocks. The large size of these single stones for the side of each window and dormer is generous to the point of extravagance. Carefully selected blocks are used for the quoins and plinth and the whole superb stone composition is stamped triumphantly with the date! Improving landlords, increasingly in the nineteenth century, were anxious to build higher quality housing for their tenants, as much for the good of the leaseholders as for the soundness of the investment. The legacy of this policy can be seen today throughout the whole country. There are considerable numbers of these solid and beautiful stone houses surviving and the type is particularly abundant in estate and market towns.

82

County Council cottages
BALLYBODEN
CO. DUBLIN 1905

FROM THE END of the nineteenth century the State, through the various municipal authorities in the cities and towns and the councils in rural areas, increasingly assumed responsibility for the housing of workers and the landless. The cottages in Ballyboden, now a suburb of Dublin, are typical of a large number of well-designed dwellings constructed in the first decade of the twentieth century in the south of the county. The single-storey versions, sometimes detached but mostly in semi-detached types, are usually faced totally in stone. The two-storeyed type usually has a buff-coloured brick facing to the upper floor. The stone is the local

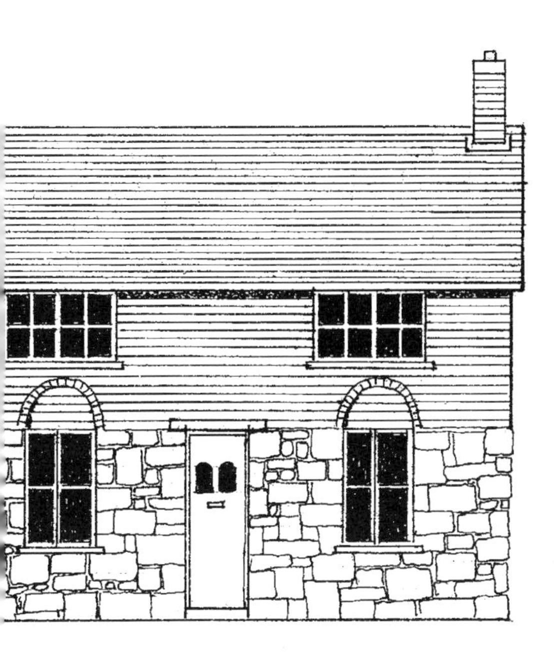

granite which was freely available in the early years of the century and the technique of masonry used is known as snecked squared rubble. The "sneck" is the small stone used to complete the pattern when unequal blocks are used together. The architect for these council houses was T.J. Byrne who was appointed by the South Dublin Rural Council to provide workers' housing in the county areas, then outside the city. A reflection of the somewhat pious, social evangelizing of the times was the instruction to provide large, narrow but long gardens at the rear so that the industrious council tenant could grow his own vegetables.

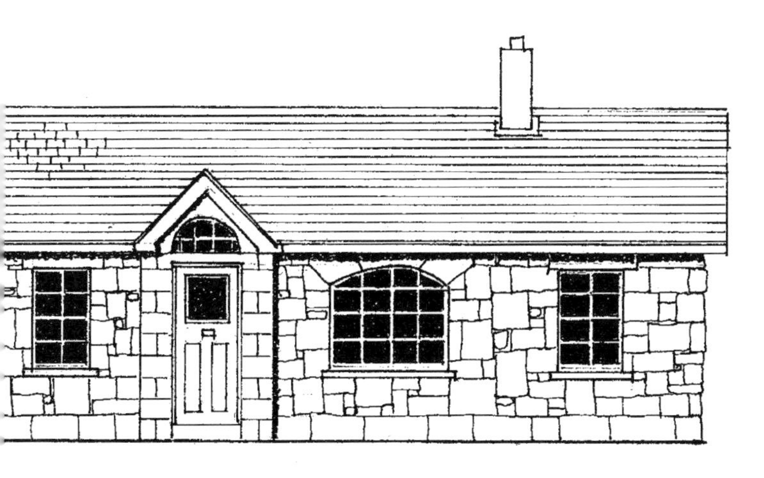

83

Sir Edwin Lutyens (1869-1944)

LAMBAY CASTLE LAMBAY ISLAND
RUSH CO. DUBLIN 1905–12

LUTYENS, ONE of the most celebrated architects of the first half of the twentieth century, designed just one country house in Ireland, which, with its integration of buildings, gardens and landscape, is among the most sublime of all of his creations. The ruins of a minute fifteenth-century castle formed the centre of a great, circular, double rampart and the new buildings were organically disposed around the converted fortification. Most of the new accommodation is arranged around the kitchen court, here illustrated. The Arts and Crafts movement of the end of the nineteenth century is evident in the sweeping clay-tiled roofs and rubble stone as well as the asymmetry of a picturesque vernacular. The gardens within the ramparts are a combination of formal planting, semi-wild landscape and tightly compartmented outdoor spaces. The stone used for the buildings was quarried on the island and is a blue-green porphyry shot with feldspar crystals. Elsewhere on the island Lutyens designed the Guest House, cottages for the farm staff, a boathouse, a chapel and rackets courts. The famous Gertrude Jekyll designed the planting.

At nearby Howth Castle, Lutyens carried out alterations and designed a new tower. His gardens at Heywood House, Ballinakill, Co. Laois, have recently been restored. The Irish National War Memorial at Islandbridge in west Dublin is one of his finest works: a tranquil, architectural garden above the dark-flowing river Liffey.

84

Suburban house

MOUNT MERRION CO. DUBLIN 1934

THE INDUSTRIAL REVOLUTION may have spurred the fast growth of cities and towns, but the twentieth century saw the eruption of the phenomenon of suburbia. In the early years of the century there was an increasing concern about the form that these new peripheral settlements should take. The various Garden city movements, inspired by the pioneer writings of Ebenezer Howard at the turn of the new century, tried to find a solution to the problems of the spreading growth of cities in lessons from a visionary view of the ideal village community. The large housing estate built on the heights of Mount Merrion in south Dublin in 1934 is a good example of this eagerness to build a new utopia, away from the perceived ills of the city. The inspiration for the architecture is the earlier Arts and Crafts movement but mixed with a nostalgic picturesque, typical of the suburban 1930s, such as sham half-timbering, leaded windows and pan-tiled roofs. The semi-detached house type predominated in the new suburbia. This was done for purely commercial reasons, to squeeze more house units onto the site, and the detached house became more rare, more expensive, and also more desirable. The detached house in Mount Merrion, shown here, is a landmark building at the entrance to the scheme and has a more successful composition than the semi-detached type could achieve. The estate, designed by the firm of Jones and Kelly, expanded continuously up to the present day.

85

Modern house
CASTLETROY
CO. LIMERICK 1938

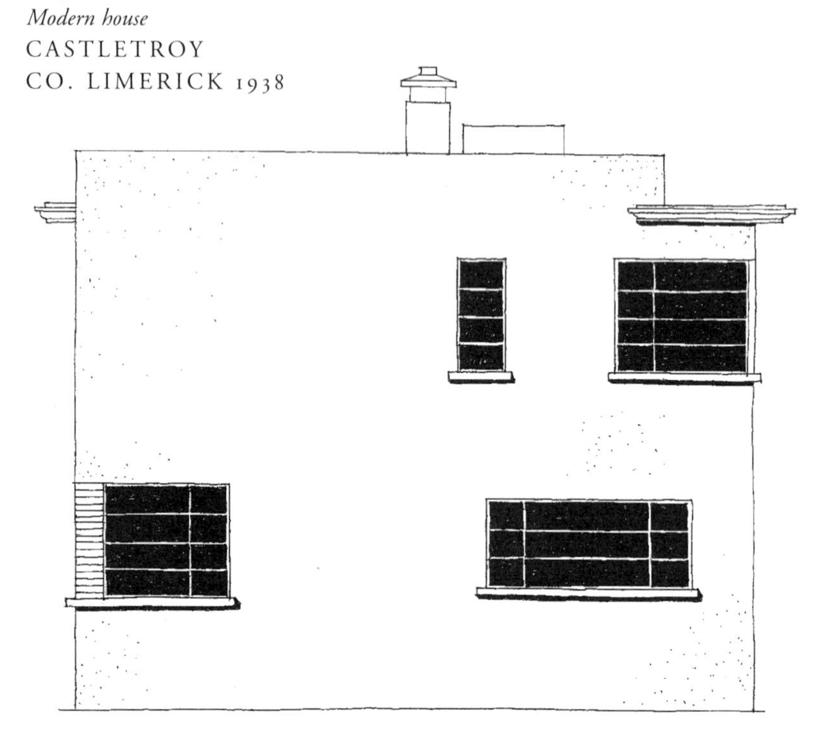

THE REVOLUTIONARY NEW architecture of Le Corbusier and the architects of the Bauhaus came to Ireland in the 1930s. Concrete was considered the ideologically correct material for the new style which was to be applied internationally. The universal language of Modern Architecture, as it was called, was to be characterized by flat roofs and cubic forms which were white-painted and in stark contrast to the old historic styles. A small group of modern houses was built at Castletroy, a suburb of north Limerick, in the late 1930s and the architects of these, the firm of Clifford, Smith and Newenham, enthusiastically embraced the trappings, if not the whole spirit, of the Modern Movement. The mandatory flat roof is combined with steel-framed windows, some placed on corners, and the glazing bars stress a sweeping horizontality, another hallmark of modernism.

The pioneers of modern architecture reacted against the continuous revivals of styles prevalent in the late nineteenth and early twentieth centuries. Ornament was to be abolished and the architecture of the brave new world was to right the ills of the dark, crowded cities by using large windows to let in the light and balconies to enjoy the sunshine. Only a few houses were built in this style in the 1930s and providers of domestic architecture continued in later years to prefer a cosy relationship with the past.

BUILDINGS OF TOWN AND VILLAGE

Towns or villages did not exist in ancient Ireland. The first settlements which could properly be called villages grew up around the Early Christian monasteries and these became larger and more formal with the introduction of the great mediæval friaries and abbeys. The buildings of these first settlements invariably consisted of small domestic dwellings. The Norsemen can be credited with introducing the concept of the town when they fortified their settlements around navigable river estuaries on the east coast in the ninth century. Dublin, Wexford, Waterford and, later, Limerick were early Norse foundations but the Irish quickly adapted to the new idea of urban habitation. After the Anglo-Norman invasion of the twelfth century the number of towns increased rapidly as the new invaders tightened their conquest of the whole country by building motes and fortified castles. Settlements grew around the castle with houses, mills, workshops, markets and churches. The great mediæval monastery also provided a focus for new settlements and thus towns spread out from the coasts, along rivers and throughout the midlands.

The plantations of settlers from England and Scotland which followed the Elizabethan wars created new types of towns and villages, particularly in Ulster, and fresh building types emerged. From the seventeenth and eighteenth century Irish towns and villages were profoundly changed by the initiatives of the wealthy landowners whose estates were the dominant force in every region. Many of these new settlements were now planned from the start, instead of the essentially random development of the past. Formal layouts such as, malls, squares, diamonds and crescents established an order and discipline to the design of the village or town, and public buildings were placed as centrepieces to vistas and architectural compositions. The streets of shops and the market house were the focus of commerce while the courthouse and the jail symbolized the power of the state. Instead of the single church of mediæval times, the spires of several denominations now vied for attention on the skylines. More building types were added in the nineteenth century, the most important architectural asset often being the commercial bank, and in the larger towns several of these competed for business with different styles and varying opulence of detail.

In the smaller settlements the village school was close to the church and during the nineteenth century national school buildings spread through the countryside until every community was served. Another new building type, although less welcome, was the workhouse of the years of the Great Famine many of which survived to evolve into hospitals, asylums and old peoples' homes in the later century. Municipal pride brought the town hall to the larger places, while philanthropy was largely responsible for the introduction of the library.

86

Deserted village

BROCAGH CO. WICKLOW

THE DESERTED VILLAGE of Brocagh lies buried in a forest on the slopes above and to the north of Laragh, Co. Wicklow. The numerous deserted villages of Ireland can often give a better picture of what these early settlements were like, since many of the surviving villages have changed so much as to obliterate their past forms. Brocagh was abandoned by the beginning of the twentieth century and by its remains it can be seen to have been a straggling collection of stone cottages and little farmhouses spread out along a track. This type of village is known as a clachan and was primarily concerned with agriculture. The buildings shown here are arranged around a courtyard with one dwelling in the centre and another on the right. The house on the right has animal quarters built on, while the range of buildings on the left are barns. A different village type was the booley which was essentially for summer use only when tending cattle on hill pastures. Simple clusters of round stone huts can still be seen in Co. Kerry as evidence of this practice. The deserted village of Slievemore in Achill, Co. Mayo, is still well preserved and many of the islands off the west coast like Gola, Co. Donegal, Inishkea, Co. Mayo, and the Blaskets, Co. Kerry, have lonely, roofless stone settlements, homes now to birds and rabbits. Throughout the west of Ireland the evidence of villages abandoned after the Great Famine can be seen when slanting sunlight reveals the straight rows of old cultivation ridges on mountain sides.

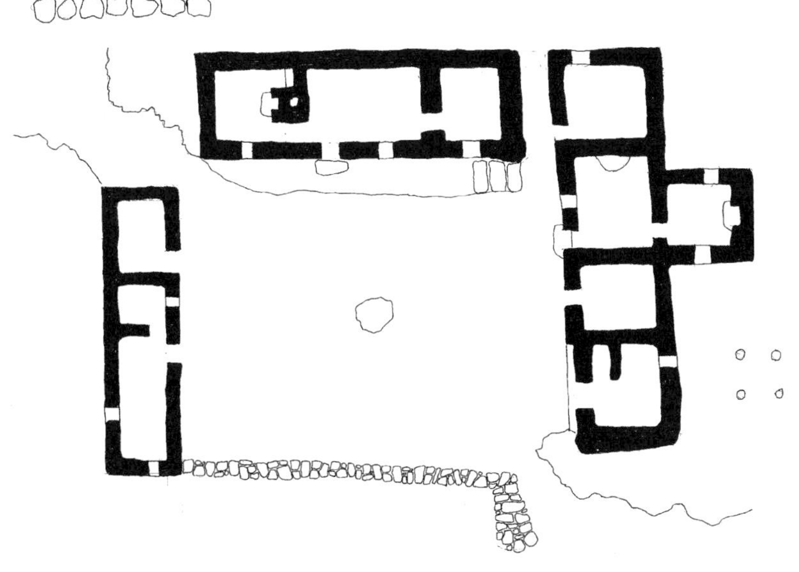

87

Estate village

BLACKSMITH'S HOUSE

ENNISKERRY CO. WICKLOW 1855

MOST OF THE land of Ireland was owned by wealthy aristocrats who inhabited the great country houses in the eighteenth century. In contrast, their landless tenantry lived in poverty outside the walls of the estates. Towards the end of the century a few humane and benevolent landlords became concerned about the conditions of their tenantry and the building of the estate village was one of the tangible responses that helped alleviate the wretched living conditions of the poor. These new settlements were well planned and provided with proper housing, often built in stone, and facilities such as schools, churches, dispensaries, courthouses and drinking fountains.

The village of Enniskerry in Co. Wicklow was built by the 6th Viscount Powerscourt below the grand entrance to his magnificent estate and Palladian house. The older village was a haphazard straggle of houses along the hill up to the gates of Powerscourt, while the new plan created a triangular space with buildings on each side and a fine clock-tower in the centre. In 1855 a forge and a blacksmith's house were added and these were built in granite using a snecked, squared, rubble. The stone bargeboards to the roof gables are carried on carved granite brackets and the horse-shoe shaped opening to the forge was a witty and favourite device of the time. The granite arch even has the square nail holes imitated!

88

Forge
ENNISKERRY
CO. WICKLOW

THE ARCHITECT FOR the forge and blacksmith's house was probably E.W. O'Kelly from Bray and the forge cost £150 and the house £200. The sturdy, plain style of these little works becomes more neo-Tudor in the terrace of buildings on the road leading up to the estate. The terrace contains an almshouse and a police barracks while farther down the hill is the tiny courthouse.

At least twenty estate villages were built up to the mid-nineteenth century although many more villages and towns show the architectural influence of the wealthy landowner. Adare, Co. Limerick, was built by the Earls of Dunraven in a picturesque style in the early nineteenth century, with thatched cottages and rustic embellishments. Tyrrellspass, Co. Westmeath, has a superb village green framed by a crescent of classical buildings and a Protestant church with an elegant spire. Blessington, Co. Wicklow, is one of several planned villages built by the Downshire estate. Abbeyleix, Co. Laois, was laid out by Lord de Vesci in the late eighteenth century with tree-lined streets and a classical courthouse. Bagenalstown (now called Muine Beag), Co. Carlow, was to be called Versailles by its enthusiastic founder, Walter Bagenal, but the result was a good deal more modest! In 1782 an extraordinary and grandiose proposal was made to settle dispossessed Swiss watchmakers at Passage West, Co. Waterford. The colony was to be called New Geneva and to stretch along the coast for half a mile. The foundation stone was laid but delays and wrangling about privileges killed the project in 1784.

89

Moravian village

GRACEHILL CO. ANTRIM 1746

THE CHURCH 1765

THE SMALL MORAVIAN village of Gracehill, Co. Antrim, was founded by Reverend John Cennick in 1746. This was one of a number of planned settlements by specific religious groups and since the Moravians did not attempt to proselytize, theirs was a successful venture. The village consists of a square of buildings grouped informally around a green space with the church occupying one side and houses, a post office and a shop on two other sides. The church presents a plain classical side to the square with three tall round-headed windows and smaller lights over the somewhat heavily framed doors. The clock tower is a modest affair and does not seek attention from the surrounding countryside, which seems in tune with the community's desire to fit in with neighbours of different persuasions. The pilasters and cornice of each door are elaborately carved in wood and the windows have stone surrounds. The placing of the doors at each end was for the purpose of separating the sexes. The walls are plastered and painted and the stone quoins rusticated with deep chamfered joints. The interior is a simple hall with galleries at each end. The church was built in 1765. On one side of the church is a school and a house, of similar size, balances this on the other side. The south-east side of the square contains a post office and grocer's shop which date from 1787 and a fine two-storey house built of black basalt stone in square blocks.

90

HOUSES 1780

THESE ARE ONE pair of houses on the north-west side of the square and the fact that they are not equal in size fits with the general informality of the village. There is a certain order in the plan around the square but this leads to no rigid application of eighteenth-century classical planning. Two of the houses in Gracehill were for the unmarried brothers and sisters and in the cemetery, behind the church, there are separate sections for males and females.

There were several other experiments in creating special settlements for religious groups in Ireland. The Quakers built Ballitore in Co. Kildare in the early eighteenth-century complete with a meeting house, school, dispensary and a savings bank. The most famous of the pupils of this school, which was founded by the Yorkshire Quaker, Abraham Shackelton, was Edmund Burke (1729–97). A much more controversial settlement was built on Achill Island in the nineteenth century for the purpose of converting the Roman Catholic islanders to the Protestant faith. The Reverend Edward Nangle set up a school and an orphanage but his religious fanaticism, expressed through a newspaper he published, failed to win more than a handful of converts and the experiment failed.

91

Industrial village

STONECUTTERS' VILLAGE BALLYKNOCKAN CO. WICKLOW
QUARRY MANAGER'S
HOUSE AND COTTAGE

*c.*1900

THE VILLAGE of Ballyknockan is situated on the east shore of the man-made lake of Poulaphuca about eight kilometres south of Blessington. It grew up beneath the stone quarry which supplied granite for buildings in Dublin, and indeed in England, up to the present day. The village, now much enveloped in modern building, provides ample evidence of the craft of the stonemason. The two-storey manager's house illustrated is the only formal building in the village and it is truly an advertisement for stone detailing. The chimney stacks are sculptural beyond mere function and the decorative stone window surrounds would do justice to a great country house. The crowning glory, however, is the astonishing doorcase – a builder's catalogue of tricks in granite – with chamfered corners and a curved pediment topped with a stone ornament. Elsewhere there is a wealth of beautiful details to be found on the little cottages, the barns and on the innumerable, carefully constructed, dry-stone walls all around. The tiny cottage illustrated, St Anthony's, is the work of a master mason. The superb stone stack is the minimum size and must have the circular flue carved from the stones – a detail that only the artist craftsman knows! The end section of the bargeboard is returned in one piece. The *tour-de-force* for the stonemason are the perfect stone-ball decorations and the carved pineapples to be seen elsewhere in the village.

92

Stone barn

BALLYKNOCKAN CO. WICKLOW LATE 19TH C.

THE MEN OF Ballyknockan all worked in the quarries, but there were many times in the nineteenth and twentieth centuries when there was no work, whether through depressions in the industry or lost contracts. Marginal farming on the poor mountain slopes was an alternative and many of the inhabitants were part-time farmers. The splendid stone barn, shown here, is undoubtedly the work of a stonemason. The large chamfer on the right corner was carefully cut as each stone course was laid and prevented the axles of farm carts from carrying away part of the corner. The painstaking detailing of granite features throughout the village point to the love of their craft which kept the stoneworkers busy in hard times.

Several other industrial villages were built in Ireland in the eighteenth and nineteenth centuries, but these were specially planned. One of the earliest was the optimistically named Prosperous, Co. Kildare, which was established in 1780 as a cotton-manufacturing centre. It was a total failure after only a few years. Bessbrook, Co. Armagh, was established in 1846 by a Quaker textile manufacturer who was a temperance campaigner and forbade any pub in the village! Portlaw, Co. Waterford, a model industrial village, was another Quaker foundation where the temperance ideal was also a premier objective. Sion Mills, Co. Tyrone, where the huge spinning factory still stands, was an industrial village founded in 1835.

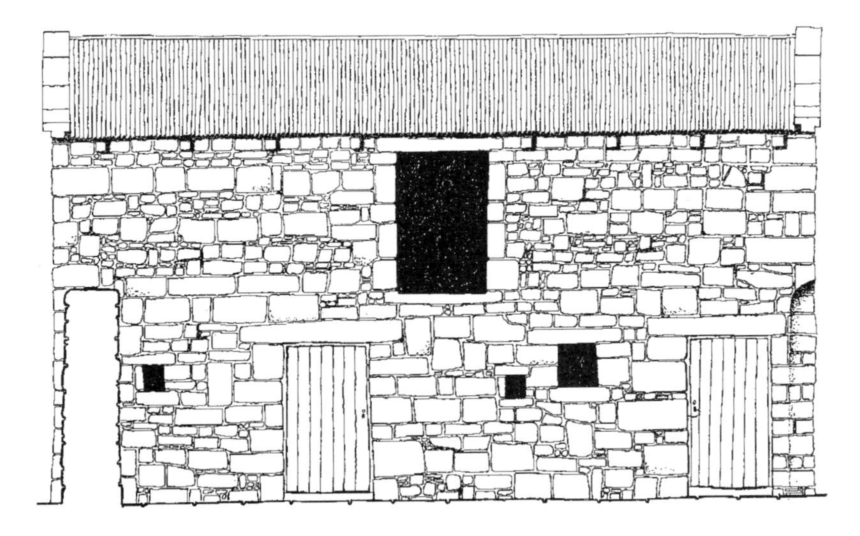

93

Town gate

WEST GATE

CLONMEL CO. TIPPERARY *c.*1830

THE TOWN GATES of mediæval times were fortified entrances to the settlements but also symbols of the power and influence of the municipalities. In Ireland these early gateways were mostly severely functional structures with little of the monumental declamation of continental towns of the Middle Ages. The burgesses of the ancient walled town of Clonmel decided in 1831 to build a new gate on the site of the destroyed mediæval west gate. Clonmel was an important town by the beginning of the nineteenth century and a courthouse, designed by Sir Richard Morrison, was built there in 1800. The Gothic and Tudor Revival styles of the times were popular when a sense of stern self-importance or an image of benevolent feudal splendour was considered proper. The town authorities borrowed mediæval military details for the new gate, including arrow loops, a look-out tower and machicolated battlements, a device to allow defenders to drop objects on to attackers of the gate. The most imposing structure in the town is the Mainguard, one of the earliest buildings specially provided for a municipality in Ireland. This dates from 1674 and was completed after the town was captured by Cromwell, whose siege of 1650 was fiercely resisted until the defenders ran out of ammunition.

94

Town hall

TOWN HALL COLERAINE CO. DERRY 1859

THE TOWN HALL in Coleraine is one of the largest and most magnificent of these public buildings to be built outside the main cities of Ireland. The town hall is the centrepiece of the Diamond in the town and the present structure replaced an older town hall which had been the work of the London architect, George Dance, the elder, in 1743. The architect of the 1859 building was Thomas Turner and the new town hall dominates the town centre. The Baroque style was selected to give this public edifice the necessary municipal importance and the solidity and power of the style is demonstrated to good effect in the end elevation, shown in the drawing. The stone used throughout is a lovely, warm-coloured sandstone which is laid in regular squared blocks known as ashlar work. The lower storey is in a manner known as banded rustication with deeply recessed joints producing a strong horizontal emphasis. The arch over the doorway is known as a segmental arch, while the round-headed window over the door has a stone surround in the manner of the architect James Gibbs. These also frame the roundels on the first storey which contain decorative shields. The building is crowned by what is known as a modillion cornice where regularly spaced brackets give a deep shadowed effect.

95

TOWN HALL
CAVAN CO. CAVAN 1908

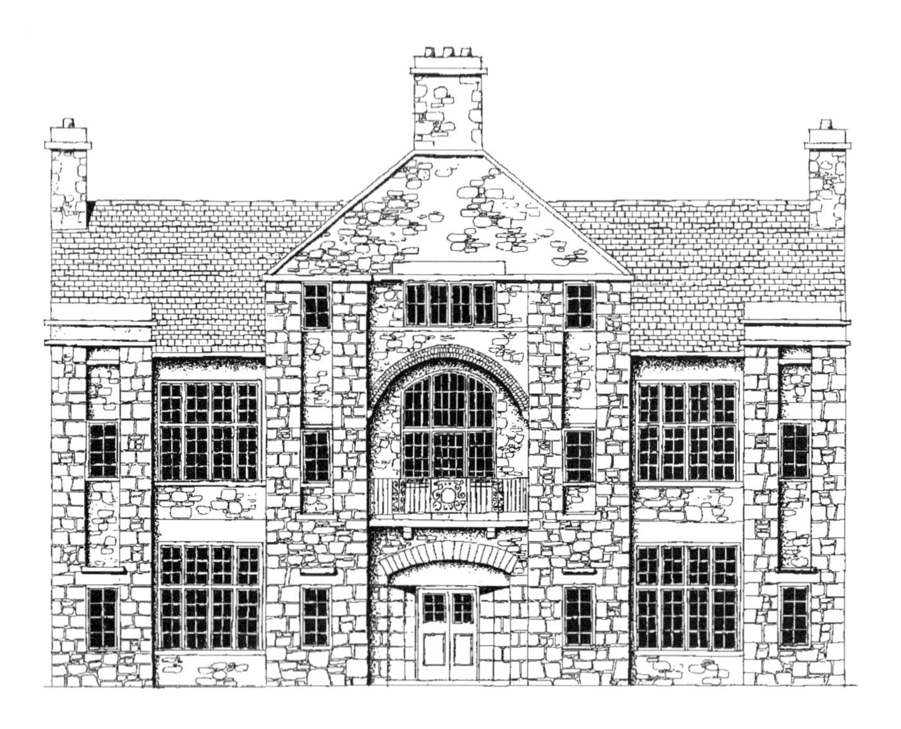

THE TOWN HALL in Cavan is the work of the architect William Anthony Scott and this building, while different in style to his church in Spiddal (illus. 36) of the same time, is a highly individualistic design which demonstrates Scott's love of expressive geometric forms. The influence of his early years in London and his exposure to the work of the architects of the Arts and Crafts movement can be seen in the roughly textured random rubble stonework, the high-pitched gabled roofs and the small-paned widows. Scott, however, arranges all of these in assertive cubes with shallow recesses beginning at first-floor level. The effect of the recesses is to produce a vertical emphasis of flat pilasters. This was to become a favourite detail of Scott and was later used dramatically in the seminary of St Mary's College, Galway, in 1912. The doorway is deeply recessed with a segmental stone arch while the large window, with French doors opening to a balcony, is arched in brick. Scott died in 1921 at the early age of fifty and while his buildings are few, all have an individual and innovatory character which make the designer one of the earliest modern architects in Ireland.

96

Town street
BALLINASLOE CO. GALWAY

THE STREETS of many Irish towns and villages, before the eighteenth century, often consisted of unplanned and straggling rows of houses, many single-storey and thatched, following the line of ancient roads or tracks. In the eighteenth and early nineteenth centuries the influence of the great estates and the model of the planned estate villages began to force some order on the architecture of the town. Main streets, squares and diamonds now had more orderly rows of terraced buildings and the familiar pattern of shops on the ground floor and domestic accommodation overhead became universal. In some towns a particular pattern of design and detail which was common to several buildings or whole terraces can be detected. In Ballinasloe there is a distinct use of little motifs from Palladian architecture visible on the main streets. The three-storey houses have Diocletian windows, semi-circular with three divisions, on the top storey and Venetian windows, three lights with the centre opening round-headed, for the first floor. These details are a delightful vernacular interpretation by the artisan builders of the correct classical form, being far too small in relation to the building and the main windows.

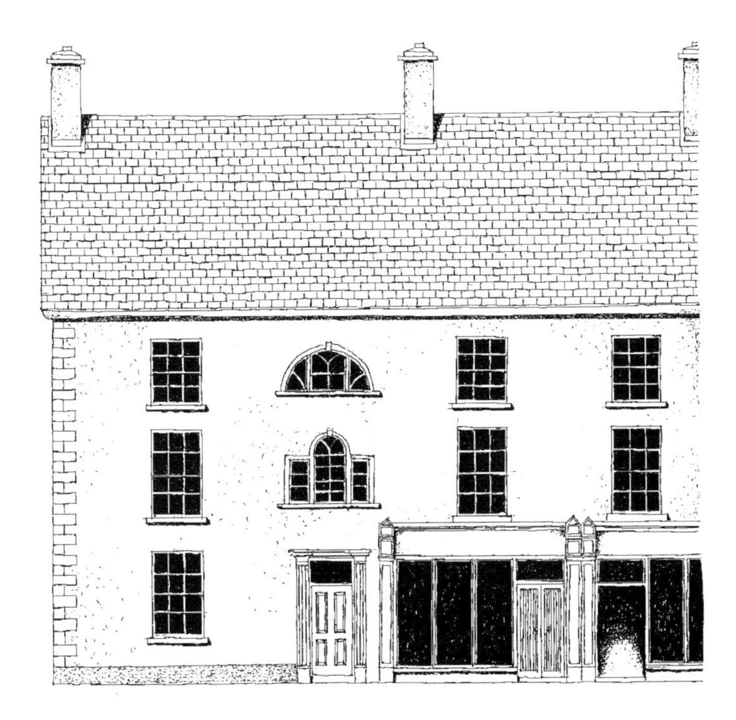

97

CASTLETOWNBERE CO. CORK

THE LITTLE TOWN of Castletownbere on the north side of Bantry bay has long been an important fishing harbour. Its sheltered waters, behind the bulk of Bere Island, made it a major anchorage for the British Royal Navy. The nearby copper mines at Allihies also brought prosperity to the town and the importance of the place in the nineteenth century is evident in the orderly rows of houses and shops in the centre. The terrace shown here is the product of a careful design and typical of a robust nineteenth-century development of the classical style. The shop windows have the graceful round-headed glazing bars which at one time were common to shops, particularly in the seaside towns of the south and south-west. The first-floor windows have segmental arches and are framed in brick to contrast with the brightly painted wall surfaces. The crowning glory of this terrace is the row of beautifully crafted bullseye dormer windows which unify the whole composition. The shopfronts were all standard at one time with matching pilasters and glazing bars but, unfortunately, the modern desire for individuality has altered many of fronts in an otherwise uniform terrace.

98

Shops
PRINTER
STRABANE CO. TYRONE LATE 18TH C.

SHOPS WERE ORIGINALLY the workplaces of tradesmen and craftsmen, the goods being made in the workplace and sold directly to customers. In time a larger window was installed to display some finished goods and the traditional shop was born. The earliest shops were open-fronted, having a counter between the shop and the street, and shops like these were standard from Roman times. Glazing of shopfronts was established by the end of the seventeenth century and Malton's prints of eighteenth-century Dublin show elegant small shops with round-headed windows. The surviving traditional shopfronts of Ireland almost all date from the nineteenth and early twentieth centuries but a few earlier examples still exist. Gray's printer's shop, 49 Main Street, Strabane, Co. Tyrone, is one of the oldest surviving traditional shopfronts in the country, probably dating from the late eighteenth-century. The slightly curved front is typical of the eighteenth century double bow-fronted shops which were abundant in London and Dublin in the Georgian period. The windows and door are framed by extremely slender Tuscan columns and the simple arrangement of cornice, nameboard and many-paned windows is typical of the earliest shopfronts. Strabane was a publishing centre in the late eighteenth century and Gray's shop has been restored by the Northern Ireland committee of the National Trust.

99

BALLYMENA CO. ANTRIM LATE 18TH C.

MONTGOMERY'S FURNITURE SHOP, 27-29 High Street, Ballymena, Co. Antrim, is another of the handful of surviving shopfronts of the eighteenth century. The town was founded by Scottish settlers in the seventeenth century and was largely Presbyterian. It was a centre for the linen industry with a flax market supplying the spinning mills. Montgomery's splendid emporium no doubt satisfied the needs of a growing middle class of millowners and the larger farmers who grew the flax. This is a large three-storey town house with the business on part of the ground floor. The fascia is taken across the whole façade and is supported on fluted Ionic columns which proudly unite the façade of shop and dwelling. The entrance doorway to the house is an elaborate classical composition with the door set in a curved recess and flanked by Ionic colonettes. The tripartite window with the frilly decorated lintel is the house living-room and the shop windows are projected forward with curved sides and glazed with small panes in the Georgian manner. The main walls of the house are built in the local black basalt, a stone peculiar to the geology of the area and the method of walling is to use squared blocks of different sizes bonded with small blocks or snecks. The use of bricks to form the lintels and jambs to the windows is a practical measure since brick is cheaper and easier to build than cut stone.

100

THOMASTOWN CO. KILKENNY LATE 19TH C.

THE BOOTMAKER'S SHOP and house in the village of Thomastown epitomizes the workplace and home of a successful tradesman whose business has been long established. The earliest shop of a country bootmaker was a simple cottage where the work was carried out on a bench in front of the window and customers called at the door. Here the ground floor is given over to the shop with large display windows and the workshop has developed into a retail establishment. O'Reilly's shop is unusual in that, while the house must date from about the mid-nineteenth century, the shopfront is in a perfect eighteenth-century style. The central doorway with the delicate traceried fanlight and the shop windows with the small Georgian glazing bars all point to an earlier period, and this shop would not have been out of place in classical Dublin. The fascia and cornice are gracefully carved with elegant curved ends in lieu of the usual consoles or brackets. A finely carved cable- or rope-moulding, so-called since it imitates a twisted rope, runs the full length of the shopfront below the fascia. This is the work of a local craftsman and there are several other examples of the same style in the village. It is interesting to speculate that the early style of the design comes from past generations of artist craftsmen who built shopfronts in the cities.

101

BAILIEBOROUGH CO. CAVAN 1826–*c.*1880

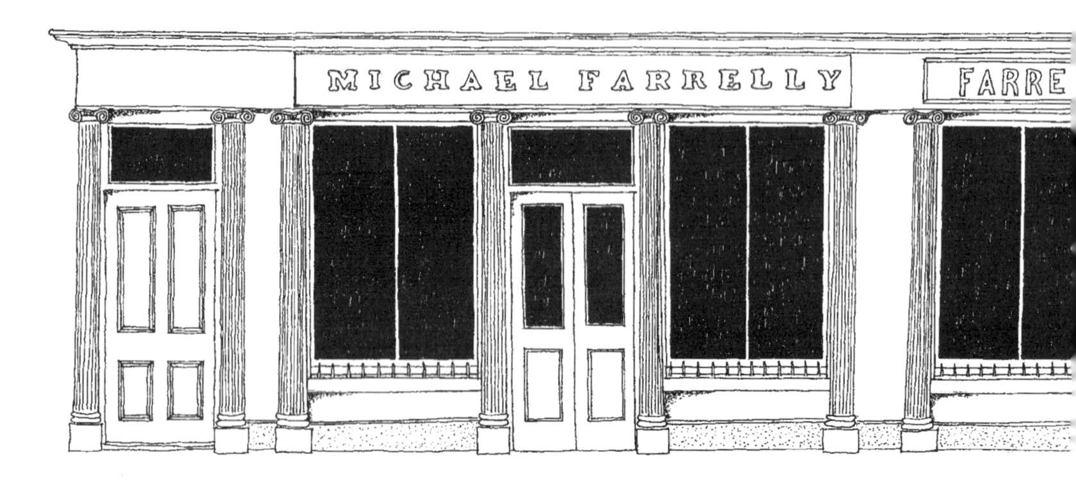

One of the outstanding features of Irish towns and villages is the small shopfront. Where many of the streetscapes followed a common logic of uniform rooflines and a loosely classical rhythm of vertical house-fronts and windows, the general impression of the street was of a lively informality within the overall order. The shopfronts may have followed a standard arrangement of cornice, name fascia and pilasters, framing the shop windows, but a wide variety of the details of each of these, combined with strong contrasting colours on the painted fronts, make for a unique Irish folk-art form. The majority of Irish small shopfronts are individual units of one shop window and a door or a central entrance framed by two windows. Occasionally several of these are combined in one architecturally composed range. One of the most satisfactory of these is the Farrelly group in Bailieborough, Co. Cavan. Different members of the family or different generations give their names to the enterprise which operated originally as a general shop for all the needs of this market town. The nameboard is common to all of the units but the most endearing feature is the triumphant use of small Ionic fluted columns, all in wood, to frame the doors and windows. The entrance doors to the dwellings are placed comfortably on each side to round off the composition.

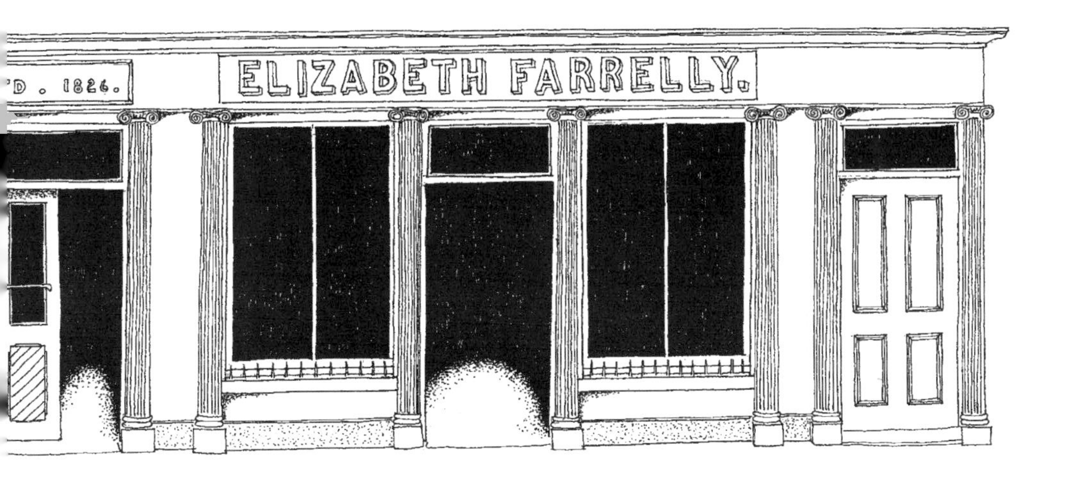

The fascia of Farrelly's is plain and without consoles or brackets at the sides, while the cornice is simple and functional, just for the purpose of shedding rainwater. Although the nameboard gives the date of the establishment of the business as 1826, these particular shopfronts are certainly of a much later date, probably towards the end of the nineteenth century. The Catholic merchant classes were becoming more prosperous in the later decades of the century and this shopfront and twin dwellings were likely to have been built at the same time. The shop windows are each divided into two vertical strips and this method, combined with the repetition of the columns, maintains the vertical scale of the street. Each shop window sill is provided with a row of metal spikes which offered a sharp message to potential idlers not to sit there! The early photographs in the Lawrence collection show many views of Irish towns in the second half of the nineteenth century, and this range of fronts in Balieborough differs little from the shopfronts of those days. The photographs often show large numbers of people on the streets, especially on market days, and the shop window must have been a major attraction for country people after their long journey to the town by horse and cart.

102

CASTLEISLAND CO. KERRY 1835

CASTLEISLAND IS a small market town in Co. Kerry, and Wren's shop and house is a representation of the emergence of a prosperous middle class and a confident merchant class in the early decades of the nineteenth century. The large plaque celebrates the establishment of the business in 1835 and that date is likely to be the actual date of the building shown. Instead of the earlier practice of making a shopfront in an existing house front, the whole enterprise is now built as one designed unit. Wren's is the work of a local artisan builder who was familiar with the rules and styles of architecture and probably had access to pattern books such as the works of the carpenter William Pain. These books appeared from the middle of the eighteenth century and the designs were widely copied by the artisan architects and builders in the towns and villages of Ireland. The three-storey house with Georgian windows is almost standard for the Irish town dwelling for the merchant class but the designer builder of Wren's gilded the lily somewhat by adopting the larger three-light window for the upper floors. The shop windows are provided with round-headed glazing in a manner common to the southern half of the country and the spandrels, or spaces, between the heads are given delicate trefoil shapes.

103

Watchmaker jeweller

BIRR CO. OFFALY LATE 19TH C.

BARBER'S SHOPFRONT in the town of Birr, Co. Offaly, is one of the most perfect and beautiful examples of the art of the wood-fronted shopfront in Ireland. The design is a product of the late nineteenth century with many of the crafts and motifs of shopfront design of the time exploited to the full. The entire front is treated as a separate composition, regardless of the rest of the building. The pilasters framing each side are taken up to merge with the consoles, or brackets, which in turn frame the nameboard. These are elaborately carved with a decoration which continues across the whole cornice. The decorative motif is known as "egg and dart", a device which originated in the architecture of ancient Greece and Rome. The glory of the shop is the superb painted lettering. This is in the manner known as "shadowed"where a three-dimensional effect is given by painting on simulated shadow. A further sophistication is added here by apparently tilting the letters to read downwards. Wooden shutters were common in Irish towns and served the dual purpose of security from theft as well as the more immediate threat of damage from rampaging cattle, when fairs were held in the town streets. Barber's was painted dark green and this colour and, more often, black were favoured for the watchmaker, jeweller and pawnbroker.

104

Chemist

MITCHELSTOWN CO. CORK EARLY 20TH C.

THE CHEMIST or pharmacy in the Irish country town constituted a distinctive type of shop and, like the watchmaker's, sober colours were generally used for the wood front. Murphy's splendid pharmacy in Mitchelstown is typical of many superb house-shops lining the main street. Many of the these have been designed as one, with the façade of the upper-floor dwelling complementing the shopfront on the ground floor. Murphy's reinforces this unifying effect by carrying narrow decorative pilasters right up to eaves' level, then joining these by another frilly decorative band across the top. The decorations are made in plaster, a method of producing economical embellishments widespread in the south and south-west of the country. The windows in the first floor have elaborate surrounds and bracketted cornices and are carefully paired to create a unified composition. The shop lettering demonstrates the influence of Art Nouveau and places this design at the beginning of the twentieth century. The little stepped mouldings under the nameboard cornice are known as dentils and are another feature from ancient classical architecture. Many chemist's shops in Ireland, even very small establishments, have the grand title of Medical Hall and demonstrate, perhaps, the growing self-importance of the profession in the late nineteenth century.

105

Draper's

NEWTOWNSTEWART CO. TYRONE EARLY 20TH C.

THE LARGE DRAPERY STORE only appeared towards the end of the nineteenth century in Irish towns. In rural areas the ordinary people either made their own clothes or went to a local tailor. In Victorian times the alleyways of the cities and large towns were crowded with second-hand clothes shops and these were the main source of clothing for the poor. The tailor's workshop, like those of other tradesmen, gradually evolved into shops selling ready-made clothes, and these stores blossomed when mass production of machine-patterned garments brought down the price of new clothes. Hood's palatial drapery store in Newtownstewart dates from the early twentieth century and the large, plate-glass display windows bear witness to this. The structural columns for the building are behind the glass, thus allowing the emerging art of window dressing to have full freedom. The nameboard here is typical of a refined type of fascia which developed towards the end of the nineteenth century. The robust, serifed lettering, and the floral decoration on each side, is cut deeply into the wood and then picked out in gold leaf. The rest of the nameboard is painted in a dark colour, often black, and the whole fascia is covered in plate glass. The result is a sparkling sign which requires little or no maintenance. Early photographs of Irish streets show many shops with awnings, which could protect the goods on display from damage by sunlight. The awning for Hood's is neatly built into a box in the cornice.

106

ARDEE CO. LOUTH *c.*1900

HAMILL'S SHOP in the busy market town of Ardee, Co. Louth, is a *tour-de-force* of the art of faience majolica. This is the use of material in the form of a glazed stoneware or terracotta, in effect tiles, to clad the entire face of a shopfront. Late nineteenth-century technology led to the mass production of ready-made decorative details which formerly had to be made laboriously by hand. This new "Majolica Ware", as it became known, was available in a vast range of sculptural shapes, designs and colours, and could be ordered from a manufacturer's catalogue. Butcher's shops, fishmongers and dairies were the main users of tiles, with the obvious desire to present a clean, fresh appearance. The tiling on the front of Hamill's is in two shades of green: light and dark. The dainty festoons of flowers, in the form of swags, interlacing the full-blooded Art Nouveau lettering, are the most striking features of one of the best shopfronts in the country. The shop was originally a grocery and pub, and the tiling would have been a cheerful and hygienic surround to slabs of yellow butter and sides of bacon. Only a few of these splendid tiled shops remain in Ireland, although fragments of tiling can still be seen on partially modernized façades. A larger number of tiled interiors survive, usually in butcher's shops. These are often decorated with homely pastoral scenes which, no doubt, were intended to soften the gory nature of the business.

107

Pat McAuliffe (1846-1921)
ABBEYFEALE CO. LIMERICK *c.*1900

EXTERIOR PLASTERING, or stucco as it was known, was used by Palladio. In later times the architects of the classical revival enthusiastically adopted the material to dress up buildings, made of cheaper materials, to imitate cut stone. Plaster had many attractions for the country artisan builder who was also invariably the architect for the houses and shops of the common people. Using plaster, he could imitate easily all of the classical detailing such as window surrounds, quoins and string courses. It was possible to produce an entire shopfront in plaster from the classical entablature, which included the cornice, consoles and nameboard, to flanking pilasters or classical columns. The strongest tradition of decorative plaster, used for shop and house fronts, is to be found in the southwest of Ireland. The most famous plasterworker-designer, whose work mostly survives in counties Kerry and Limerick, was Pat McAuliffe. This eccentric artist craftsman was born in 1846 and before he died in 1921 he left an extraordinary, exotic and fascinating legacy of exterior plasterwork in these counties. Listowel, Co. Kerry, is where the bulk of McAuliffe's work can be seen, but O'Mara's front in Abbeyfeale is one of several superb designs in this town. The decorations are an eclectic mixture of Celtic interlacing, classical egg and dart and one of the artist's own inventions, strange arrows penetrating a circle.

108

ABBEYFEALE CO. LIMERICK *c.*1900

DALY'S HOUSE and shopfront in Abbeyfeale is another of Pat McAuliffe's whole façade creations. Only the nameboard looks bare and this is likely to be the result of the later removal of some of his ornamental details which may have been considered too ostentatious. McAuliffe loved to cram as much variety as possible onto a single façade and was never content with restraint as a virtue in design. The quoins of each storey are treated differently. Corinthian pilasters are used on the ground floor, eighteenth-century arabesque decoration on the first-floor and giant, diamond-pointed rustication on the top storey. The Hiberno-Romanesque style supplies the human heads over the windows as a final touch to this confection. McAuliffe's *tour-de-force* in carrying out a total façade design must be O'Connor's building on the opposite side of the street to Daly's. Two sides of this house shop are embellished with folk art, including biblical scenes and mottoes in three languages, Latin, French and Irish!

109

Banks

BANK OF IRELAND

36 SCOTCH STREET ARMAGH CO. ARMAGH 1812

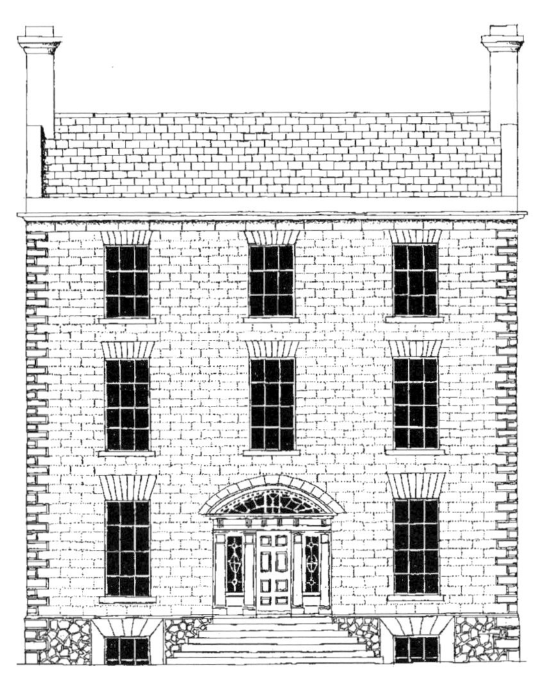

The history of the architecture of banks has its beginning in the Renaissance with the construction of exchange buildings but the start of banking as a business in Ireland belongs to the eighteenth century. It was not until the end of the century that buildings specially designed to serve as banks began to appear. These were few in number until a huge bank-building boom took place in the mid-nineteenth century.

The Bank of Ireland existed since 1783 and this branch of the bank was built in the city of Armagh in 1812. The building was erected for Leonard Dobbin who, as well as being Sovereign of the city, was the agent for the Bank of Ireland. The tall, well proportioned classical design is possibly the work of Francis Johnston, architect of the beautiful observatory in Armagh (illus. 141–2). The building is raised on the usual *piano nobile* and the main walling is in a fine ashlar with strongly chamfered quoins. The simplicity of the Georgian windows focuses full attention on the superb doorway. This tripartite arrangement of a solid door flanked by sidelights, with a shallow segmental fanlight embracing the three elements, is to be found in many Irish towns. The delicate tracery of the sidelights and the fanlight, with its built-in lantern provides a nice contrast to the plain glazing-bars of the windows.

110

BELFAST BANK DUNGANNON CO. TYRONE 1855

REGIONAL BANK companies developed rapidly in the early nineteenth century. The Belfast Bank began in 1827 and this branch in Dungannon was built in 1855 to the designs of William Henry Lynn. This was an early work by the accomplished northern architect, later to be one of the partners in the famous firm of Lanyon, Lynn and Lanyon. The branch bank shows the influence of the architectural critic and writer John Ruskin, whose espousal of Venetian Gothic had a profound effect on the architecture of the later nineteenth century. The close grouping of the windows, which can be seen in the Dungannon bank, is a common feature of the typical palazzi along the Grand Canal in Venice. The round-arched windows have sharp, ogee-shaped Gothic mouldings overhead and decorative colonettes between the windows. Unlike the typical classical façade, the cut-stone blocks in the quoins are underplayed and used merely to achieve structural stability when building in the squared rubble-walling method. An extra refinement is the use of a delicate vertical moulding on the corner, further distancing this design from the plain solid architecture of the eighteenth century. The cornice is light and graceful with a decoration of dentils which, together with the corner mouldings, frame this delightful composition as in a painting. Most of the regional banks were taken over by larger groups in recent times. The Dungannon branch is now the Northern Bank.

III

NATIONAL BANK BALLYMAHON CO. LONGFORD 1860

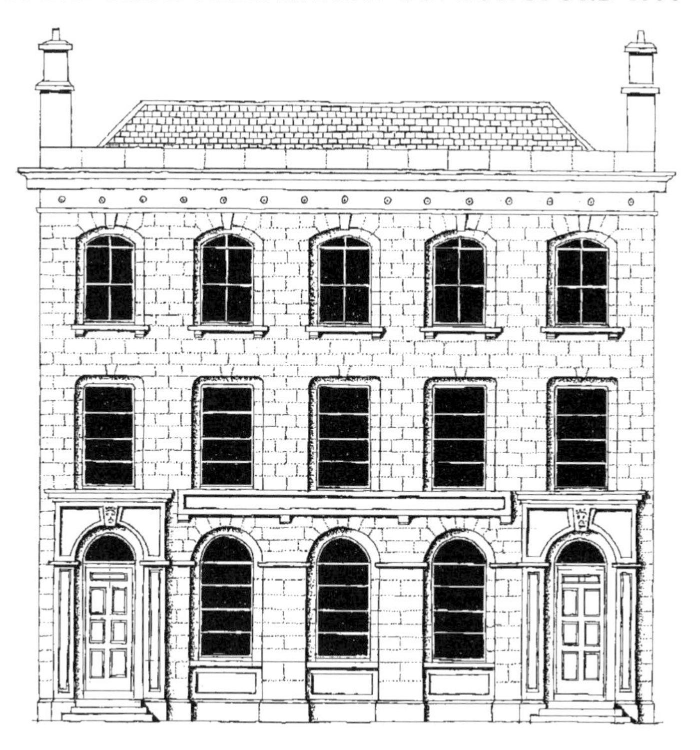

THE NATIONAL BANK, founded by Daniel O'Connell, was one of the banks established in the early years of the nineteenth century which relied heavily on English capital. This branch of the National is an extraordinarily powerful piece of architecture in such a little town in the midlands. The architect was William Caldbeck who from 1852, when he was appointed as architect to the company, designed no less than twenty-six branches of the National. Caldbeck adopted a formula for all of his bank designs and the Ballymahon branch demonstrates some of the elements which make up this formula. The building has five bays in three storeys and there are three windows for the central ground-floor banking hall. Unlike many of the other branches, however, the Ballymahon branch is entirely stone-fronted and the imposing limestone ashlar walling gives this building the real and impregnable look of a Renaissance palazzo. The round-headed ground-floor windows are slightly recessed giving the appearance of being an arcade, a favourite device of the architect. The cornice is a robust feature to cap the building but the small decorative medallions are the only frivolous touch on this massive façade. Other banks by Caldbeck in the midlands are in Roscrea, Co. Tipperary, Longford town, Moate and Mullingar in Co. Westmeath, Dundalk, Co. Louth, and Kells, Co. Meath.

112

ROYAL BANK DONEGAL CO. DONEGAL 1860

THE ROYAL BANK was, like the National, set up with English capital and established in 1836 when the company took over Shaw's bank of 1799 in Foster Place, Dublin. The branch in Donegal town dominates the diamond in the centre and is another grand stone palace. Although only two storeys high, the massive stone chimney stacks, paired towards the centre, make this one of the most imposing buildings in the town. The classic formula of five bays is adopted with the entrance squarely in the centre. There is a gesture of a regal balcony over the entrance hinting, perhaps, at the bank's stately title! The round-headed windows on the ground floor lighting the banking hall are in the Italian manner which is now, in mid-century, commonly accepted as the correct style for the main banks. The finely dressed ashlar stone used for the main walling, and the stone window surrounds and prominent keystones in this design, show how the many competing banking companies in the mid-nineteenth century wanted to advertise and demonstrate the security of their capital. The former Royal Bank in nearby Ballyshannon, Co. Donegal, is a spectacular design and the bank's inclination to commission eclectic styles is evidenced in the former Royal Bank in Sligo, now the headquarters of the Yeats Society. The Royal was one of the three banks which merged to make the new Allied Irish Bank.

113

PROVINCIAL BANK OMAGH CO. TYRONE 1864

THE PROVINCIAL BANK was set up in the early decades of the nineteenth century and while its finances were British, most of the staff of the Irish branches were Scottish. Scotland pioneered branch banking and the Provincial's vigorous intention to promote this system throughout Ireland was largely responsible for the proliferation of branch banks throughout the land. By 1846 the Provincial had established the huge number of forty-two branches. This number was cut, however, to thirty-eight in 1850 due to a slump in agricultural prices. The Provincial in Omagh is one of a number of distinguished banks on the High Street and the style is a full-blooded Venetian Gothic, designed by W.G. Murray. The twin windows light the banking hall and the large door on the right gives access to the rear. Round-headed windows on the ground and first floors are framed with tiny colonettes and the upper windows have chamfered jambs. This was a refinement of the expert stone mason who considered that a sharp arris to a window was too abrupt. The cornice is magnificently sculptured and medallions decorate the frieze (the flat space below the cornice). The Provincial was the second bank to become part of Allied Irish.

114

PROVINCIAL BANK
COOTEHILL CO. CAVAN LATE 19TH C.

THE PROVINCIAL BANK in Cootehill, Co. Cavan, is in the familiar form of five bays with the entrance placed centrally. The five arches on the ground floor form a splendid Italian arcade and the proportions of the building, with one storey over the arcade, make it very similar to the earlier Irish market houses. Unusually, instead of a fanlight over the main entrance, there is a monumental double door which opens into a lobby. When the doors are opened for business the effect of the open arcade is more evident. The building is built in the lovely warm, golden sandstone from Donegal but unfortunately this has deteriorated considerably over the years. There is no parapet, as they became less fashionable towards the end of the century and the use of the more practical and more trouble-free eaves became popular. It was still considered important to create an interesting capping to the building and this was achieved by strongly modelled brackets to the eaves board. The branches of the Provincial were more numerous in Munster, where there were eighteen, and in Ulster, which had fifteen. The bank was called the "landlord's bank" in the nineteenth century since it held accounts from many important landowners.

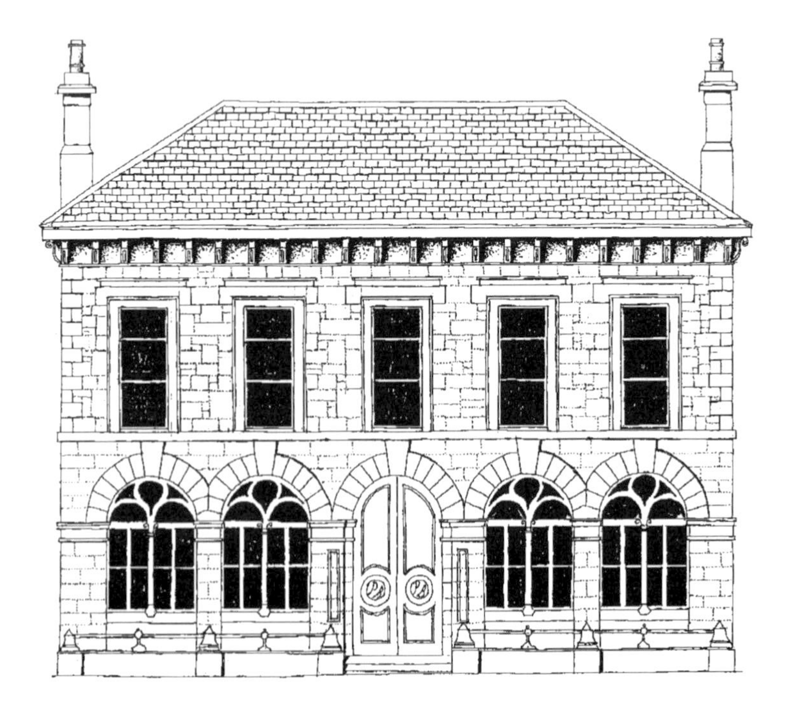

115

THE HIBERNIAN BANK
LETTERKENNY CO. DONEGAL 1874

THE HIBERNIAN was another of the banks set up in the early nineteenth century which determined to open branches in the country towns. The branch bank in the important market town of Letterkenny is one of the most exotic and interesting architectural works in the place. The architect was the Belfast-born Timothy Hevey who, as a Catholic, had worked in his younger days for the High Gothic firm of E.W. Pugin and George Ashlin. The façade of the Hibernian in Letterkenny is ornately textured and richly coloured in the fashionable Victorian Gothic manner. Red sandstone embellishments set off the grey-blue snecked rubble walling and polished granite is used for the little columns. The eaves is a riot of foliated sculpture while the twin doorways, with mock balconies over, would not be out of place on a royal palace. The Hibernian is now part of the Bank of Ireland group. Unfortunately both major banking groups removed old names from the branches when mergers took place. In many cases the lettering was part of the architecture as well as an essential part of the history of banks. Old names can still sometimes be detected, as here in Letterkenny where the original Hibernian plaque exists.

116

MUNSTER AND LEINSTER BANK
SCHULL CO. CORK 1932

THE MUNSTER AND LEINSTER is the third of the banks which have now amalgamated to form the Allied Irish Bank. The Munster Bank was founded in 1864 and was outstandingly successful in its early years, taking over the branches of the older Union Bank in the province of Munster. Its success was partly due to the prosperity of the dairy industry in Ireland at this time. The Munster had 48 branches at the height of its early growth and these were mainly concentrated in the southern province. In this great expansionary period for banks up to 1878 there were 403 branches opened by the different groups in Ireland. In 1885 the Munster Bank became the Munster and Leinster and by 1930 was the third largest bank in Ireland, after the Bank of Ireland and the National. It now had branches in every one of the thirty-two counties of Ireland, 115 in total. The Munster and Leinster in the south-western town of Schull was built in 1932 and still presents the image of a little palazzo. One of the few changes from the designs of the previous century is the adoption of steel windows, which were now mass produced and available from catalogues. The beautiful lettering was in bronze and is now sadly removed. The design of the Schull branch was by the Cork architect B. O'Flynn.

117

Post office

WESTPORT CO. MAYO 1899

MANY OF THE larger towns of Ireland began to be provided with purpose-built post offices towards the end of the nineteenth century. In previous years and in the smaller towns and villages the post office was usually only a space or a separate counter in an existing shop or house. The busy town of Westport acquired this lively design in 1899. The new building fitted in to the tree-lined mall of this planned eighteenth-century town with its simple classical buildings, despite being definitely horizontal in character in contrast to the generally vertical emphasis of the older architecture. The three semi-circular arches on the front elevation are in the tradition of the early arcaded market houses, but here the size is far greater and they dominate the façade. The influence, along with the powerful feeling of horizontality, is from the new spirit of modernism which pervaded contemporary architectural journals at the turn of the new century. Reminders of the classical past, however, are deliberately inserted by the use of great blocks of rock-faced stone in Gibbs-style arches, the robust plinth and quoins. The beautiful serifed lettering was in bronze and this was mass produced and available from manufacturer's catalogues. The architect was Howard Pentland who designed several post-office buildings for the Office of Public Works.

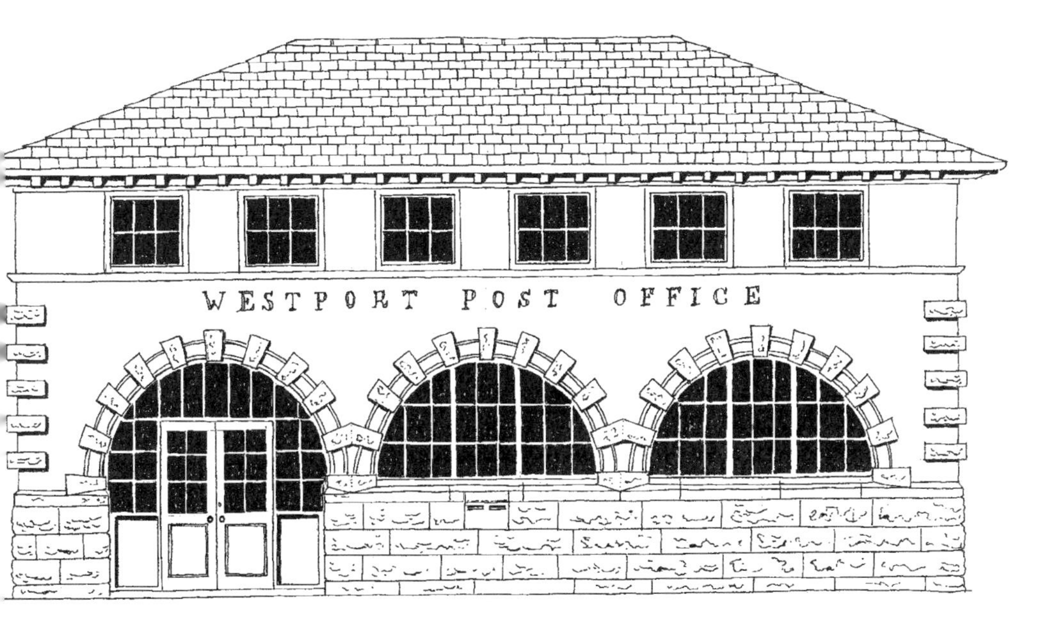

118

Schools

CHARTER SCHOOL MONASTEREVAN CO. KILDARE 1758

SCHOOLS, as a distinct building type, did not emerge in Ireland until the seventeenth century and the earliest of these were the Royal Schools in the province of Ulster. Charter Schools were promoted to protect the Protestant faith in 1730 and it was in this century that many new schools were built in the cities and country towns. The schools built during the period of the Penal Laws were exclusively Protestant and Catholic children were educated either in any existing building which they could avail of or in the open air, in the "hedge schools". The architecturally grand Blue Coat School was built in Dublin in 1723 but the smaller Charter Schools were more modest in character. The school in the small town of Monasterevan is a plain and even severe classical block. The tiny windows, although in character with the authoritarian philosophy of the time which held that children should not be distracted by a view of the outside, are in fact the result of a later conversion to a warehouse when the school closed and the canal brought business to the town. The stone-framed entrance and the bull's eye window in the pediment, or triangular gable, are typical of classical architecture of the eighteenth century. The two smaller side doors were to provide separate entrances for the boys and the girls. The Sunday School was a new evangelical project in the late eighteenth century and the first of these, as a special building type for inter-denominational education, appeared in Ireland. This first purpose-built Sunday School in the world was erected in School Street, Dublin, in 1798.

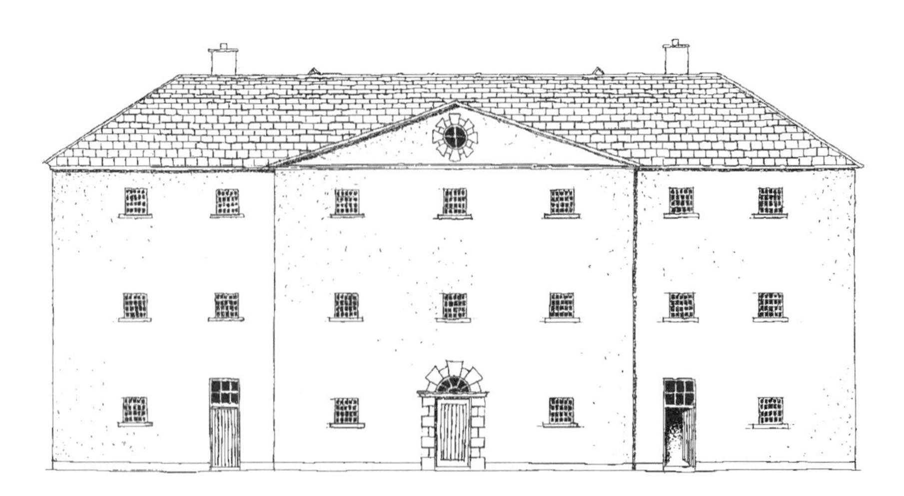

119

NATIONAL SCHOOL
MASTERGEEHEY CO. KERRY

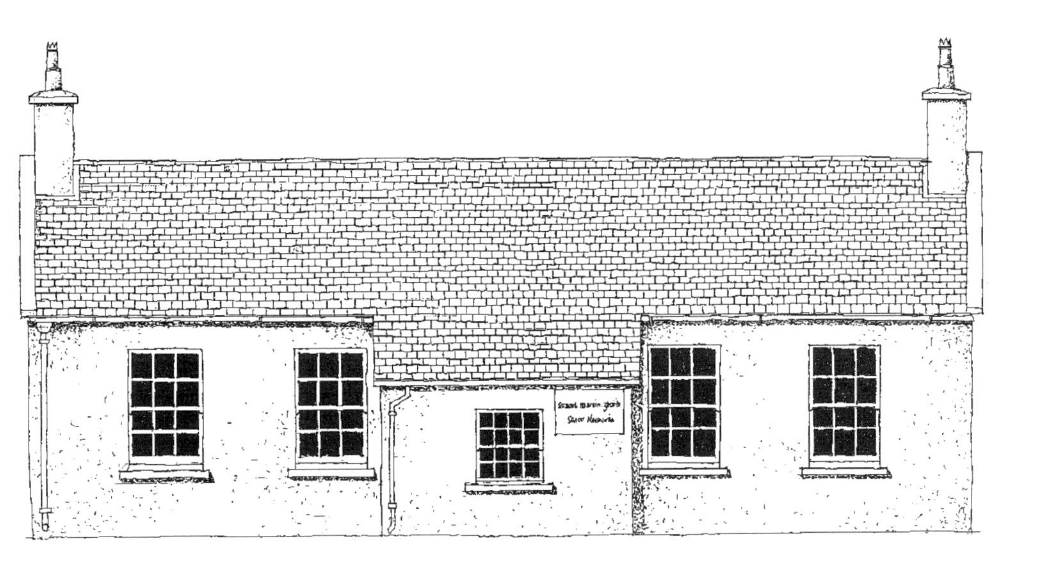

When the force of the Penal Laws against Catholics faded towards the end of the eighteenth century there was a growing official concern about the lack of proper schooling for the children of the majority religion, particularly for the poor. A National Board of Education was formed in 1806 and from this the National Schools were set up in 1831. One of the most ubiquitous building types in the Irish countryside today is the rural National School, although many of the smaller ones have closed and have been converted to other uses. Most of these modest buildings followed a simple formula which was mainly based on a single-storey, two-classroom, block. Within this there were many variations to be played out and in this version in the rural area of Mastergeehey, near Waterville, Co. Kerry, a small porch is economically formed by continuing the roof pitch and providing separate entrances for boys and girls. Separate classrooms were also decreed and the division of sexes was continued with two play-yards, each with its own privy. Most of the small rural National Schools were provided with a stone plaque which had lettering cut in giving the name of the school and sometimes the date. This can usually still be seen in the abandoned or re-used school buildings in the countryside.

120

NATIONAL SCHOOL
BALLINASLOE CO. GALWAY

THE LARGEST LANDOWNER in the area of Ballinasloe was Lord Clancarty whose Garbally House and estate were close to the town. Many of the big landowners of the time were keen to demonstrate their desire to improve the lot of the common people of the area and to this end Clancarty donated a site for the building of one of the new National Schools. The Ballinasloe building is somewhat bigger than the standard country school and the architect here has made a deliberate effort to overcome the major design problem of creating a unified elevation when the separate education of the sexes requires a doubling of the accommodation. By placing the twin entrances, and their windows overhead, close together and then projecting the large classrooms forward the design is neatly unified. The composition is then more strongly emphasized by using a much larger window in each end. The style of architecture adopted was the then fashionable late mediæval, with the characteristic hood moulding which was used originally to throw rainwater clear of openings. In the nineteenth century this was an architectural device to give a look of antiquity. The diamond-paned windows were for the same purpose but in this era after the Industrial Revolution the window framing was made of cast-iron. The Ballinasloe school is built in the famous local limestone which has a blue-grey colour and gives fine sharp joints.

121

BUSH NATIONAL SCHOOL CO. LOUTH

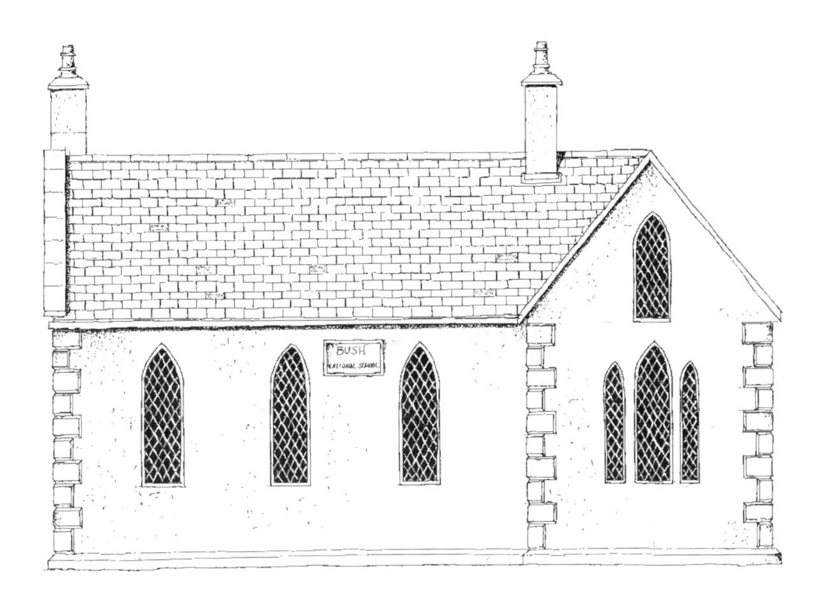

THE NATIONAL SCHOOLS were obliged to provide separate religious instruction and therefore, in Ireland, most were for Catholic children. This tiny school on the Cooley peninsula, near Carlingford, Co Louth, however, was to serve the small Church of Ireland population. The school is situated just behind and to one side of the little Gothic church and the style of the school was in keeping with the style of the church. The classrooms were lit by three tall lancet windows and a triple light on the gable projection, which gave an appropriate ecclesiastical look to the educational establishment. This was in line with the educational ideology of the time where, for instance, one author of a book of designs for schools stated that school buildings should "partake of a semi-religious or semi-ecclesiastical character". Curiously, but possibly in deference to the widespread local classical tradition in Ireland, the rusticated stone quoins are in the older style. The attic space, lit by the smaller window, was to accommodate frugal living quarters for the schoolmaster. The only heating in these small country schools was by open fire and in the poorer parts of the country, particularly in the west or the mountainous regions, each child was expected to bring a sod of turf for the day's heating.

122

NATIONAL SCHOOL
MOUNTSHANNON CO. CLARE

THE NATIONAL SCHOOL in the village of Mountshannon, Co. Clare, is built to a far higher standard than many of the small, two-classroom schools of rural areas whose architecture was generally plain and unpretentious. The Mountshannon building is a clever composition of schoolmaster's house and the two classrooms of the school. The house was placed in the centre and the classrooms were arranged at right angles to each end, making a neat entrance court which was also a front garden for the master. This plan allowed a rigid separation of the boys and girls as well as producing a highly satisfactory solution to the design problem of the composition of the front elevation. The front door to the house was now the main focus while the separate entrances to the schoolrooms were discreetly hidden away to the left and right of the entrance court. The drawing shows the schoolmaster's house with the gables of the schoolrooms outlined on each side. These were lighted by large windows in each gable. The style used for the school and house is Tudor and the treatment for the door and windows is extremely elaborate for such a small building. The ogee-shaped fanlight over the door has delicate tracery while the stone arch is beautifully sculptured with a deep recess. Single stones are used for the window surrounds and neatly carved Tudor hood mouldings are built over the windows. The walling is a richly textured random rubble, using a warm, multi-shaded local stone.

123

VICARSTOWN SCHOOL CO. LAOIS 1868

THE TINY VILLAGE of Vicarstown, just six kilometres north-east of the town of Stradbally, Co. Laois, would seem an unlikely place for such a grand piece of architecture as this school. Vicarstown was to benefit, as did many other small villages which were situated close to great estates, from the generosity of a local landowner. The Grattan family built the Vicarstown school and employed the architect Charles Geoghegan who completed the work in 1868. The designer here triumphantly solved the usual problem of twin entrances and twin classrooms by the bold device of creating a dominant centrepiece to concentrate attention, the classrooms then appearing as simple supporting wings. The powerful central chimney stack and the other two stacks which are turned at right angles and grouped towards the centre all reinforce this inexorable symmetry. The use of red brick for all of the door and window dressings is a practical and economical stratagem and is a colourful contrast to the plastered walls. Stone is used for the little Gothic buttresses and brackets to the front gable bargeboards and this, in conjunction with the pointed arched doorways, gives the desired ecclesiastical touch to the school. The schoolmaster's or schoolmistress's quarters were accommodated in the central block while the children were firmly separated, with classrooms and play-yards for boys and girls on opposite sides.

124

NATIONAL SCHOOL
CLONSILLA
CO. DUBLIN

CLONSILLA IS a little village situated on the Royal Canal in the west of Co. Dublin. The National School is two-storeyed here, in contrast to the generally single-storey arrangement seen elsewhere in the country. The separation of boys from girls is vertical, with boys on one floor and girls on the other. This building is unusual in that there are actually three floors, with a gloomy basement providing quarters for the schoolmaster. There is only one classroom on each floor and the entrance to the upper room is by the doorway on the left. This leads into a narrow hallway and stairs up to the top classroom, which is large and very well lit with windows on three sides. The pine trusses supporting the steep-pitched roof are exposed and this room is quite a splendid space. The lower classroom is of similar size and also well lighted but has a much lower ceiling. There is a grimly ecclesiastical look to the school with the Gothic doorways and steep pointed gables. Each classroom was heated by a closed stove located on one of the long sides of the room.

125

NATIONAL SCHOOL
SANDYFORD
CO. DUBLIN 1936

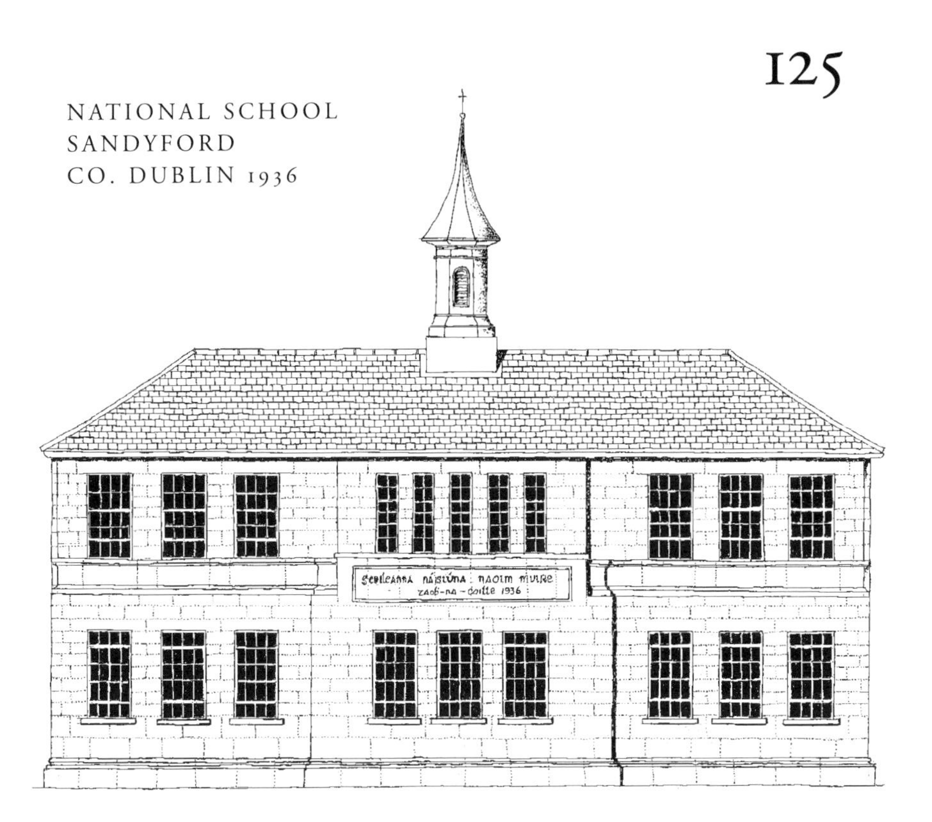

THE ORIGINAL National School at Sandyford, in south Co. Dublin was built in 1840 and was a gaunt utilitarian structure where the infant classes were marshalled on tiered benches to the side of one enormous classroom. This was heated by an ancient pot-bellied stove with the coal stored under the wood floor and reached by a trapdoor. The old school was demolished in 1935 and a resplendent modern building, by the architect Arnold Hendy, replaced the Victorian pile. The policy of the newly independent Irish state in the 1930s was to push forward a programme of new housing, hospitals and schools, and St Mary's in Sandyford was one of the larger county schools of the period. Barnacullia, the linear stonecutters' village on the hill behind the school, supplied many of the pupils and the sole local industry was granite quarrying. The white stone from this area was particularly prized for building and the new school was faced in sparkling local granite in deference to the indigenous craft. The walling is in a fine ashlar and the centre of the block is projected slightly forward. Originally the girls and boys were separated vertically, with the girls accommodated on the top floor and the problem of a single play-yard solved by separate playtimes. Each floor could be one huge space with sliding and folding partitions creating three classrooms on each floor. The copper-clad graceful spire made this a local landmark.

126

Carnegie Libraries

LIBRARY BALLYDUFF CO. WATERFORD 1910

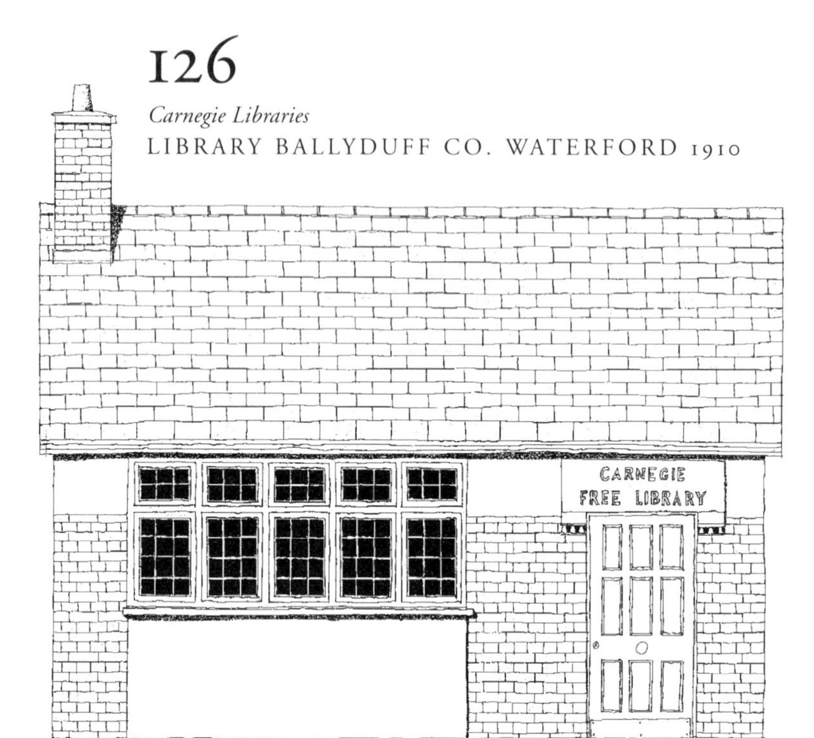

In the early years of the twentieth century the wealthy American industrialist and steel magnate Andrew Carnegie offered a scheme of grants to build public libraries in Ireland. These were to be designated "Free Libraries" and the intention was that ordinary people would have easy and free access to books and journals, and a pleasant and comfortable place in which to relax and read. The Carnegie Library in the village of Ballyduff, Co. Waterford, is one of the smallest of the buildings which received grants from Carnegie. The main room was the reading room and this was supervised by the librarian from his glass-partitioned office. The library is economically built in red brick with plaster panels and a limestone panel over the entrance. The tiny carved decorations under the panel on either side of the door are known as Doric *guttae*. The architect for the Ballyduff library was George P. Sheridan. At least sixty Carnegie Libraries were built in Ireland up to 1918 but the distribution of these throughout the country is anything but even. They are thickly clustered in the counties of Limerick and Kerry and again in Co. Dublin and Co. Wicklow. A smaller number were built in counties Down, Armagh, Cork and Waterford. Most of the rest of the country had no free library and it seems that it was up to an enterprising county or borough council to apply for a grant. The fact that acceptance of a grant meant a commitment to adopt the Library Acts, provide a site and levy a rate meant that many councils in the poorer areas were not willing to proceed.

127

LURGAN CO. ARMAGH 1906

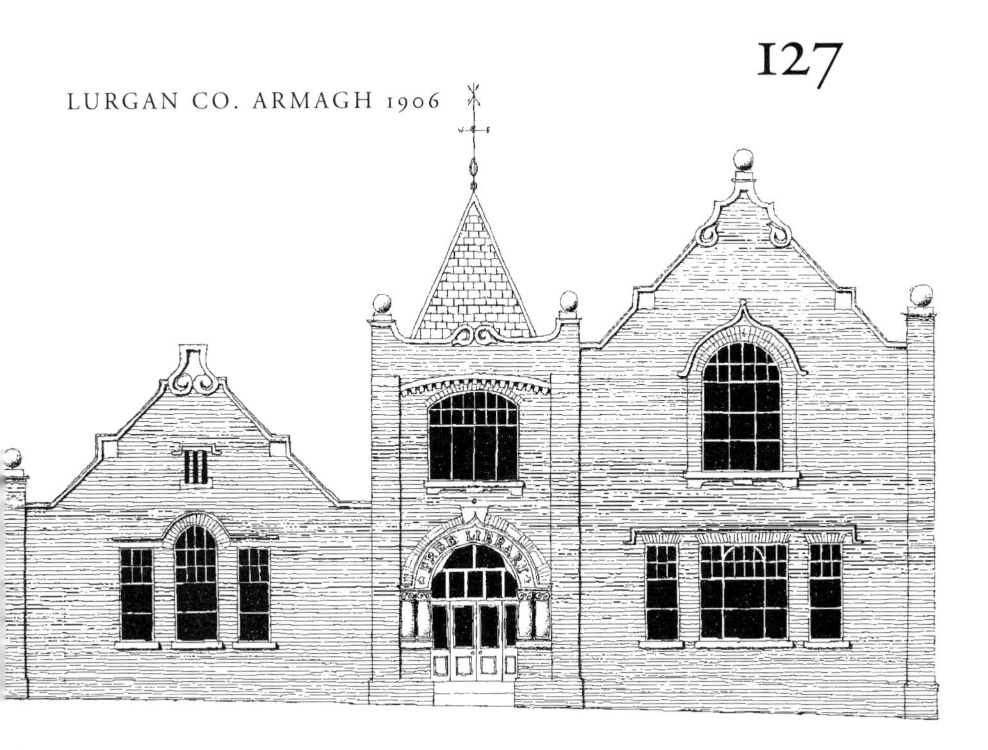

THE LIBRARY on Carnegie Street, Lurgan, was one of the larger free libraries and the grant for this was £2000. The architect was Henry Hobart and he seems to have been given a free hand with this flamboyant design. A mish-mash of influences is evident with borrowings from several of the architects of the late Victorian period whose works were regularly illustrated in the architectural press. The Dutch gables and heavy brick pilasters were popular with famous architects such as Norman Shaw, and Hobart uses these motifs heavily in the Lurgan building. The main lending library was on the first floor and originally the timber roof trusses were exposed. The single-storey block on the left was called the "Boys Room" on the drawings and since no room is similarly labelled for girls it seems that young females were not to have a special area! The doorway is a delightful fantasy with stumpy columns and Ionic caps and the lettering is boldly raised. The building is in red brick with sandstone used for the convoluted copings and decorations. Unusually, the library is well supplied with lavatories for both sexes, on different floors. These facilities were roundly discouraged by library committees for later buildings since they were perceived to cause a nuisance! Other Carnegie Libraries in the area are at Portadown, Co. Armagh, and at Newry, Banbridge, Downpatrick, Newtownards and Bangor in Co. Down.

128

KILKENNY CO. KILKENNY 1910

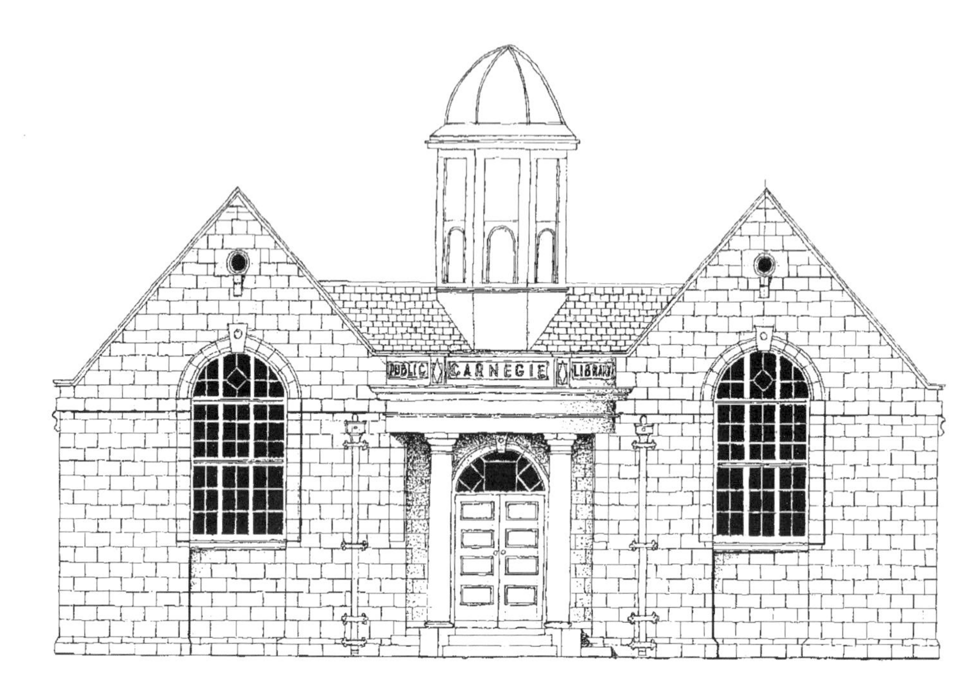

THE PUBLIC library, on John's Quay, Kilkenny, is one of the more interesting schemes produced for this building type, which resulted in a rich variety of designs from nearly twenty different architects. The Kilkenny Carnegie Library was by the architectural firm of E. Stewart Lowrey & Son with Tyars and Jago, and was completed in 1910. The plan of the building was almost square with the reading-room on the left of the entrance and a large lending area with a counter on the right. There was also a small reference area, a librarian's office and, oddly, a small room labelled "Gymnasium". This was, apparently a trick to ensure that a half penny should be struck from the rates under the Gymnasium Act "legally and beyond question"! There was no intention to use the room except for library purposes. A small "Ladies" reading-room was provided and this had a discreet lavatory. The main elevation to the river is largely classical with a fine semi-circular front porch supported on Tuscan columns in limestone. Although the walling looks to be in ashlar stone masonry, it is in fact built in a very well-made concrete block. The negotiations concerning a grant for the library were conducted with James Bertram, who was private secretary to Carnegie. Bertram was annoyed at requests for extra money and queried the cost of the central cupola, calling it an "unsightly object"!

129

Courthouses and market houses

COURTHOUSE

KINSALE CO. CORK 1706

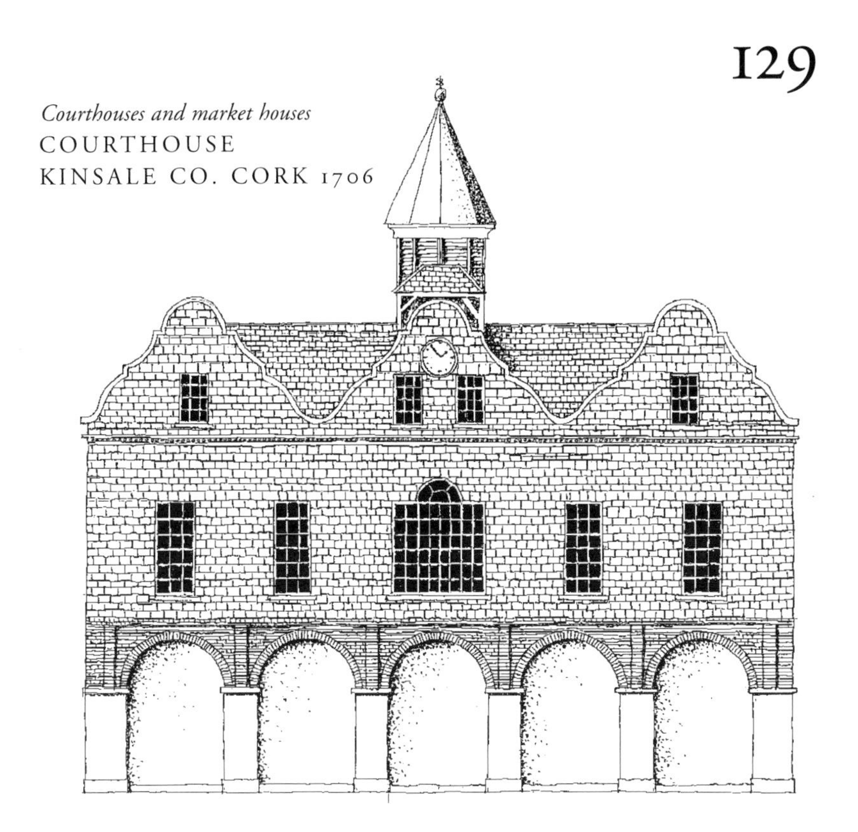

NEW TOWNS were founded and older towns expanded in the early eighteenth century and this period saw the arrival of a new type of public building variously titled Tholsel, Exchange, Guildhall, Market House or Court House. One of the oldest of these is the Tholsel or Court House in Kinsale, an old harbour town in Co. Cork. The main building, as illustrated in the front elevation here, dates from 1706 but the white-painted rear is of a far earlier date, probably *c.*1600. The arcaded ground floor was for a market and the court rooms were on the first floor. The Venetian window, tripartite with the central section round-headed, is one of the oldest in Ireland. The other windows are tall and narrow, a feature of early eighteenth-century architecture in Ireland. The beautiful curve-linear gables are evidence of the strong Dutch influence on Irish building at this time and it is likely that the bricks used in arches, and the spandrils between the arches, came from the Netherlands, possibly as ship's ballast. The slate-hung façade is another feature of a maritime town and the use of slates for wall cladding is common in Kinsale. The central bellcote is louvred and its conical roof is crowned by a weather vane in the shape of a salmon.

130

MARKET HOUSE
BALLYJAMESDUFF CO. CAVAN 1813

THE EARLIEST MARKETS were in the open air and were usually held in some clear space in the centre of the town. The regulation of the markets was soon recognized as a source of revenue to the Crown and the special building type called the market house was soon to appear in most Irish towns. Many of these were simple two-storey buildings with the markets accommodated in an arcaded ground floor. In some of the smaller places a court room or an assembly room was placed on the upper floor. The market house in the centre of Ballyjamesduff was built in 1813 and is a particularly handsome example of the type. The plain block is enhanced by setting back the three-bay arcade and emphasizing the granite quoins of the end bays. The circular openings over the arcade are known as oculi. The plaque in the centre is inscribed "Erected in MDCCCXIII A year memorable for the Glorious Achievements of Marquis Wellington". Decorative niches and small Georgian windows set off the end bays. The drawing shows the arcade as it would have appeared when it was used as a market house. A door has been placed in the centre arch and the other openings have been filled in when the building was converted to another use: a fate which has befallen many of the surviving small market houses.

131

MARKET HOUSE
NEWTOWNBUTLER CO. FERMANAGH 1830

THE MARKET HOUSE in Newtownbutler is one of the best buildings in the town. The design was by the architect W.D. Butler and the building was completed by about 1830. The architecture of the front elevation was carefully considered and the standard formula of a solid block over an open arcade was skillfully varied here by reproducing the arcade again on the first floor, thus achieving a subtle and lively rhythm to the whole façade. Four bays, as distinct from five or three, created an immediate problem of duality, which is a problem for designers since there is no obvious point of focus on the façade of the building. The classical solution here was to create a triangular pediment over the centre and the circular oculus completed the centre of interest. The building is now used as a church or community hall and unfortunately as a result the lower openings of the arcade have been filled in, with doors and windows inserted. The drawing shows the open arcade as it would have appeared originally. The nearby courthouse is also a design by Butler and was completed in the same year. The town of Lisnaskea, just north of Newtownbutler, had a similar market house which was probably by the same architect.

132

MARKET HALL
ATHY CO. KILDARE *c.*1856

THE BUILDING of market houses declined in the later half of the nineteenth century. This was possibly caused by the effects of the Great Famine and also by the coming of the railway system, which encouraged the transport of produce to the bigger markets in the cities. The market house in Athy is one of the last of this distinctive building type and its unusual, not to say bizarre, style of architecture owing to the fact that it was commissioned by the powerful Duke of Leinster. Wealthy landowners often requested striking works of architecture for quite everyday buildings as symbols of their power and influence. Frederick Darley was the architect to the duke, designing two churches and the Model School in Athy, and he may also have been the architect for the market house. The style is a revival of Tudor and the curving gables are certainly Dutch. The building has arcades on both sides. The walling is in a rough rubble of small local stones which create a rich texture. The wall surfaces are nicely framed by cut limestone quoins and the beautifully shaped corner brackets, under the stone barges, are a particular delight. The chimney stack is also in cut stone and the separation of the flues, each given an octagonal shape, is a characteristic device of this revival style.

133

COURTHOUSE DUNDALK CO. LOUTH 1813–19

FROM THE LAST decades of the eighteenth century and into the early part of the nineteenth a series of magnificent courthouses were built in the major towns of Ireland. These buildings were the responsibility of the Grand Juries, bodies which in this period were made up of people of wealth and property. The interests of the landed gentry and aristocracy were thus solidly represented.

Dundalk Courthouse is one of the most impressive examples of this type of public building in Ireland. The architects were Edward Parke and John Bowden, and the courthouse was opened in 1819. The style is Greek, favoured for establishing an image of stern and righteous justice. The portico could be that of a Greek temple with Doric columns and a grand procession of triglphs, with triangular little guttae under each motif, along the frieze, or in a broad band above the columns. The flanking walls are blank, which heightens the mystery and majesty of the dark entrance behind the portico. This is a building which overawes and is to be to be respected, like the law. The portico is built in a lovely white Portland stone, which was easily carved. The main walling is in superbly crafted, granite ashlar blocks. The Carlow courthouse of 1830, by the architect William Vitruvius Morrison is possibly the most magnificent of all of the courthouses of the time. A superb Ionic portico sits on a high podium with twin polygonal courtrooms. Morrison's court-house in Tralee, Co. Kerry, is similar but has semi-circular courtrooms.

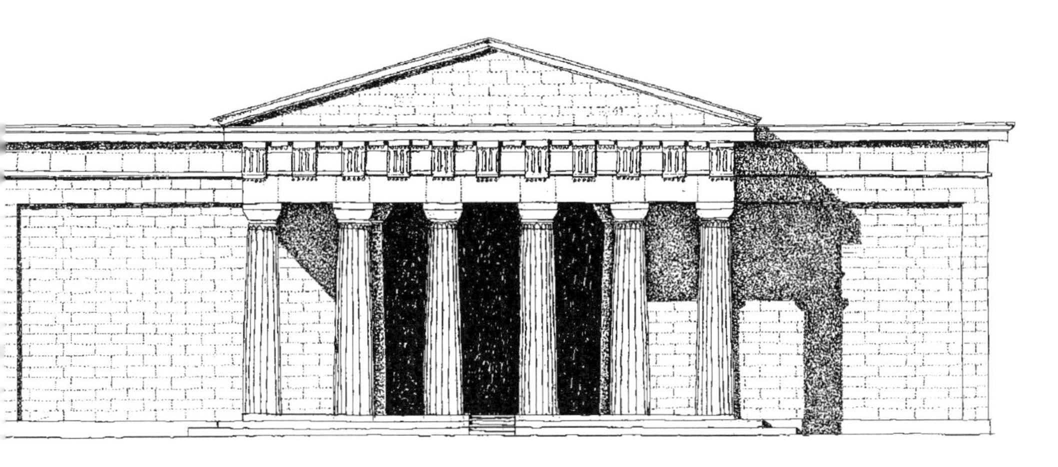

134

COURTHOUSE SKIBBEREEN CO. CORK 1828

THE MONUMENTAL COURTHOUSES were reserved for the larger towns and cities of Ireland but many smaller places were provided with more modest buildings for the administration of justice. The Grand Juries were concerned with more than just simple administration of the law since in large parts of the country they were effectively the local government. They remained in this position until county councils were established in 1898. Small courthouses were built in any town of reasonable size; many of these still exist and most are still used as public buildings. The Grand Juries also appointed the architect and the builder for the court buildings and in the early nineteenth century they also had responsibility for roads and bridges of the region.

The small courthouse in Skibbereen, Co. Cork, is one of a number of similar designs carried out in the southern county in the mid-nineteenth century by the architect George Pain. The massive, fortress-like walling had the dual purpose of supplying the appropriate image of majesty and the practical function of soundproofing the courtrooms from a noisy street. The Venetian window is set high up to achieve a degree of privacy and the twin solid doors, each with a triangular pediment, are set in the solid granite wall. There are similar courthouses in Midleton and Bantry, Co. Cork.

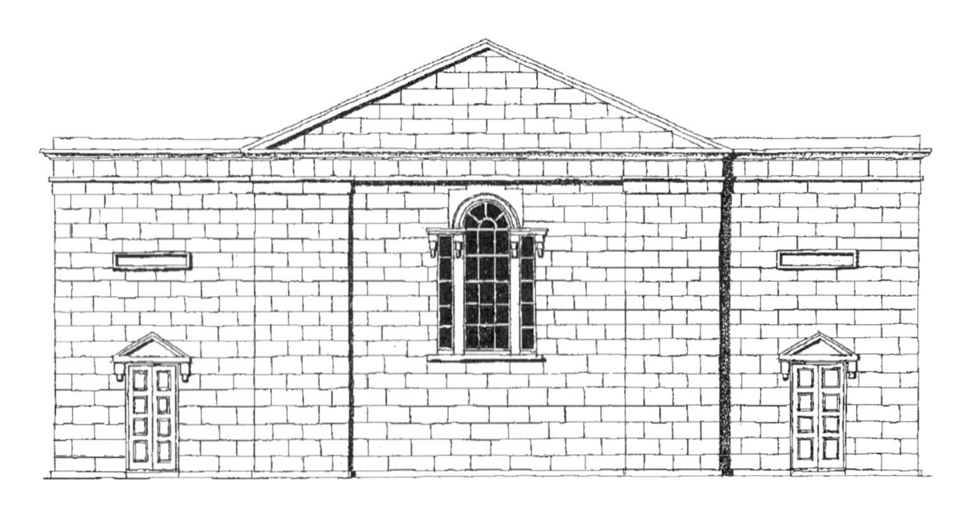

135

COURTHOUSE DUNDRUM CO. DUBLIN 1855

THIS IS A building by one of the most original designers of the nineteenth century, Benjamin Woodward. A remarkably gifted architect, he was a partner in the firm of Deane and Woodward and in his, sadly, short life he produced a series of unusual and brilliant works. His court house in Dundrum, in south County Dublin, was built in 1855 and the design is far removed from the serene and often plain classical used for the majority of the court houses of the country. Woodward was one of the most creative practitioners of the style which came to be known as Ruskinian Gothic which was perfected triumphantly in his greatest work, the Museum at Trinity College, Dublin. The Dundrum building is a highly original adaptation of Gothic with steep pitched roofs and embryonic buttresses. The windows are an ingenious amalgamation of mediæval details. The high pointed brick arches are filled with a thin stone panel out of which is cut a quatrefoil opening, while the jambs and mullions are carefully chamfered. The walling is local granite which is built in the polygonal rubble form, adding to the originality of this lively building.

136

Workhouse

DUNFANAGHY WORKHOUSE
CO. DONEGAL 1841

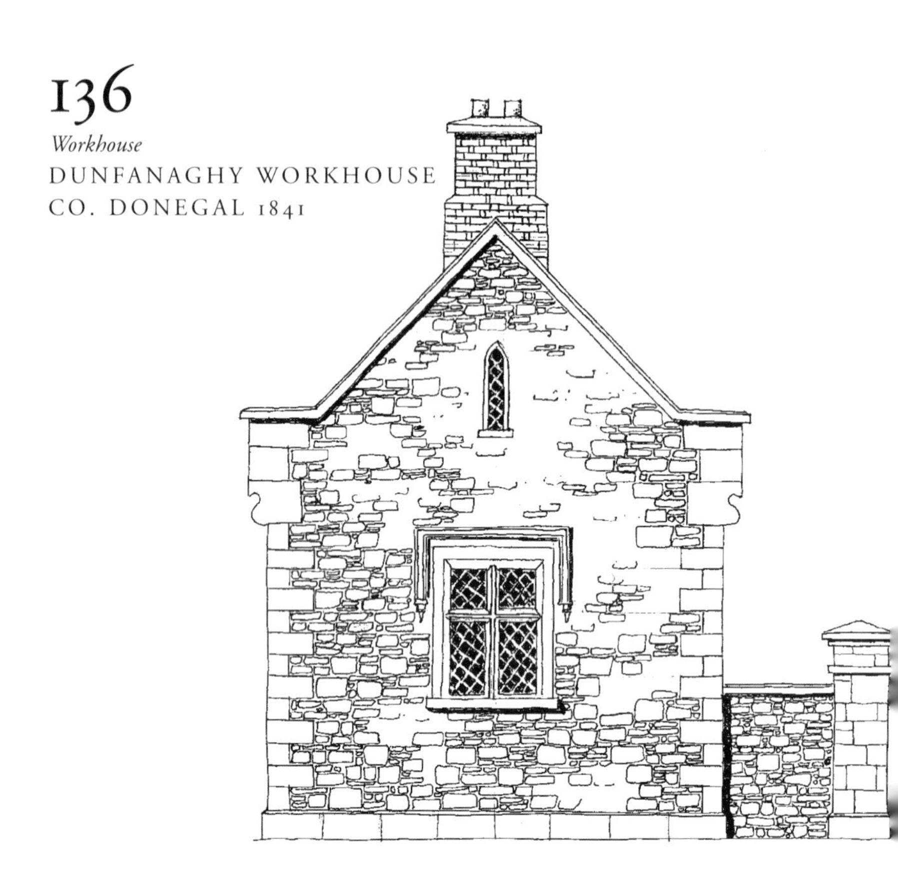

THE IRISH POOR LAW ACT was passed in 1838 and a system of providing relief for destitute people now existed for the first time in the country. Critics of the Act stated that what the poor in Ireland needed most was employment and public works. The Act, however, allowed for charity to be dispensed only through being housed in a workhouse which, in effect, was little different from being imprisoned. The country was split up into 130 areas and these Unions, as they were called, were given the responsibility of building workhouses and administering the system of relief. An English architect, George Wilkinson, who had experience of designing workhouses, was given the job of designing these new buildings for housing the impoverished. From 1840 large numbers of these grim reminders of total dependency arose in every area of Ireland but the Great Famine of 1845 to 1848 filled the already overcrowded buildings beyond capacity. Most of the workhouses had standard plans with sleeping wards, a laundry and kitchen, and sometimes a separate infirmary or fever ward. The complex of buildings was surrounded by a high wall and the analogy to a prison was inescapable. Wilkinson adopted a simplified version of Tudor for all of his workhouse designs, a style in sympathy with the repressive regime imposed by the institutions themselves.

The workhouse at Dunfanaghy in remote north-west Donegal is typical of the smaller institutions in rural areas. This was intended to house 300 inmates and separated males from females in opposing blocks. Families were split up as soon as they entered the gates of the workhouse. Males went to one side and females to the other. A further splitting occurred when boys were separated from their fathers and girls from their mothers. There were adult wards and children's wards and even separate exercise-yards for men, women, boys and girls. There was usually a common dining-hall, although the sexes were separated on opposite sides. Raised platforms were constructed in the wards for sleeping purposes instead of beds, and the degree of overcrowding in famine times has to be imagined. The lavatory provisions consisted of placing of a single privy in the corner of each open yard. The Dunfanaghy design shows Wilkinson's favourite Tudor window with hood moulding and diamond-paned windows. His tiny lancet window is almost a trademark, as is the S-shaped detail of the corbel stone supporting the gable coping. The Dunfanaghy Workhouse lay derelict for many years and parts of the building have long vanished, but the remainder, including the two blocks shown here, were recently restored and are a reminder of a terrible time in Ireland's history.

137

LETTERKENNY WORKHOUSE
CO. DONEGAL 1844

THE LETTERKENNY WORKHOUSE held 500 inmates and the building shown here was the entrance block which in most cases was placed well in front of the main workhouse. This entrance building held the offices with the board-room on the first floor. The architecture of the entrance block is quite benign and its almost domestic character could not prepare the unfortunates who entered the doors for the scale of the great forbidding structures which lay behind. The sharp gables, each with their carved corbels, and the Tudor windows are typical details of Wilkinson's workhouses. The original building had tall chimney stacks on each side of the central recessed section. Each of these may have had up to four flues so this entrance block at least had reasonable heating. Drawings and old

photographs show few chimney stacks on the main workhouse blocks and it would seem that this luxury was not for the paupers. The entrance building to the workhouse in Antrim is almost exactly identical to Letterkenny. The smallest workhouses were to cater for 200 inmates but a great many of these institutions were built to house over a thousand. It is estimated that at the height of the Great Famine over 900,000 destitute and starving people were crowded into the workhouses of Ireland. Many of these buildings became district hospitals or old peoples' homes in the twentieth century and parts of them, at least, still survive in many areas. Letterkenny Workhouse is now a museum.

138

Prisons

CORK CITY GAOL

SUNDAY'S WELL CORK 1822

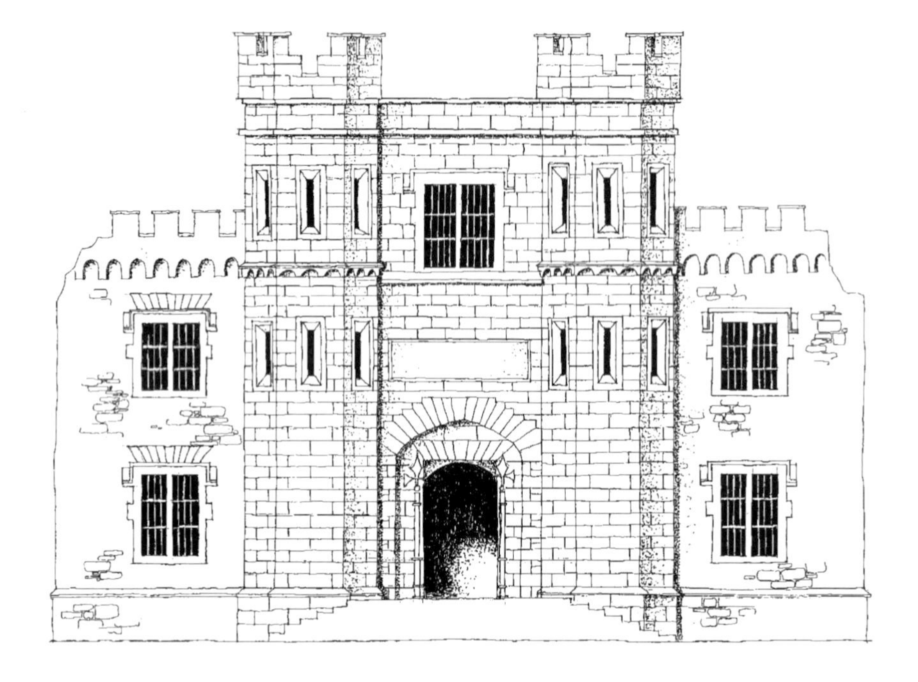

AFTER THE WORKHOUSE the other symbol of repression in Ireland was the prison and large numbers of these were also built throughout the country, particularly in the early years of the nineteenth century. Cork city had a number of prisons; the grim Greek Doric gaol was designed by the Pain brothers and built in 1818. The city Gaol, completed in 1822, used a different imagery to convey respect from the citizenry and possibly terror from the convicted felon. The entrance gates of these prisons was where various stylistic devices were employed to convey the appropriate message. One author of a work on the improvement of prisons suggested that the entrance portal should convey an aspect "as gloomy and melancholy as possible". The gateway of the city Gaol in Cork is designed to imitate the entrance to a mediæval castle and the twin towers, complete with sham arrow loops, framing the narrow cavernous doorway, conveyed an awful prospect of the dungeons within. The iron feature on each side of the door is known as a fasces and spear, and is a symbol of authority. The designer of the City Gaol was William Robertson, who was also the architect for alterations to Kilkenny Castle. The ruins of this magnificent castellated gaol have been recently restored and are open to the public.

139

GAOL
NEWPORT CO. TIPPERARY EARLY 19TH C.

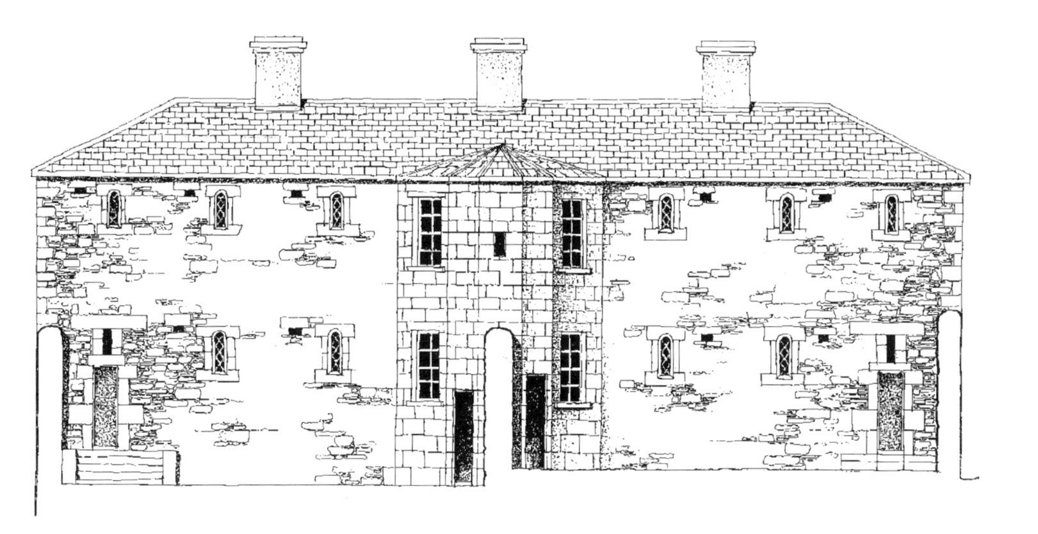

THE PRISONS in the cities and larger towns were for the convicted felons. Here strict solitude and hard labour were prescribed, by the so-called prison reformers of the day, for the rehabilitation of the criminal. The smaller gaols in country towns were intended for the petty offender and were mostly simple places of incarceration where there was little attempt at any kind of reform.

The tiny gaol in the little town of Newport, Co. Tipperary, is a poignant symbol of the harsh regimes which dispensed justice in the nineteenth century, when a place as small as Newport could boast its own gaol. The cells are arranged on two floors and each is supplied with a minute round-headed window with bars in diamond shape, and high up on the wall, an open square hole for ventilation. The cell doors were solid cast-iron and each cell had an iron bed. The central polygonal-shaped block contained rooms for the warders and a spiral stairs to take the top-floor prisoners down to the exercise yard which was entered through a narrow iron door. Males and females were to be accommodated, hence the twin yards which were surrounded by a high wall. Random rubble is used for the main walling while the central block is finished in good quality ashlar with Georgian windows. This is one of the few surviving small-town gaols and it is still largely intact. The drawing is a cross section through the twin exercise-yards with the dividing wall between males and females in the centre.

140

BRIDEWELL TARBERT CO. KERRY

The bridewell was also called a house of correction and was used for locking up the petty offender as well as the vagabonds and disturbers of the peace. The bridewell at Tarbert, on the estuary of the Shannon, is possibly as small as any prison could be. Despite its diminutive size the architect managed to give it a pompous and self-important image. The outer gate with the heavy stone surround was intended to overawe and the language of classicism was used here to convey the image of authority. The outer gate led into a tiny entrance court and then to the door to the prison hall. Most of the larger prisons had this progression from the freedom of the outside world through a number of spaces, each increasingly controlled until the final destination of the cell is reached and the iron door clangs shut. The central block at Tarbert held the warders' quarters and the group of cells for male and female prisoners are arranged on either side. The magnificent array of chimney stacks over the warders' block and the lack of any for the cell blocks, demonstrate the gulf between authority and the prisoner. The semi-circular cell window shape, when provided with heavy bars, was another favoured device to convey the appropriate oppressive image. The exercise-yards for males and females are well separated and help to give the little building an air of civic importance by increasing the length of the front elevation.

141

Francis Johnston (1760-1829)
OBSERVATORY ARMAGH
CO. ARMAGH 1791
ENTRANCE FRONT

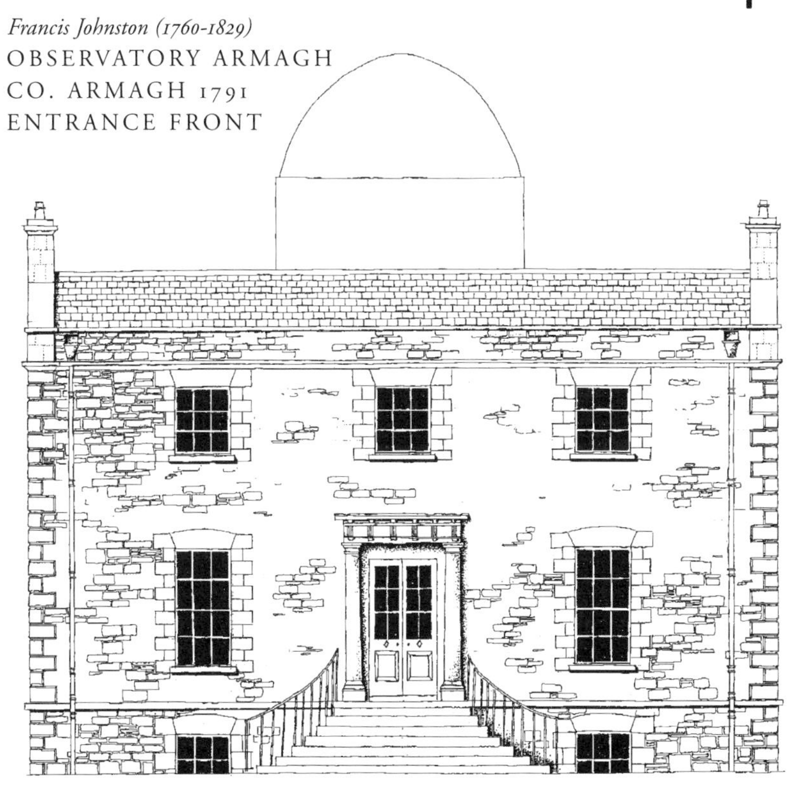

FRANCIS JOHNSTON was one of the most celebrated architects of the late eighteenth and early nineteenth centuries. He was born in Armagh in 1760 and the Observatory in the town of Armagh was completed in 1791 and is therefore one of his earliest works. Until his death in 1829 Johnston carried out a large number of important commissions including houses, churches and large works of civic architecture. As was fashionable at the time, Johnston was adept at both the Neo-classical style as well as castellated Gothic. In the observatory in his home town he employs a version of the classical style which could be identified as personal to him. As in his later classical designs Johnston relies on simple proportions and carefully reduces the amount of ornament on the buildings to the absolute minimum. His great house at Townley Hall, near Drogheda, Co, Louth, is an austere plain cube enriched only by the splendid interiors. One of the earliest observatories in Ireland was the Trinity College Observatory of 1785 at Dunsink, Co. Dublin. The Armagh design comprised a main house with low blocks connected to the east side which housed various astronomical instruments. The only decoration is around the entrance which has a plain Doric entablature supported on columns.

142
OBSERVATORY
ARMAGH
REAR ELEVATION

THE REAR of the building is dominated by the beautiful circular tower surmounted by a dome. The circular form was a favourite of Johnston best seen in the superb central rotunda at Townley Hall. The tower had a massive central pillar around which wound the spiral staircase. The main purpose of the central pillar, however, was to provide a solid foundation and base for the astronomical instrument known as an "Equatorial" which was used to observe the motion of the stars. The dome was revolving and was one of the earliest astronomical domes to survive in Europe. The main walling of the observatory is a richly textured random rubble with the ubiquitous rusticated granite quoins of the country house. The architect, however, recognizes the special and precise character of the pure geometry of the circular tower and gives this a smooth surface with finely bonded ashlar blocks.

A selection of Francis Johnston's most famous buildings would include the Chapel Royal in Dublin Castle, St George's Church and the General Post office in Dublin. When the Bank of Ireland bought the old Parliament House in College Green, Dublin, in 1802 Johnston was appointed as architect for extensive alterations and additions.

BUILDINGS OF THE ESTATE

THE GREAT IRISH country estate existed for about two hundred years, at least in terms of the power and influence exercised by the large landowners in the widespread regions where estates developed. The country houses ranged from the great mansions of the aristocracy to the smaller, solidly built and classically formal farmhouses of the prosperous landowner. In addition to the main house there was a wealth of smaller structures built by the landowner either for his tenants or for the everyday business of the estate. Another and quite disparate class of buildings, but peculiar to the great estate, is the extraordinary array of garden buildings and architectural follies for the enjoyment of the estate owners and their guests.

The estate villages have already been mentioned and although many of these grew out of genuinely philanthropic motives it cannot be denied that a neatly planned village gave prestige to the great estate. Village houses, churches, schools and almhouses were all small, architectural set-pieces, which adorned the approaches to the gates of the estate.

These entrances also provided wonderful opportunities for architectural experiment and sometimes grandeur, and many estates had several entrances widely spaced around the walls of the demesnes. The gatelodge is a special building type and vast numbers of these were built throughout the country. Although many have disappeared a large number of these delightful architectural foibles still exist to be enjoyed countrywide. The province of Ulster is the only region where gatelodges have been surveyed and nearly one thousand are reckoned to survive. Gatelodges were often ingeniously, or more often inconveniently, built on to a monumental gate or built separately as were the houses for the various estate workers, stewards, farm managers or tenants.

The farm buildings themselves constitute another and very interesting building type which has received little study or recognition. These were often included as formal outbuildings attached to the main house or, as in the larger estates, special planned farm complexes, well removed from the main building.

The architectural styles adopted for the small buildings of the estate were as diverse as were the building types themselves. Where the great house was in a formal classical style, some of the buildings, such as the farms, were carefully matched with the architecture of the house. For the gatelodges and the garden buildings, however, imagination was often given full rein and exotic, even bizarre designs flourished. The rich variety of these designs, which can be seen in every county of Ireland, is an indication of the pleasure which the commissioning of these little buildings gave to the architects in the Ireland of the eighteenth and nineteenth centuries.

143

Gateway
CLONGOWES WOOD COLLEGE
CLANE CO. KILDARE *c.*1800

THIS MONUMENTAL, castellated gateway is the main entrance to Clongowes Wood College, a Jesuit boarding-school near the village of Clane, Co. Kildare. The estate was originally Castle Browne, where a Gothic Revival castle was built in 1788. In 1818 it was sold to the Jesuits and substantial additions were made for the building of the school. The twin towers, framing the arched opening, act as a dramatic portal to the start of the long tree-lined avenue up to the main building. The strict symmetry displayed by this gateway was usually employed when a dramatic, direct axial approach was required for the main house, and the language of classical architecture was normally the vehicle for this formality. The Gothic Revival style was popularly deployed at the end of the eighteenth century to achieve a picturesque effect, and the castellated gateway here was an attempt to imitate the formal entrance portal of a mediæval castle. The architect, however, was playing with the language of mediæval architecture and this is not a gateway to intimidate but instead is for the visitor to enjoy the allusions to what is in effect only a sham – a piece of theatre! The towers are too thin, the machicolations are false and the arrow loops, bartizans and battlements are all part of the game of illusion.

144

BRYANSFORD GATE TOLLYMORE PARK CO. DOWN 1786

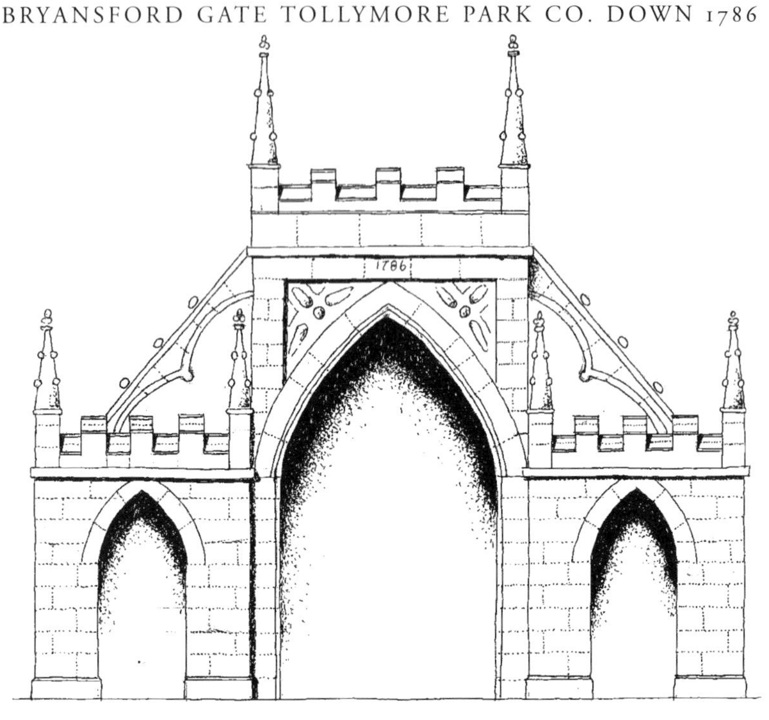

THIS SUPERB Gothic gateway leads from the little village of Bryansford, near Newcastle, Co. Down, into the magnificently forested Tollymore Park. This was originally one of the estates and deer parks of Lord Limerick and was established in the mid-eighteenth century. Romantically sited on the lower slopes of the Mourne mountains, it fulfilled all of the requirements of the picturesque. The original house was demolished in 1952 but most of the large collection of Gothic gates, lodges, bridges and other buildings of the estate survive, to be enjoyed in this forest park which is open to the public. The Bryansford Gate is the most elegant of the structures and its sharply pointed main archway gives intriguing views into the beautiful forest. The flying buttresses, along with the battlements and the pinnacles adorned with little crockets, help to create the agreeable effect of picturesque Gothic. The gateway known as the Barbican Gate is an altogether less-refined structure imitating, as it does, the entrance to a mediæval castle with over-sized arrow loops and rough rubble stone. Among the delights of the estate is the church-like Clanbrassill Barn and a series of romantic bridges in totally different designs. These are called Horn Bridge, Ivy Bridge, Foley's Bridge and Old Bridge. There is also a series of little structures known as Lord Limerick's Follies which are placed outside the estate and along the Hilltown road.

145

Gate and gatelodge
SHANKILL CASTLE
PAULSTOWN CO KILKENNY MID-19TH C.

THIS WONDERFUL castellated gatelodge and gateway constitutes the main entrance to Shankill Castle near the village of Paulstown, some sixteen kilometres east of Kilkenny city. The castle was created from an early eighteenth-century house which was remodelled in the early part of the nineteenth century and given the fashionable mediæval look. The architect for the alterations was the exponent of Gothic conversions, William Robertson, but the gateway is attributed to the later Daniel Robertson. This is a very refined interpretation of mediæval architecture and instead of the rugged, random rubble stonework which could be expected, the entire gate screen and lodge is built in fine ashlar blocks. The lodge is accommodated in the tower which is crowned with miniature battlements. The windows are in the Tudor style, each provided with a hood moulding. The projected window to the first floor is known as an oriel window. The four-centred Tudor arch of the main gate is a more sophisticated version of the Gothic pointed arch. Four arcs, each with a separate centre, are used to describe the curves instead of the normal two centres. The turrets, in diminishing sizes, to the left of the main gate, are references in miniature to the look-out posts of the great castles. The gatelodge to Johnstown Castle, Co. Wexford, is very similar and could be by the same designer.

146

GATELODGE SLANE CO. MEATH MID-19TH C.

THE TINY, Tudor-style gatelodge is in the centre of the village of Slane, Co. Meath. This was the estate village for the great Slane Castle whose demesne is above the River Boyne and borders the village. The cross-roads in the centre of the village is a formal set-piece with four classical-style houses placed precisely at the angles of the cross. The architecture of the gatelodge, however, is influenced by the early Gothic Revival of Slane Castle, designed by James Wyatt and Francis Johnston. The screen wall of attenuated battlements is taken up partly to hide the lodge and focus attention on the gateway. This was often the fate of the actual living-quarters of the gatekeeper with the lodges totally hidden away and dominated by the monumental gateway. The main gateway to Slane Castle, close by and near the river bank, is a magnificent castellated screen with twin turrets and flanking walls, stepped to suit the slope of the roadway. The gatekeeper's lodge is hidden behind and is completely invisible from the approach. Francis Johnston was the architect for this gateway and for the second entrance, designed in the form of a barbican gate to a mediæval castle. These barbicans straddled the entrance and had holes in the floor for dropping rocks or hot liquids on attackers below. The gatelodge accommodation here was partly in the barbican above the gate.

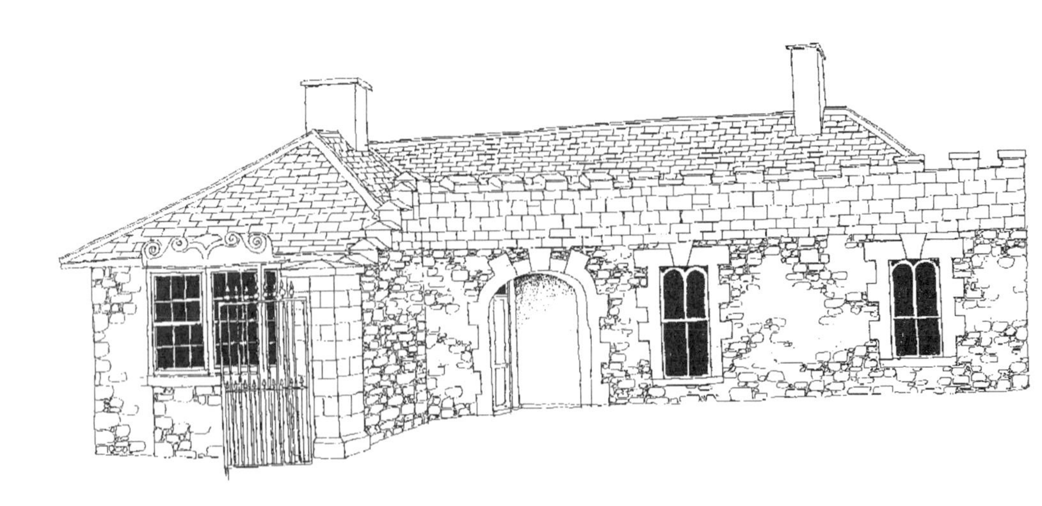

147

GATELODGE AND GATES
FOTA ISLAND CO. CORK *c.*1820

AN EARLY HUNTING lodge on Fota Island in Cork harbour was considerably enlarged in the 1820s by the celebrated architect of nineteenth-century country houses, Sir Richard Morrison. The delightful classical gatelodge and twin gates are almost certainly the work of Morrison. As in so many gatelodges, the architect manipulates the plan of the little house to produce a highly dramatic centrepiece, in the form of a polygonal tower crowned by a central chimney stack. Although the lodge is given three Georgian windows on the ground floor, the domestic nature of the building is deliberately obscured by placing blank panels on the upper storey. The gates are particularly magnificent and obviously intended to impress. The round stone piers carry the wrought-iron gates and infill screens in a superb horizontal sweep. The spear-headed railings, doubled for the lower parts of the gates, were intended to give a firm warning of private property within.

Almost exactly similar gates were built at Killruddery estate, near Bray, Co. Wicklow, and for the magnificent Ballyfin House at Mountrath, Co. Laois. Both were built in the early nineteenth century and designed by Sir Richard Morrison.

Fota demesne encompasses the whole island and contains one of the most famous gardens in Ireland. The warm waters of the southern harbour of Cork encouraged keen horticulturists of the nineteenth century to create gardens of exotic trees and shrubs. The arboretum at Fota is world famous and contains many rare specimen trees.

148

GATE AND GATELODGE
BEARDIVILLE BUSHMILLS CO. ANTRIM *c.*1810

THE GATELODGE provided for the unfortunate gatekeeper at Beardiville, near Bushmills in the north of Co. Antrim, must be the one of the most inconvenient homes ever to be devised. The living quarters here were in two sections, separated by the arched gateway. Each single-storey block was lit by a huge Diocletian window, only the centre section of which was glazed. Since the lodges are no longer occupied, the centre sections, as shown in the drawing, are built up in polygonal masonry. This is almost a vernacular classical composition as the elements are not matched in scale with each other. The arch and Diocletian windows are too large for such a tiny assemblage and the pediment is too small. The result, however, is playful and firmly in the sometimes frivolous tradition of minor estate architecture. The rubble stonework is the local black basalt, peculiar to Co. Antrim and seen to great effect at the nearby Giant's Causeway. Granite is used for the stone dressings and quoins. Great ingenuity was employed to disguise the domestic content of the gateway when the chimney flues on each side were laboriously bent around the archway to emerge in the centre and well behind the pediment as a small stack. This stack has now been removed. The nearby lodge at Ballylough, Bushmills, is another highly inconvenient place for living as practical considerations were all abandoned in favour of producing a completely circular two-storey building to ornament the entrance gates to the estate.

149

GATELODGE
GOATSTOWN SOUTH CO. DUBLIN LATE 19TH C.

THE ESTATE at Goatstown is mostly swallowed by the relentless spread of suburbia but one startling reminder of the nineteenth century era of the great house remains. The gatelodge on Mount Anville Road is a typical High Victorian extravaganza. The sheer quality of the work, however, raises it head and shoulders above the dreary and repetitious speculators' sham Victorian of modern times. The main walling is a pure white limestone, laid in a surprisingly large, snecked, squared manner with red brick used to form the essential vertical corners and arched openings. Pressed bricks are laid head on to give a rich adornment at window-arch level. A popular decorative idea at the time was the use of polychromy; the placing of materials which had several different colours in close relationship with each other. This little lodge is a riot of colour and contrasts with no less than three colours of brick; rich red for the quoins and arches with horizontal bands of white and blue bricks in the chimney stacks. All of this contrasts superbly with the white stone. Even the roof slating is decorative with two shades of light and dark and a band of scalloped slates. A timber roof truss is taken out to adorn the gable and this is crowned with a wood finial. A graceful wrought-iron railing sits on top of a dwarf, stone-capped wall.

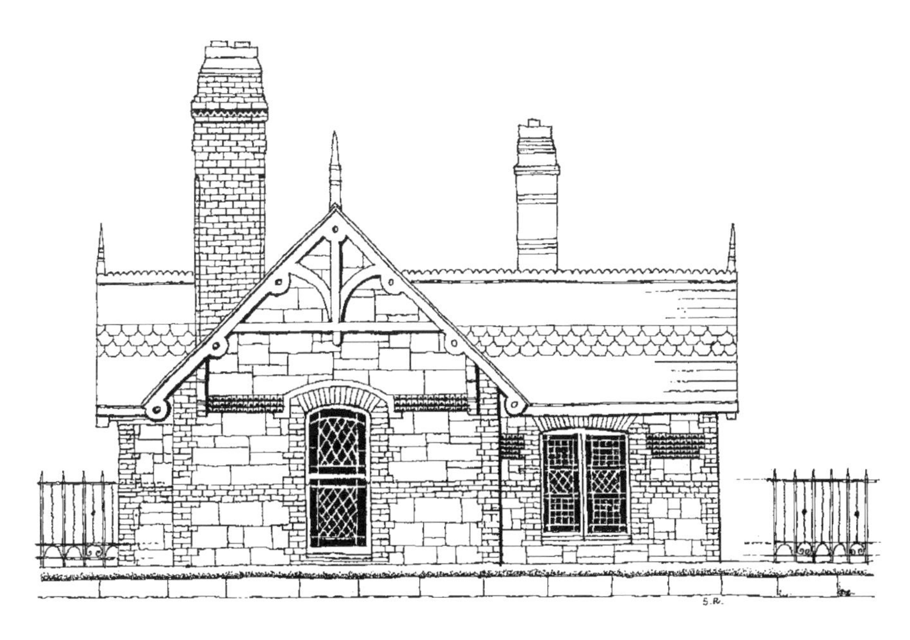

150

GATELODGE TULLOW CO. CARLOW 1859

ONLY A SAD ruin remains of the country house, St Austin's Abbey, close to the town of Tullow, Co. Carlow. The house and various buildings on the estate were the work of the celebrated architect Benjamin Woodward. The robust gatelodge survives intact, however, and is an example of Woodward's wonderful manipulation of geometry to produce arresting architectural forms. Even for a commission as small as a gatelodge the architect gives a unique identity and sense of importance to the building. The steep roof with its asymmetrically placed dormer window sits on top of a solid stone block. The stonework is a finely bonded squared rubble and the quite large stones are bonded without any obvious pattern and without regular quoins, giving a textural effect very different from a formal classical design. The dramatic chimney stack is a contradiction of this with its bold chamfers and ashlar masonry.

Near Thomastown, Co. Kilkenny, about forty kilometres south-west of Tullow, Woodward designed a country house called "Brownsbarn", which is one of the best of his smaller works. One of his grandest houses is "Glandore" in Monkstown, Co. Dublin, another exercise in Ruskinian Gothic with dramatic, tall chimney stacks. His prettiest domestic work must be "Clontra" in Quinn's Road, Shankill, Co. Dublin, where he uses an exotic mixture of pointed brick arches and steep dormers in a rich granite walling.

151

Estate houses

ARDAGH CO. LONGFORD 1862

THE ESTATE VILLAGE of Ardagh in Co. Longford is a very late example of the work of an improving landlord in Ireland. Sir Thomas Fetherston employed the Dublin architect, J. Rawson Carroll, to design the complete village, and the result is a Victorian ideal of pastoral living. Single- and two-storey cottages are grouped around two sides of a triangular green which has a Protestant church on the other side and a clocktower acting as a focal point for the village. The cottages have the steep pitched roofs which were commonly used for Victorian housing. The prominent timber barge-boards, which are decorated by cut-outs and curves, are devices borrowed from mediæval architecture. The popular revival of these styles lasted well into the later years of the nineteenth century. The diamond-paned windows are again a reminder of past styles but in the mid-nineteenth century the windows could be purchased from a builder's catalogue in standard sizes and made in cast-iron. The walling is a beautiful, snecked, rubble limestone in random patterns. The stones around the windows and porch are carefully dressed and the sharply angled chamfer to the window jambs and lintel adds a stylish detail. The clocktower is a Gothic design with pinnacles and an inscription dedicates it to the original landlord, Sir George Fetherston, for his "life-long devotion to the moral and social improvement of his tenantry".

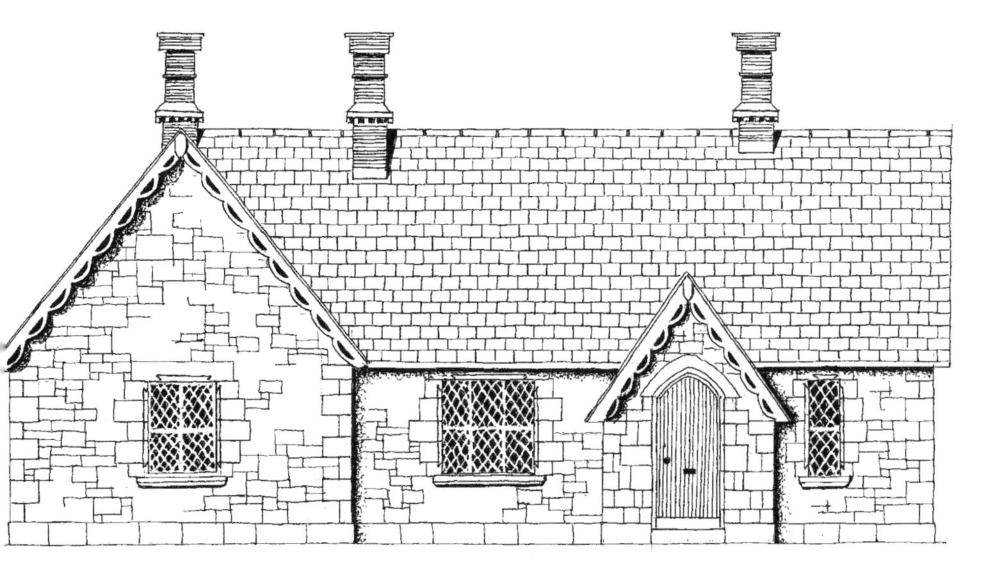

152

ESTATE COTTAGES
POWERSCOURT CO. WICKLOW *c.*1860

THE GREAT ESTATE of Powerscourt in north Co. Wicklow was planned and laid out in the years after the completion of the Palladian mansion in 1740. A vast programme of work was initiated to create an extensive landscaped park along the romantic, winding river Dargle and culminating in the sublimely picturesque waterfall in the mountains to the west. In the mid-nineteenth century a later Lord Powerscourt, in addition to creating the planned village of Enniskerry, continued the development of the estate with the construction of the superb terraced garden to the south of the house and other massive works of roads, waterways, demesne walls, gates and farm buildings. Contemporary accounts of the work in the early stages mention the employment of "great numbers of labourers". In addition to half-a-dozen gatelodges, a number of houses were built for the estate workers at Kilmolin, to the north of the estate and outside the walls of the demesne. These were both two-storey and single-storey in semi-detached form and the design produced shows the care taken by the designers to resolve the problem of uniting the elevation of two identical units. The plan of each house was "handed" which pushed the entrances apart and concentrated the windows towards the centre. The carved barge boards are a delight and the walling is a wonderful mix of random rubble with cut granite for the quoins and brick employed for the infills and surrounds. The Tudor window hoods echo the antique image of the planned village in the valley below.

153

VIRGINIA CO. CAVAN MID-19TH C.

THE PRETTY VILLAGE of Virginia on the shores of Lough Ramor in the south of Co. Cavan was a plantation village founded in the reign of King James I. The Marquis of Headfort built a hunting lodge on the lake shore in the early nineteenth century and this building and accompanying lodges were in the fashionable picturesque style. These semi-detached cottages in the main street of the village also followed this romantic style which was widely promoted by writers in the early years of the century. Pattern books illustrated designs for ideal cottages and the rustic appearance was especially praised. The frilly carved barge-boards over the dormer windows and porches are combined with the rustic posts, interlaced over the doors. The picturesque movement, in so far as it affected the design of villages, was in many ways a reaction to the Industrial Revolution and the rise of the industrial, unplanned city. Nostalgia for a lost rural past ,in addition to a re-discovery of the beauties of nature in wild landscapes, encouraged an enthusiasm to re-create these ideals in humble cottages, cottage gardens and village churches, with chimney smoke rising above screens of trees. There are several picturesque gatelodges nearby, on the banks of the lake.

154

Gamekeepers' lodge

DOWNHILL CO. DERRY *c.*1854

AN ARMY OF SERVANTS and workers was needed to run the great estates during the eighteenth and nineteenth centuries, when their influence was strongest. Not the least important member of the staff was the gamekeeper since it was his work which ensured the main entertainment for the landowner and his guests. The Keeper's Lodge, illustrated here, is an imposing-looking structure with its gabled front and bullseye window. The house has two storeys but the entrance front is designed for effect and only the ground floor has windows on this side. These are placed in recessed arched openings to pretend that this is a single hall with a high ceiling. The walling is in the local black basalt with brick used for the arches and the horizontal band.

The Earl Bishop of Derry's great estate at Downhill, near Coleraine, stretched along the north coast and today only the ruins of the huge country house survive. The Earl Bishop was a compulsive builder and the demesne, which was developed from the end of the eighteenth century, acquired an extraordinarily diverse collection of temples, follies, gates and lodges. The most romantic estate building is the Mussenden Temple, built in 1785 and in a spectacular location on the edge of a sea cliff. The temple along with the mausoleum and the two entrances, the Lion Gate and the Bishop's Gate, are designed in the style of the Renaissance.

155

Farm steward's house

COOLATTIN SHILLELAGH CO. WICKLOW MID-19TH C.

THE HOUSE for the farm steward at Coolattin is the dominant feature of an extensive planned farm layout in this heavily forested part of south Co. Wicklow. The farm buildings are now neglected and partly ruined but the façade, at least, of this sturdy house survives intact. The design is unusually monumental for a member of the staff of the estate and was no doubt mainly intended to stress the importance of the landowner. The house gable is turned to the road to form the entrance front and the gable itself is fashioned into a classical pediment with a prominent bulls-eye window. There are heavy stone barges to the eaves forming the top of the pediment, but the rest of the front is totally devoid of ornament. The entrance door surrounds are in large, dressed stone blocks with a shallow hood. The main walling is in a high-quality granite ashlar which would not be out of place on a grand courthouse or Palladian mansion. The high stone stacks have no less than eight flues which meant that each of the rooms had a fireplace. Coolattin Park was the estate of the Earl of Fitzwilliam whose house was built in 1804.

156

Estate farm

THE GRANGE CASTLEWELLAN CO. DOWN *c.*1750

VERNACULAR FARM BUILDINGS in Ireland were almost always small and the layout of the various buildings was not formally planned. The simplest farm buildings were merely additions to the traditional long house with the animals and feed kept in thatched extensions to the domestic part of the house. In some areas a fall in the ground allowed for loft storage over a byre but the buildings were essentially utilitarian. On the eastern side of the country, and notably in Co. Wexford, there was occasionally a conscious effort to arrange farm buildings at right angles to form a courtyard, with the main house occupying one side. These arrangements were always practical and there was no attempt to make an architectural composition. When the great estates were laid out in the eighteenth century almost all of these had farm buildings, some attached to the main house. The strong influence of Palladianism on the architecture of the country house was reflected in the design of the farm buildings. Simplicity, formality and perfection of proportions were guiding principles, and the farms which were attached to the mansions were designed as parts of the overall composition with pavilions, connecting arcades and formal courtyards. The planned courtyard, with buildings reserved for different functions or housing stock, became commonplace for the estate farm and the court arrangement was also used for farms constructed away from the main house. In the larger estates there were often several farm complexes at different ends of the estate.

The planned farm for the estate at Castlewellan, Co. Down, is a very early example of the type and it is possible that it may date from even earlier than 1750. The farm is built separately and well away from the castle. It consists of three formal courtyards, each linked to the other, and the drawing shows the south-east side of the first court. There are eight segmental arched openings for the stables and the louvred openings overhead provided ventilation and may also have been used as pitching holes for getting hay to the loft. The architecture is plain and simple, and although adhering to Palladian principles the rough white-washed walls place the buildings close to the vernacular tradition. The second courtyard also has two-storey buildings and the gateway leading into the third court has a bellcote. The third courtyard walls have been largely demolished but the stone gate piers remain. A dovecot (illus. 160) is placed on the axis of the entrances to the courtyards. The grange may have originally included living-quarters but the present castle was built in 1858. The demesne contains several other interesting buildings including one of the most handsome gatelodges in Ireland. The lodge is at the Castlewellan gate and was designed by William Burn in 1861. The design is a full-blooded example of the picturesque with three extravagantly carved gable barge-boards. Castlewellan is now in public ownership and has been opened as a forest park.

157

Farm buildings

TIGLIN ASHFORD CO. WICKLOW 1866

THE TIGLIN farm buildings were built on the estate of Glanmore Castle, the home of Francis Synge MP, great grandfather of the poet and playwright J.M. Synge. The castle was built in 1804 to the castellated designs of Francis Johnston. This farm was situated high above the Devil's Glen, a popular scenic spot in the nineteenth century and now buried in the shade of a state forest. The buildings of the farm were laid out in a strictly formal and geometrical plan. This consisted of two walled rectangular spaces of equal size, set out side by side and separated by a roadway. The entrance gates to each walled courtyard were from this road. The sides of each yard were lined by buildings with pitched slated roofs consisting of stables, byres, barns, animal houses and accommodation for farm workers. The steward's house completed the side of one rectangle. The range of buildings shown here occupies the short side of one courtyard and housed stables with lofts for feed and fodder overhead. Access for loading the loft was provided by the small square openings over the doors. The circular windows, or bullseyes as they were called, are a recurring motif at Tiglin. The lattice glazing-bars of the window openings are in sympathy with the fashionable antique style of the time and were made of cast-iron.

158

TIGLIN ASHFORD CO. WICKLOW

THE LONG SIDE of one of the rectangles consisted of a forge and a pigsty. The forge had a horseshoe-shaped entrance in cut granite with the date of the farm cut into the arch. The architectural indulgence of the forge entrance is matched by the luxury of the cut-stone arched openings to the pigsties! In mediæval times pigs were allowed to roam widely and forage in the woods for food. By the middle of the eighteenth century selective breeding produced the farm animal which needed to be housed in sheltered conditions. Each pigsty had a little walled yard which contained the feeding trough which could be supplied from outside. Strong wooden gates were fitted to each pig yard and the round openings overhead were for ventilation. Specially designed pigsties were popular in the planned farms of the nineteenth century and there are many surviving examples of little architectural gems like the set at Tiglin. The walling is a wonderfully rich mix of local stone, the light-coloured blocks of granite contrasting with the dark shades of mica schist: the two stones of the Wicklow mountains. A bright-red brick was used for the arched openings and the surrounds to the windows. As well as creating a nice effect this was a wholly practical device for quick and easy construction. Tiglin now houses a Youth Hostel in one courtyard and an Outdoor Education Centre in the other.

159

Courtyard farm

NARROW WATER CO. DOWN LATE 19TH C.

THE COURTYARD FARM at the Narrow Water estate near the town of Warrenpoint, Co. Down, is a surprisingly modest Georgian design, when contrasted to the Tudor picturesque of the house and its marvellous castellated gateway. The range of plain buildings here may have housed farm workers as well as a stable, behind the triple-arched opening. The central classical pediment, with its blank bullseye decoration, gave a simple dignity to this modest range of buildings. The walling is in rough random rubble with selected larger squared stones used for the quoins. This range of farm buildings has now been converted into housing which demonstrates how successful the old courtyard farm can be when restored to new uses, since modern farming methods have made such worthy buildings redundant.

Possibly the most splendid of all of the courtyard planned farm buildings in Ireland is the stables at Carriglas, Co. Longford. The work of the celebrated architect James Gandon, the stables date from about 1795 and consist of a perfectly proportioned walled rectangle, divided into two courts. Kilcarty, Kilmessan, Co. Meath, is a country house of about 1780 and the farm buildings here form a great courtyard behind the house with the gable ends of the barns designed as part of the composition of the front façade.

160

Dovecote
THE GRANGE
CASTLEWELLAN
CO. DOWN
EARLY 19TH C.

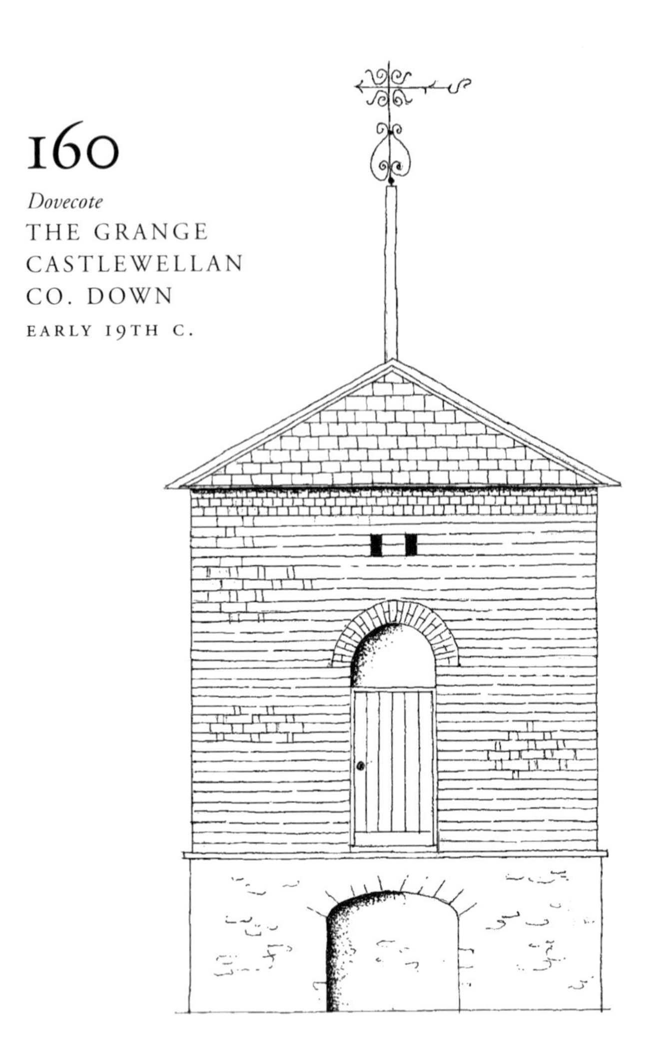

THE DOVECOTE or columbarium is a building type which has existed since mediæval times. Before the advent of modern farming methods there was a shortage of fresh meat at certain times and a supply of pigeons for the table bridged the hungry gap. In Ireland the mediæval monastic foundation developed this special building for the housing of large numbers of pigeons which could be harvested for food. A small number of these early dovecotes survive: notably at the Augustinian monastery of Ballybeg, just south of the town of Buttevant in Co. Cork. These early dovecotes were small round structures, roofed with stone domes, and the interior of the wall had hundreds of holes and roosts for the birds. The great estates of the eighteenth century usually provided a dovecote for the production of a table delicacy rather than an essential food. The dovecote at Castlewellan is aligned with the farm buildings at the Grange and is a simple, square brick building and crowned with a pretty weathervane. The pigeons entered through the small holes and the interior walls were lined with brick roosts.

161

Picturesque farm buildings
BARN CAVANGARDEN
BALLYSHANNON
CO. DONEGAL
EARLY 19TH C.

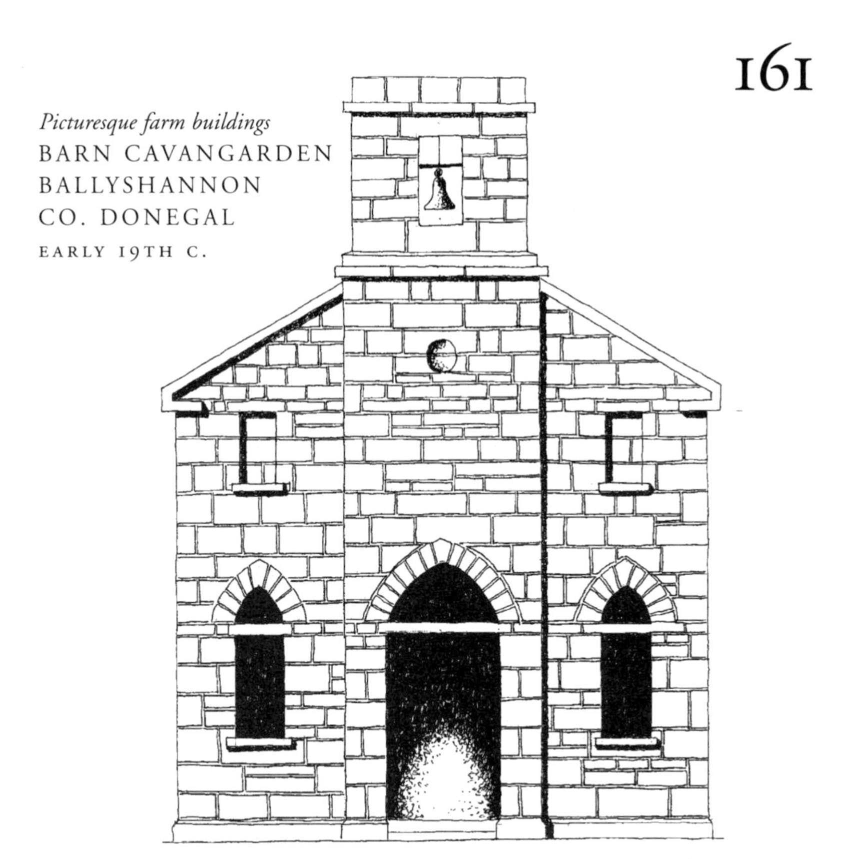

TOWARDS THE END of the eighteenth century the buildings of the large country estates were strongly influenced by new interest in the romantic aspect of landscape which led to the style known as the picturesque. It was no longer enough to design farm buildings in a plain and simple version of the Palladian or classical style of the main house. The farm buildings were now to be given belfries or spires and even to be totally disguised, as in the treatment of the barn gable at the estate of Cavangarden, four kilometres north-east of Ballyshannon, Co. Donegal. The image of a little Gothic church was adopted here to give the desired romantic feeling to a utilitarian building. Walks or carriage driveways were planned so that these picturesque structures could be viewed or glimpsed through the trees, thus recreating the arcadian scenes of contemporary painters of the romantic landscape. The estate and house of Cavangarden date from 1770. The most extraordinary barn built in a great estate is the aptly named Wonderful Barn on the Castletown demesne, near Leixlip, Co. Kildare. Built in 1743, this bizarre conical tower with a winding outside stairs may have been commissioned more for the purpose of supplying a romantic landmark than to have any practical use for storing grain.

162

Gazebo

GAZEBO AND BOATHOUSE
LEIXLIP CO. KILDARE

MID-18TH C.

TO ENJOY the romantic landscape properly and in comfort a suitable vantage point was all important. The little buildings known as gazebos were erected for the dual purpose of providing shelter at a viewing point on the estate and also to act as an appropriate arrival destination for a excursion or picnic. Although often classed as a folly, since the gazebo could be described as a frivolous building, it did have more of a practical function than many other follies which were totally ornamental. The gazebo at Leixlip Castle is superbly sited on the river bank at the meeting of the waters of the Liffey and Rye and near the village of Leixlip, just west of Dublin. The look-out chamber is a hexagonal-shaped room roofed with a dome and built over a boathouse. A small-sized random rubble is used for the chamber and a larger and more rugged rubble for the base. Red brick provides neat and precise angles. Another garden building which served the same purpose as a look-out was the belvedere, a term originating in Italian landscape design.

163

Folly
PEBBLE HOUSE
RUBANE KIRCUBBIN
CO. DOWN *c*.1740

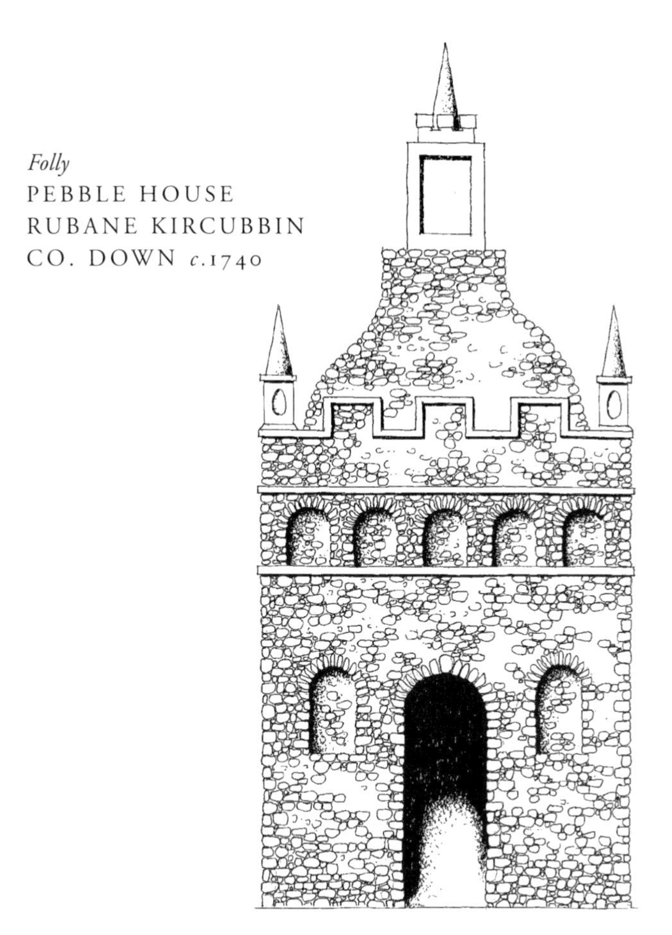

THE ULTIMATE FOLLY in terms of fantasy building is the grotto. In complete contrast to the belvedere or gazebo, the grotto was intended to be a place of mystery and even of delicious terror. Grottoes were always dark and gloomy places and almost every estate had some form of this building for the entertainment of the guests. Unusual and even grotesque materials were invariably used in the construction of the grotto to conjure up disturbing feelings and shivers of apprehension when entering the forbidding portal. The Pebble House on the estate of Rubane, Co. Down, is more ornamental than many grottoes which were often constructed as rocky caves, but the use of bizarre round pieces of volcanic stone and the dark interior fulfilled the desired purpose. Exotically shaped pieces of rock which had been eroded into fantastic shapes by wind or water were a favoured material for grottoes. The Hermit's Cave was a type of grotto popular in the Irish country estate and could evoke feelings of horror at the possibility of a wild-looking denizen with matted hair! Less terrifying were the grottoes designed as shell houses where the interior of the building was decorated with thousands of colourful shells. The most famous of these is at Carton, near Maynooth, Co. Kildare.

164

EYECATCHER
LAWRENCETOWN CO. GALWAY LATE 18TH C.

THE LANDSCAPE OF IRELAND was covered in ruins in the eighteenth century. The stark remains of destroyed monasteries, castles, tower houses, early churches, round towers and the huge legacy of megalithic monuments and pre-historic forts were to be seen everywhere. In these circumstances to build a deliberate ruin would seem to be a pointless exercise, but the very presence of real ruins acted a spur to the romantic spirit. Everybody wanted a ruin to grace the landscape of the estate and these eye-catchers, as they were called, helped to create agreeable scenic compositions. The estate of Bellevue, near the village of Lawrencetown in south county Galway, is long vanished and this Gothic ruin stands incongruously in a field near a little country road. With flying buttresses, pointed windows and pinnacles, it is a piece of theatre scenery: the front wall of a building which never existed! The largest Gothic sham ruin in Ireland is at Belvedere on the shores of Lough Ennell, near Mullingar, Co. Westmeath. This enormous structure is known as the "Jealous Wall" since it was reputedly built by Lord Belvedere to blot out the view of his brother's house!

165

Gothic cottage

LAWRENCETOWN CO. GALWAY LATE 18TH C.

THIS FOLLY is a contradiction since a two-storey house is concealed behind the Gothic extravaganza which constitutes the gable wall of the dwelling. Ambiguity and contradiction were employed enthusiastically by garden and landscape designers, as demonstrated by the wealth of miniature temples, sham castles, toy forts and hermits' caves built for the great gardens of Europe since the Renaissance. Follies, like the grotesque assembly of bits of mediæval architecture as illustrated here, were also popular in this game of illusion. The cottage, on the old estate of Bellevue, was placed at right angles to the road so that the folly on the gable end would disguise the dwelling, until revealed to the visitor's amazement when viewed from the side. The flying buttresses jut out at an angle and are far too big for the little building but are part of the pleasure and fun which follies were intended to provide. The building has suffered in recent years with the loss of some of the pinnacles, the cross and the stepped gables, and also from being painted over in whitewash. The drawing shows the original folly with the missing elements as depicted in old photographs. Bellevue estate was also called Lisreaghan and was famous for its great woodlands of ilexes and cedars of Lebanon, but little remains today and the old house with its Doric portico has long vanished.

166

Triumphal arch
VOLUNTEER'S ARCH
LAWRENCETOWN CO. GALWAY 1782

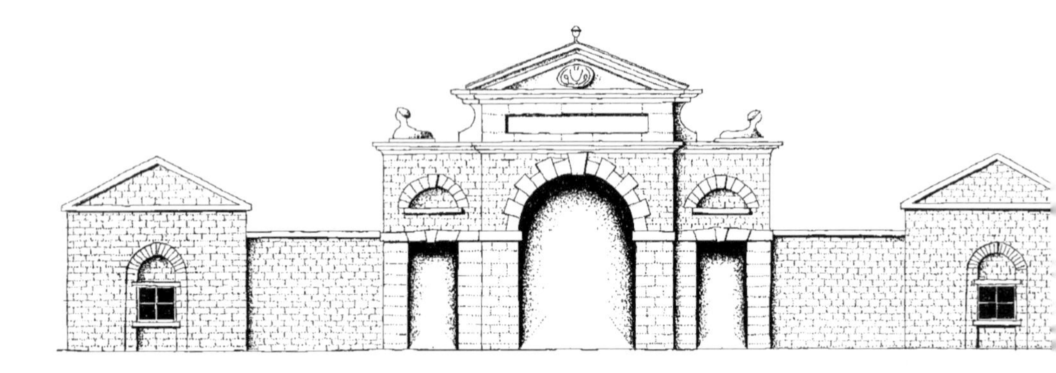

THE MONUMENTAL or triumphal arch has been one of the most enduring architectural symbols since it was invented by the Romans in the first century BC. From the Arch of Tiberius to the Grande Arche in Paris the celebration in stone of the passage through a portal has been revived endlessly for some two thousand years.

The monumental gateway at Lawrencetown is called the Volunteer's Arch and was built by Walter Lawrence to commemorate the Irish Volunteers of 1782. The arch was also the main entrance to the old estate of Bellevue and the avenue to the house swept grandly up from the gates. The gates and the avenue are now gone and the beautiful arch stands neglected and forlorn across a minor country lane. The small pedimented pavilions on either side of the screen walls housed tiny two-roomed gatelodges, each with a window to the outside world set in deep recesses. The triumphal arch is decorated with a medallion in the centre of the pediment and two sculptured sphinxes stare out at the countryside.

Irish country estates are well endowed with monumental gates and triumphal arches. One of the oddest is at Bantry House, Co. Cork, where the arched opening is surrounded by a magnificent two-storey gatelodge. At Mote Park, near Ballymurray, Co. Roscommon, the original house of 1787 has vanished but a magnificent triumphal Doric arch survives, surmounted by a stone lion.

BUILDINGS OF INDUSTRY AND TRANSPORT

THE INDUSTRIAL REVOLUTION in the eighteenth century saw the beginnings of an architecture of industry and most Irish industrial buildings date from the middle of that century. Industrial activity, however, had far older origins in Ireland, stretching back to pre-historic times with mining and fabricating metals.

Water power was harnessed by the early monasteries but there was no special architecture for industry until comparatively recent times. The eighteenth century, which was a period almost free of war, saw a great industrial expansion in Ireland. The Dublin Society was founded in 1731 with the aim of promoting industry and advancing the practice of agriculture. Water power was harnessed far more efficiently with the development of advanced gearing systems. Mills for corn and flax scutching and for smaller rural industry such as saw mills, maltings and spade-mills appeared all over the country. Water also provided the first modern transport system with the development of canals, and these in turn linked up with the new mills and other industrial enterprises and encouraged new settlements. A distinctive architecture developed to serve the waterway network and many of the buildings, locks and bridges of the age of canals still exist.

Roads were a far older transport system and many roads in Ireland today still follow the line of ancient tracks and drovers routes. With the obvious exception of bridges, there is little architecture associated with the road system. Small toll houses were, however, built to serve turnpike or toll roads and the earliest of these roads, dating from 1729, were from Dublin to Kilcullen in Co. Kildare, and from Dublin to Navan in Co. Meath. At least two good examples of toll houses survive; at Blessington, Co. Wicklow, and at Leixlip, Co. Kildare.

After the first railway in Ireland was built from Dublin to Dun Laoghaire in 1834, a rail network spread rapidly throughout the whole country from the major towns to the remote north-west of Donegal and south to the end of the Iveragh peninsula in Co. Kerry. There was a huge volume of building associated with the railway companies, from stations to engine sheds, water tanks, hotels and workers' housing. The architecture of railways was more ostentatious than the architecture of the older canal system and reflected the aggressive spirit of enterprise of the nineteenth century.

This century also saw the development of mining with the importation of modern methods of metal extraction and the large-scale use of steam power pioneered by the railway inventors. Many of the old industrial buildings in Ireland became redundant in the mid-twentieth century and were left as ruins. The countryside is still dotted with these reminders of an older industrial past and most of them are worthy works of architecture and deserve preservation and conversion to new uses.

Mill and water wheel

CASTLEBRIDGE CO. WEXFORD EARLY 19TH C.

WATER POWER, in the form of a primitive horizontal water wheel, using a fast-flowing mountain stream, was used by Early Christian monks to grind corn. The invention of the vertical water wheel, combined with new forms of gearing which enabled the power to be transmitted to several sets of millstones, encouraged the building of large-scale mills for a fast-growing industry in the late eighteenth century. There were three basic types of water wheel, described as undershot, overshot and breast-shot, classified by the point of contact of the water flow. The earliest and simplest type was the undershot which required a fast-flowing stream. With the overshot and breastshot types the water could be fed from a dam through a controlled mill-race to contact the wheel at the top or above the axle. The waterwheel shown here in the village of Castlebridge, four kilometres north of Wexford town, is known as a high breastshot type. This large waterwheel is constructed in cast-iron but many of the wheels used at the time were made of wood. This medium-sized mill was a development from the many small stone-built vernacular structures which were widespread in the countryside for small-scale industry and milling. The slate-hung wall is common in Wexford. Simple sheds, with the waterwheel alongside the gable walls and dwelling-houses for the miller built on, can still be seen in many parts of the countryside. A small vernacular mill and house is located just north of Castlebridge.

168

Castellated mill

LEVITSTOWN CO. KILDARE 1790–1813

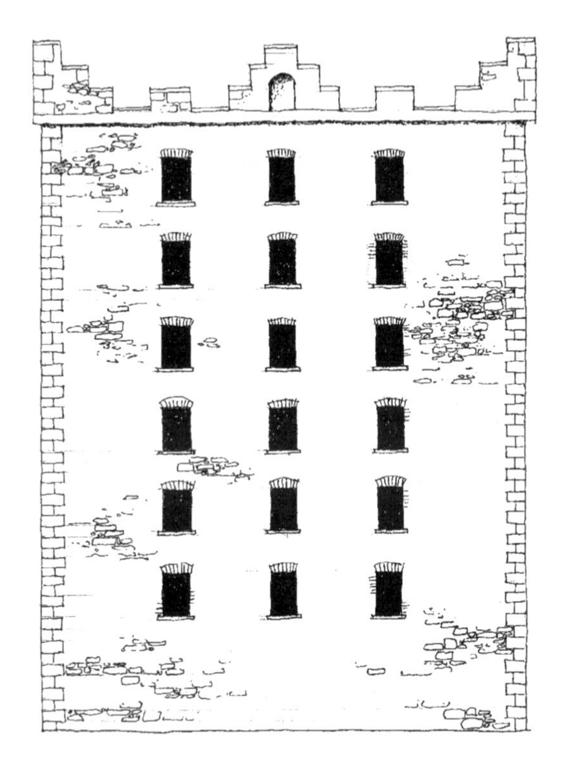

THE GREAT CASTELLATED mills on the river Barrow were constructed during the period towards the end of the eighteenth century when optimism in an industrial future for Ireland was at its highest. This is the end elevation of one of the surviving mills on this important waterway which linked with the Grand Canal. The façade seems to be modelled on the style of a mediæval tower-house but on a giant scale. Two similar structures are at Milford, south of Carlow town. These buildings are high, multi-storey, rectangular structures and the castellations on top followed the popular fashion of changing country houses into Gothic castles. Another fine stone-built, castellated mill is the Newhaggard flour mills near Trim, Co. Meath. This building is six storeys high and the huge brick chimney on one corner was added when steam power was installed. The earliest multi-storey mill in Ireland was at Slane on the river Boyne. Built in 1763, this industrial building was designed almost exactly like a classical country house but far taller, with five floors, than any great house in Ireland. The mill complex, complete with a splendid millowner's house, still stands.

169

Distillery

MONASTEREVIN CO. KILDARE EARLY 19TH C.

DISTILLING AND BREWING are very old industries in Ireland. The earliest surviving distillery is the famous Bushmills in north Co. Antrim. This may have been founded in 1608 and is reputedly the oldest distillery in the world. The largest distilleries and breweries were in the cities of Dublin and Cork, and these industries have left a rich legacy of architecture. Most of the early buildings for distilling and brewing are now redundant and a few major examples of industrial architecture in the cities have been preserved for new uses. John's Lane Distillery in Thomas Street, Dublin, has been partly converted into the National College of Art and Design, while the magnificent Lee Maltings in Cork are used by the university there. The Guinness Brewery in Dublin has some of the finest monuments of industrial architecture in the country, including the early steel-framed Market Street Store House of 1903 and the superb, nineteenth-century Robert Street Store House, which has cast-iron columns.

There were many small-scale distilling enterprises throughout the country and the distillery in the town of Monasterevin, Co. Kildare, is a good example of the simple vernacular which developed for small industries. Locke's Distillery in Kilbeggan, Co. Westmeath, founded in 1757, is a good example of the smaller country distillery and the original buildings, complete with waterwheel, are now preserved. Many of the older buildings of the maltings at Tullamore, Co. Offaly, are still intact and give a distinctive industrial skyline to parts of the town.

170

Mining

ENGINE HOUSE ALLIHIES CO. CORK 1862

MINING IS ONE of the oldest industries in the world and in Ireland the activity was practised from Bronze Age times. None of these ancient mines left any evidence of building and although some commercial mining for copper began in Ireland in the last quarter of the eighteenth century, in tandem with the larger enterprises in Cornwall, no significant development took place until the beginning of the nineteenth century. The wild and savage landscape of the remote Beara peninsula in Co. Cork saw the first large-scale copper-mining venture from about 1811. John Lavallin Puxley was the originator of the enterprise and the Allihies mines were dominated by the Puxley family until their decline in 1886. The building shown was known as a Winding Engine House and its purpose was to raise copper ore by steam power from depths as great as 250 metres. The profile of this building with its tall, steeply tapering chimney is

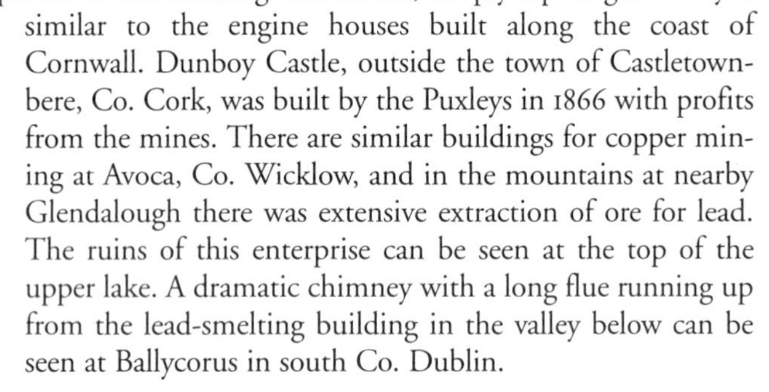

similar to the engine houses built along the coast of Cornwall. Dunboy Castle, outside the town of Castletownbere, Co. Cork, was built by the Puxleys in 1866 with profits from the mines. There are similar buildings for copper mining at Avoca, Co. Wicklow, and in the mountains at nearby Glendalough there was extensive extraction of ore for lead. The ruins of this enterprise can be seen at the top of the upper lake. A dramatic chimney with a long flue running up from the lead-smelting building in the valley below can be seen at Ballycorus in south Co. Dublin.

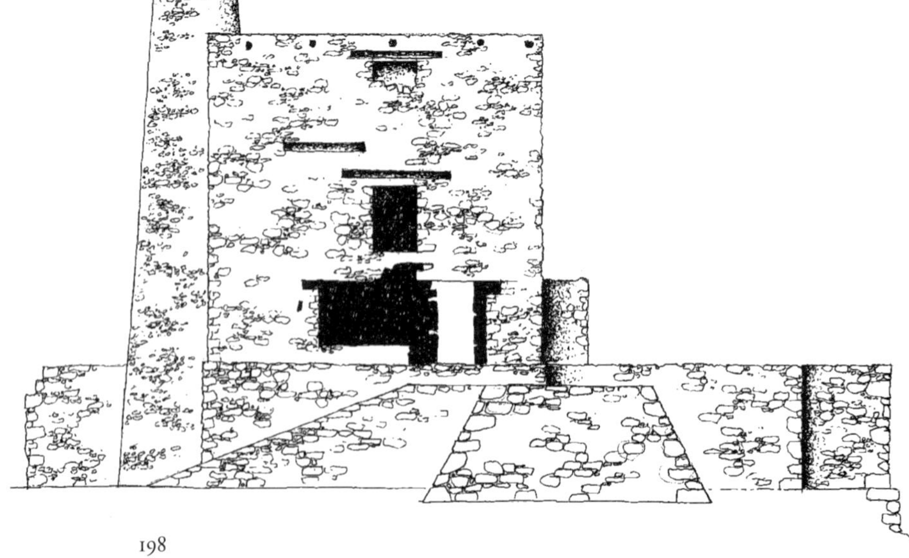

171

Canal buildings
LOCK-KEEPER'S HOUSE
GRAND CANAL *c.*1780

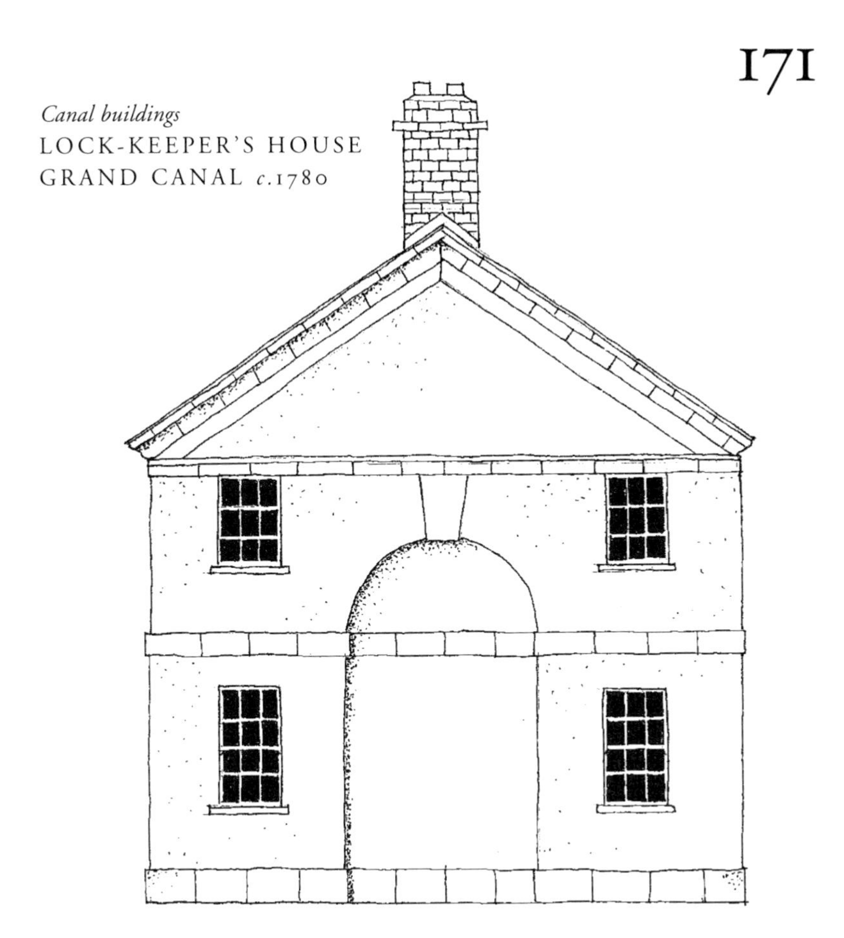

THE FIRST canal to be built in Ireland was the link from Lough Neagh to Newry in 1731, the purpose of which was to exploit the coalfields of Co. Tyrone. In the last quarter of the eighteenth century, canal building was at fever pitch with the construction of two competing waterways to connect Dublin to the river Shannon. The Grand Canal was the earlier of the two and a link was made to connect the canal into the improved navigation of the river Barrow, making a grand waterway towards the west and the south-east. The Royal Canal was completed in 1817 but ran into trouble when the railway alongside it competed for business. Canal architecture was generally small scale and modest but the strong influence of the classical tradition and the employment of architects left a legacy of delightful stone bridges, locks, harbours and lock-keepers' houses. The design shown here was probably the work of the canal architect Thomas Omer and this standard pattern was repeated on the Grand Canal, the Royal Canal and on the Lagan Navigation. The little houses all present the pedimented gables to the waterway and the round-arched blind recess in the centre is a common detail.

172

LEVITSTOWN CO. KILDARE EARLY 19TH C.

THIS PAIR OF COTTAGES for lock-keepers is at Levittstown on the Barrow navigation. The river Barrow provided the line for a waterway from the inland town of Monasterevin and the Grand Canal as far as the sea at Waterford. The sheltered harbour and several river systems here were used from early times. Stretches of canal linked the navigable sections of the river and locks usually controlled the water flow to these. The cottages are in a simple vernacular style but the owners have added their own vernacular decoration in the form of the black-painted surrounds and painted pediments to the windows. The Barrow Navigation has many splendid stone bridges and the narrow, multi-arched bridge at Athy, with its beautifully curved approaches, was intended for packhorses and is one of the best. At nearby Vicarstown there is another finely cut stone bridge with a single round arch and curved parapets sweeping to each side. The most monumental piece of bridge architecture is at Monasterevin, where a superbly detailed aqueduct was constructed in 1827 to link the Barrow Navigation with an extension to Mountmellick.

Warehouse

MONASTEREVIN CO. KILDARE EARLY 19TH C.

MONASTEREVIN was one of the most important canal towns in the early nineteenth century and a large number of warehouses were built to cater for the commercial traffic to and from Dublin. This three-storey warehouse is built right at the edge of the quay where cut stone copings protected the top of the canal walls. The building is simply built, with stone dressings to the quoins and openings and a plastered finish to the rough rubble walling. There are several of these long rectangular buildings, each with its gable end facing the waterway and with openings for direct loading and unloading of the barges. The town also contains well-built, plain merchants' houses but an unusual delight of the place are the elegant lifting bridges, made of metal.

174

GRAND CANAL HOTEL
ROBERTSTOWN CO. KILDARE 1801

THE CANALS were important routes for passenger travel as well as the transport of freight. A number of hotels was built along the lines of both the Grand canal and the Royal Canal, and this large building at Robertstown was constructed in 1801. The village of Robertstown grew up as a canal town with the hotel as the main focus. The style is that of a country house with a *piano nobile* and a pedimented front. Apart from the doorway and its graceful fanlight, the building is quite plain and functional and the canal company did not overspend on architectural frills. Despite this obvious economy the hotel was not a commercial success and after various uses it is now a canal museum while the Grand Canal is now a waterway for pleasure boats. Shannon Harbour, where the canal reaches the river, was a large and busy staging place for canal traffic. As well as substantial stone-built warehouses and Georgian houses there was a huge

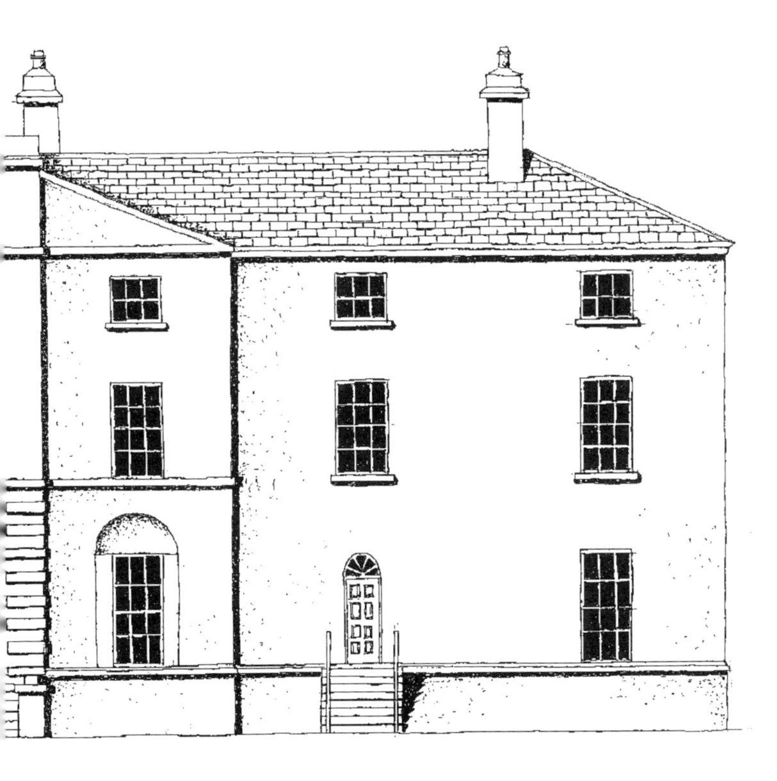

Canal Hotel which was opened in 1806. Tullamore, Co. Offaly, also boasted a harbour and a hotel, and the fourth hotel on the waterway was the elegant building by the small canal harbour at Portobello, Dublin. This is now restored and has been converted into an educational institute. The Royal Canal had two hotels, one in Dublin, at Broadstone, and another at Moyvally, Co. Kildare, which was built in 1806. Both are gone.

175

Railway buildings

BALLINASLOE STATION CO. GALWAY 1851

THE LARGER MARKET TOWNS like Ballinasloe needed a greater range of buildings to deal with increasing number of passengers and a wide variety of freight, and consequently longer platforms. The solution for many of these stations was to line the platform with buildings in a long horizontal line. The architectural problem was to create a coherent elevation and a satisfactory composition. The architect, the prolific George Wilkinson, created a centrepiece which projected slightly and was further emphasized with stone barges, massed chimney stacks and a pointed dormer. The style adopted was Tudor and many variations of this were employed for stations. One reason for this choice was the vogue for mediæval and Tudor which allowed for greater flexibility in contrast to the discipline imposed by classical. The stone used is the lovely local limestone and snecked, squared rubble is the walling method employed. The wonderfully sculptured chimney stacks are the glory of the building along with the elegantly detailed oriel dormer window. Wilkinson employed the classical style, however, for his best work, which is the terminus at Harcourt Street, Dublin, for the Dublin to Wexford line, completed in 1859. One of the stations in Athlone is also the work of this man, who had designed a prodigious number of workhouses in the previous harsh decade of famine.

After the opening of the first railway in Ireland, from Dublin to the harbour town of Kingstown (now Dun Laoghaire) in 1834, the network of railways by different companies spread rapidly throughout the country. The first line was eventually extended down the east coast to Wicklow, Wexford and Waterford. In the north the first railway was the Ulster Railway, from Belfast to Portadown which was opened in 1842. The first railway to the west of Ireland was the Midland Great Western and this was incorporated in 1845 to link Dublin with Galway through the large market towns of Mullingar, Athlone and Ballinasloe. The magnificent station at Ballinasloe, Co. Galway, is a good example of the way the early railway companies promoted high-quality architecture to create a respectable image for their service. All of the companies comissioned architects for the large volume of building needed over a short space of time. The great termini in Dublin were designed as monumental buildings and continued the classical, eighteenth-century tradition of architecture in the city. The hundreds of small stations throughout the country provided marvellous opportunities for architects to range widely through the styles, and the challenge of this new building type produced some of the most interesting buildings of the century.

176

PORTARLINGTON STATION CO. LAOIS 1851

THE GREAT SOUTHERN and Western Railway was founded in 1844 and initially the line was from Dublin to Cashel, Co. Tipperary. The station at Portarlington is one of the most splendid of all of the country stations and has recently been beautifully restored. The main station building is on one side of the platform with a smaller, less elaborate but matching building on the other. An elegant cast-iron footbridge connects the two platforms and successfully unites the station complex. The architect for the station was Sancton Wood and the style adopted was an imaginative interpretation of mediæval or Gothic. The asymmetrical composition with the two-storey station house on one side is cleverly balanced by the tall slim tower on the left. This has no function and is in fact only a façade but contributes to the spiky liveliness of the rooflines. The barges and eaves boards are elaborately carved and false timber roof trusses are exposed on the gable ends. The random rubble, limestone walling is neatly detailed around the windows of the two-storey section and the recesses have a stairs slope expressed on the outside. The tall chimney stacks, in stone with brick extensions, advertise the presence of the station. These buildings were often on the edge or even at a distance from the towns they served, so an assertive presence may have been a consideration of the designer.

Sancton Wood was an English architect who won the competition for the design of the terminus of the The Great Southern and Western Railway

at Kingsbridge (now Heuston Station) in Dublin. The building was completed in 1846 and is by far the most lively of the city's main stations. It stands in a commanding position at the edge of the river Liffey to the west of the city, and its extravagant Renaissance excess contrasts splendidly with its early classical neighbour, Dr Steevens' Hospital. After he had won the competition for the terminus Wood was appointed architect to the company and over the next few years designed most of the stations for the line from Monasterevan to Limerick Junction. The earlier stations as far as Kildare on the line were the work of Sir John MacNeill, the chief engineer for the company. Wood's station at Monasterevan is mainly a two-storey building with sharp gables and tall chimneys, and the picturesque outline, as at Portarlington, is continued for the others. At Dundrum, Co. Tipperary, the formula is similar to that used for Portarlington, with steep gables and carved barge boards and even a similar tower, but the elements are mixed in a delightful variation. At Thurles, Co. Tipperary, the same formula is again used but little castellated windows are added so that each of Wood's stations on the line has a different identity.

177

GREENORE CO. LOUTH *c.*1874

THE DUNDALK, Newry and Greenore railway was completed in 1874, linking the port with Dundalk and Newry around the Carlingford peninsula. The line was created by the London and North Western Railway Company which decided in the 1860s to open a new route to the northern part of Ireland from its rail-head in Holyhead, Wales. A substantial little village was developed to serve the port and Greenore is in many ways a planned railway village. The rail-workers' housing consists of substantial terraced dwellings in rubble walling with stone quoins and barges. The windows and doors are dressed in yellow brick and the soldier arches, where the bricks are vertical, over the openings have a bull nose or rounded edge. The Georgian windows are quite large and these were houses of some quality for workers in Victorian times. A fine brick and stone school was also provided in the village and this has now been converted into a pub. Housing was often provided for rail-workers, from simple cottages for crossing keepers to imposing villas for the managers, and many of these dwellings still survive.

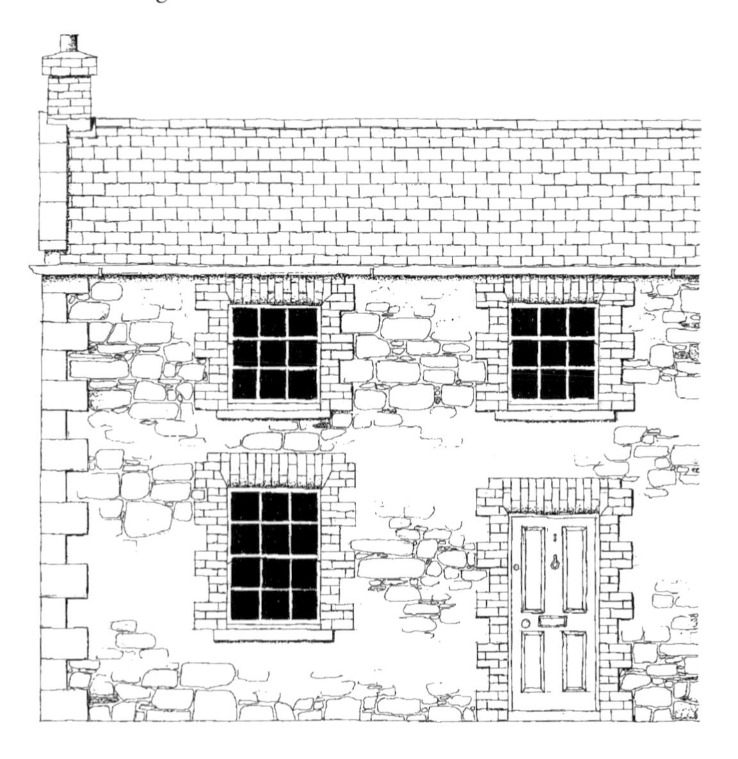

178

CARLOW STATION CO. CARLOW 1845

THE FLAMBOYANT, Tudor Revival station buildings at Carlow were the work of Sir John MacNeill or one of his assistants, since he was the busy chief engineer who laid out the whole line for the Great Southern and Western. MacNeill was one of the most distinguished figures in railway engineering in Ireland and had, in his earlier years, worked for the famous Thomas Telford. The drawing shows the road and entrance front to the main building, which is dominated by three steep gables embellished with fine stone barges, each is crowned by a finial. The subsidiary buildings on either side are treated as little pavilions with ogee-arch gables. The chimney stacks are exceptionally tall and slim and, in keeping with the desired picturesque image, the symmetry of the elevation is deliberately broken by the single dominant oriel window on the first floor. This station is built in brick with stone dressings but the façade to the platform is plastered. The line to Carlow was a branch and the Carlow station was intended to be a terminus.

MacNeill was responsible for all of the stations from Dublin to Carlow. There are many small railway stations remaining in country towns and villages and although the vast network of lines has been drastically reduced, from the high point in the late nineteenth century many old stations survive, some as ruins and many more converted to other uses.

179
WATER TANK
GREENORE
CO. LOUTH *c.*1874

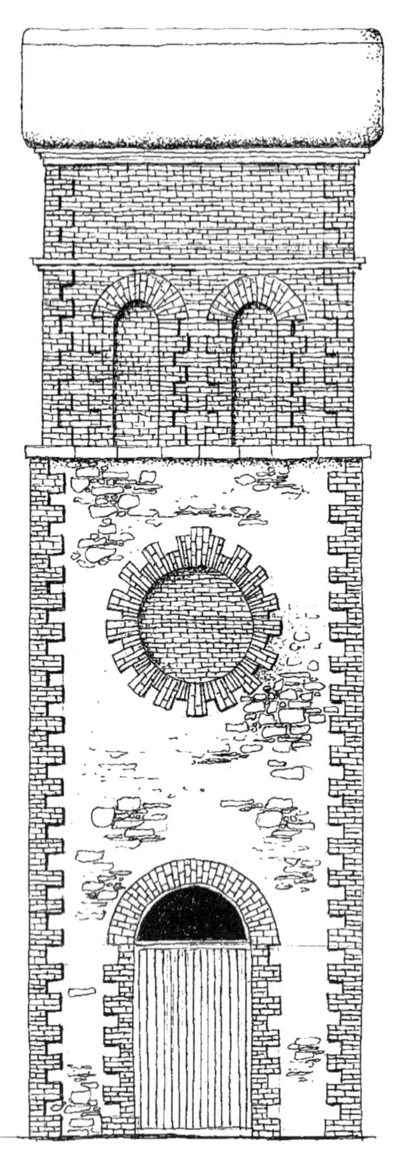

A GREAT NUMBER of utilitarian structures were erected to serve the railway networks of Ireland, including engine sheds, signal boxes and water tanks. These practical buildings were still considered to be important enough to merit careful design and high-quality materials were always used. Most of these functional structures are now redundant but many remain as testimony to the rich legacy of railway architecture. The water tank shown here is at Greenore, Co. Louth, and is unusually tall. The architects designed it as a tower in classical style, with two colours of brick, red and yellow, and rubble walling.

180

BRIDGE OPERATOR'S COTTAGE PORTUMNA EARLY 19TH C.

THE RIVER SHANNON is by far the largest waterway in Ireland. Stretching from Battlebridge in Co. Leitrim to Limerick, the waterway has only seven locks in over 200 kilometres. Although parts of the river and the large lakes were navigable from ancient times it was made into a continuous route in the 1760s and further improvements were added in the nineteenth century. The large bridge over the river at Portumna, Co. Galway, is an important road crossing and the centre portion of this was constructed with an lifting section. The little cottage shown here was for the housing of the bridge operator who could respond to signals from the larger boats. The building is constructed in a heavy and ponderous style, in keeping, perhaps, with the responsibility of the bridge keeper. The front is in fine ashlar granite blocks framed with pilasters and neat, squared stone brackets support the eaves and gutter. The simple porch has a miniature pediment, carved from a single stone. There are many interesting bridges on the stretch of the Shannon between Portumna and Athlone including a fortified bridgehead at Banagher and the seventeen-arch bridge at Shannonbridge which was built in 1700. The huge fortifications from Napoleonic times at Shannonbridge have already been mentioned (illus. 52).

181

Waterworks buildings

DRAW-OFF TOWER

VARTRY ROUNDWOOD CO. WICKLOW 1868

THE HISTORY of a public water supply stretches far back to ancient Egypt and Assyria. In the second half of the nineteenth century, with the growth of urban populations and demands of industry, a stable source of clean water became an necessity. The early water supply to Dublin was largely haphazard and came from the small rivers of the city and was stored in little reservoirs. Vartry Reservoir at Roundwood was constructed from 1862 to 1868 and was the first large-scale attempt to provide a stable storage and distributing system for Dublin's needs. A thirty-five-kilometre pipeline took the water from the high level at Vartry to the city.

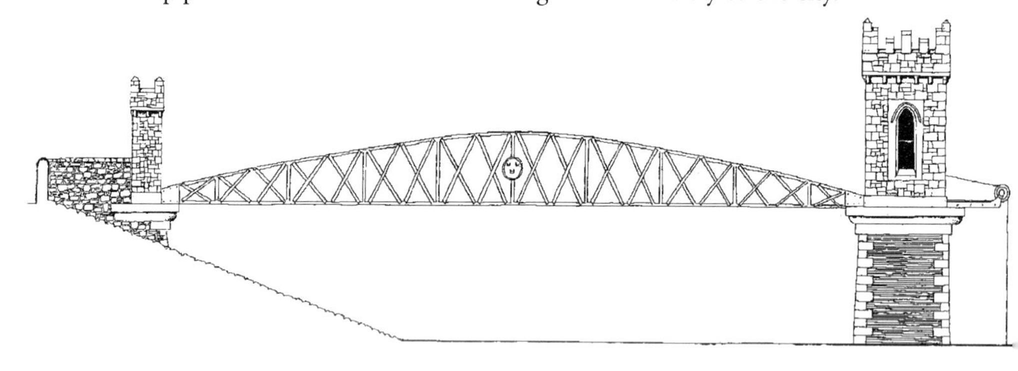

The drawing shows the draw-off tower on the upper reservoir at Vartry. The purpose of this is to take water from the lake at different levels and then to convey it through the dam to a lower level for treatment and filtering. A castellated Gothic was considered the proper architectural style for these worthy public works, and when carried out in a rugged stonework an image of power and permanency was conveyed. The draw-off chamber itself is built in granite random squared rubble with mock machicolations and battlements, and sits on a base of thick granite slabs. The base which supports the foundation tower is built in brick with granite dressings. A miniature Gothic gateway leads from a roadway which is on top of the dam, and a delicate cast-iron footbridge spans to the draw-off tower. The Vartry scheme is possibly the only water supply system to be mentioned in a major literary work. In James Joyce's *Ulysses* Leopold Bloom fills an iron kettle from the tap: "Did it flow? Yes. From Roundwood reservoir in county Wicklow of a cubic capacity of 2,400 million gallons, percolating through a subterranean aqueduct of filter mains of single and double pipage constructed at an initial plant cost of £5 per linear yard by way of the Dargle, Rathdown, Glen of the Downs and Callowhill to the twenty-six-acre reservoir at Stillorgan."

182

SILENT VALLEY CO. DOWN 1893–1933

THE SUPPLY OF WATER from the Mourne mountains to the city of Belfast had a long history. The earliest phase of this work, carried out for the Belfast city and District Water Commissioners, began in 1893 with the construction of weirs across the Annalong and Kilkeel rivers. A tunnel through the mountains connected these two rivers and a pipeline led the water to a reservoir near Belfast. The main phase of the work began in 1923 when the great reservoir called "Silent Valley" was constructed in a mountain basin above the town of Kilkeel. There were many difficulties with the work and the reservoir was not completed until 1933. The engineer for the works was F.W. McCullough. The dams and various building works were carried out in local Mourne granite and the architectural style used was a plain and robust classical. The overflow outlet from the main reservoir is a round arch with a prominent keystone and *voussoirs*, or wedge-shaped stones. A classical pediment and simple pilasters frame the opening while twin curving granite staircases lead up to the control building. The octagonal valve tower and circular overflow conduit, both constructed in beautiful stone, are fine exercises in simple geometry. The splendid Water Commissioners' gates were built in the first decade of the twentieth century and these are also unadorned cubes of cut granite. The massive gate piers are surmounted by sharp pyramids and strange lumpy capstones. The battlemented screen walls hark back to the mediæval revival styles of the previous century.

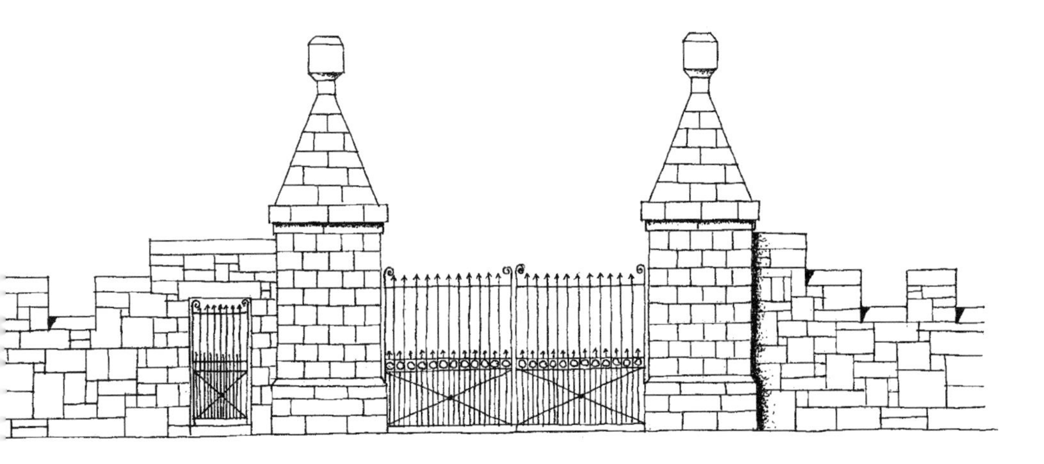

183
WATER COMMISSIONER'S GATELODGE SILENT VALLEY 1900

THERE ARE SEVERAL gatelodges controlling the entrances to the Silent Valley water scheme. This one is just north of the seaside village of Annalong and was constructed during the early phase of the works. The detailing of the stonework is remarkably robust and powerful with little concern for refinement. Such serious engineering as a waterworks demanded no frivolities. The stone barges are in great blocks of granite and the squared, snecked walling is strong enough for a castle. There is a tiny relaxation in the statement of solid permanence with the delicate chamfering to the window jambs, although this is likely to be at the insistence of the stone mason who knew how granite jambs should look! The loggia with its delicate cast-iron columns and frilly arches is another indulgence on this commanding building set high above the road.

BUILDINGS OF THE COAST

OF ALL THE BUILDINGS of the coastline, lighthouses must be the most evocative. Standing all around the coast of Ireland, on headlands, isolated rocks and harbour mouths, they mark the boundary of land and ocean. Their unique shapes create an unmistakable image and no other building type is more associated with the seaboard. Except for the ancient light at Hook Head, at the mouth of Waterford harbour, the history of lighthouses begins about 1665 when Sir Robert Reading, a member of the Irish Parliament, was granted a patent to erect lighthouses at Howth, the isle of Magee near Carrickfergus, the Old Head of Kinsale and at Barry Oge's Castle, within the harbour of Kinsale. Reading was authorized to levy tolls on all outward- and inward-bound ships in return for his costs in erecting the towers. In 1704 these lighthouses were taken over by Commissioners appointed by the government. All of these early towers were on the east coast and the only building in the west was Loop Head tower built in 1704. By 1875 the number of lights greatly increased to serve the entire coastline.

Irish maritime towns are little different from their inland or riverside counterparts in terms of their architecture and layout. Notable exceptions to this are the old towns of Kinsale and Wexford. In Wexford the "slips" or narrow alleyways, which led into the old town from the sea, follow the direct routes taken by the Vikings who beached their longships on the shore. In Kinsale the narrow streets leading up from the harbour and the tiered terraces of houses with their slate-hung walls have a maritime flavour. Most maritime towns may have harbours and quaysides, but the majority of buildings do not reflect the proximity of the sea in terms of their architecture. Sligo was a busy port from late mediæval times until well into the nineteenth century, but the town hardly reflects a maritime character. In Wine Street, however, well back from the sea, there is a shipping office which was built about 1840 with a look-out tower on the roof where the ship-owners could watch for the arrival of their vessels.

The development of resort towns in the nineteenth century saw the construction of seaside terraces which took advantage of the view, but again the architecture was not unique to the maritime site. Resorts such as Portrush in Co. Antrim, Warrenpoint in Co. Down and Dun Laoghaire, Co. Dublin, have fine Victorian terraced houses and villas with bay windows facing the sea. Bray, Co. Wicklow, was one of the most important seaside resort towns which had a planned face to the sea. A long promenade is backed by a linear green park, complete with bandstands, while an extended row of Victorian hotels and villas creates a sea front. Gaunt, ruined warehouses often remain as ghosts of a thriving shipping past in many smaller seaside towns. The coastguard stations and the numerous martello towers and signal stations, already described, remind us of smugglers and the threat of invasion and naval warfare.

184

Lighthouse
HOOK HEAD CO. WEXFORD 1170

THE LIGHTHOUSE on Hook Head is the most interesting example of the type in Ireland. It is the oldest lighthouse which is still in use in these islands and was built by the Norman invaders between 1170 and 1182. The original tower was a defended lighthouse which had bonfires and open braziers, showing a light at night and smoke by day. When Sir Robert Reading was given the job of erecting and maintaining lighthouses in 1665 he is credited with repairing the old tower at Hook Head and adding a glazed lantern to enclose the coal fire. The earliest enclosed lanterns were necessary safety devices to prevent the danger of the wind scattering sparks and burning coals from towers on exposed headlands. In 1822 Fresnel revolutionized lighthouse optics with the introduction of his annular lens. The turret on top of the old tower was completed in 1863 but the Hook lighthouse already had large convex lenses in its lantern in the late eighteenth century.

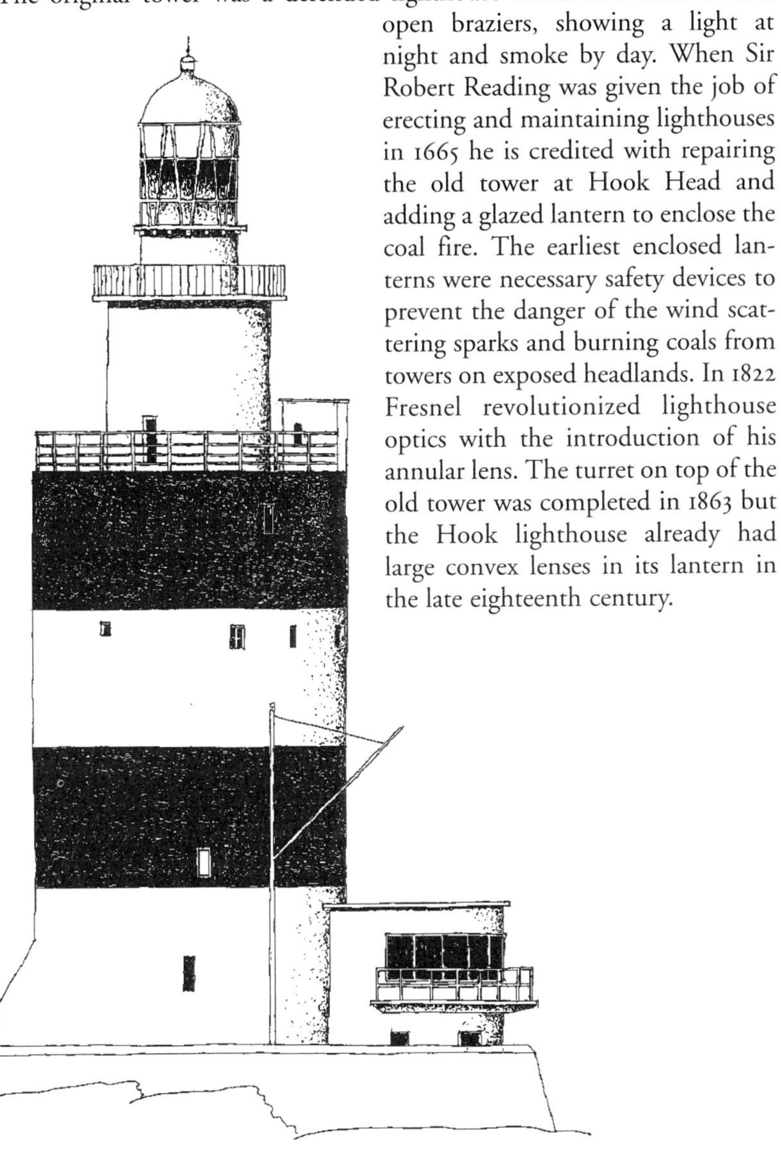

185

WICKLOW HEAD CO. WICKLOW 1778

THE SPLENDIDLY classical lighthouse on Wicklow Head dates from 1778. It was designed by John Trail, architect to the Commissioners of Revenue. In plan the building is an octagon with the ground-floor walls over two metres thick. The strongly expressed, dressed stone quoins, combined with tapered walls, give a soaring effect to the shaft. In its day the tower was crowned by an octagonal lantern with the glazing facing out to sea; the light source was ten candles boosted by reflectors. Long disused, the tower now survives as a navigation point.

186

YOUGHAL CO. CORK EARLY 19TH C.

IN MEDIÆVAL TIMES a light is reputed to have been kept by the nuns of St Anne's Convent in Youghal, near the present lighthouse. The earliest lighthouses were almost certainly beacons or bonfires placed on prominent landmarks and were already known in the ancient world. The mediæval Church was responsible for the display of many of the early lights around the coasts of Britain and Ireland, and only a handful of Irish lighthouses existed up to 1800. The shapes of the light towers vary in accordance with their elevation above sea level; from tall elegant shafts – contoured for wave action – at low level and on jagged rocks, to stumpy cones on high promontories. The existing lighthouse at Youghal was built in the early nineteenth century. Since the building was sited on rising ground there was no need for a tall tower, and the stumpy design is typical of many land-based Irish examples. The design of the lantern of this lighthouse is particularly interesting and there are many similar models around the coasts of Ireland. Curved-iron bracing struts, intended to withstand great wind pressure, were fixed to the gallery floor and to the top of the glazing.

187

Lighthouse and keeper's cottage

GREENORE CO. LOUTH EARLY 19TH C.

THE LIGHTHOUSE at Greenore was intended to mark the opening to the important navigable Carlingford Lough as well as the new port on the south side. The light tower and lantern are of the standard design which became almost universal in Ireland for the squat, land-based towers. The curved-iron wind bracing was used in conjunction with plain rectangular glazing bars and this method continued to be adopted in Ireland when lighthouses in England and Scotland changed over to diagonal glazing-bars, or astragals as they were called, to resist wind forces. The cottages for the keepers are ranged alongside the tower, and the walls, boundary and shaft are painted white, with the roofs and chimney stacks in jet black. This highly contrasting painting scheme was intended to provide a daytime navigation mark.

The Greenore lighthouse was designed by George Halpin senior and there are many exactly similar towers, including one on the approaches to Larne harbour in Co. Antrim. On the opposite side of the mouth of Carlingford Lough Halpin built one of his elegantly curved and tapered tall towers. This is known as Haulbowline Rock and the light is thirty-four metres over a dangerous shoal which is only exposed at low tide. The tower was completed in 1824.

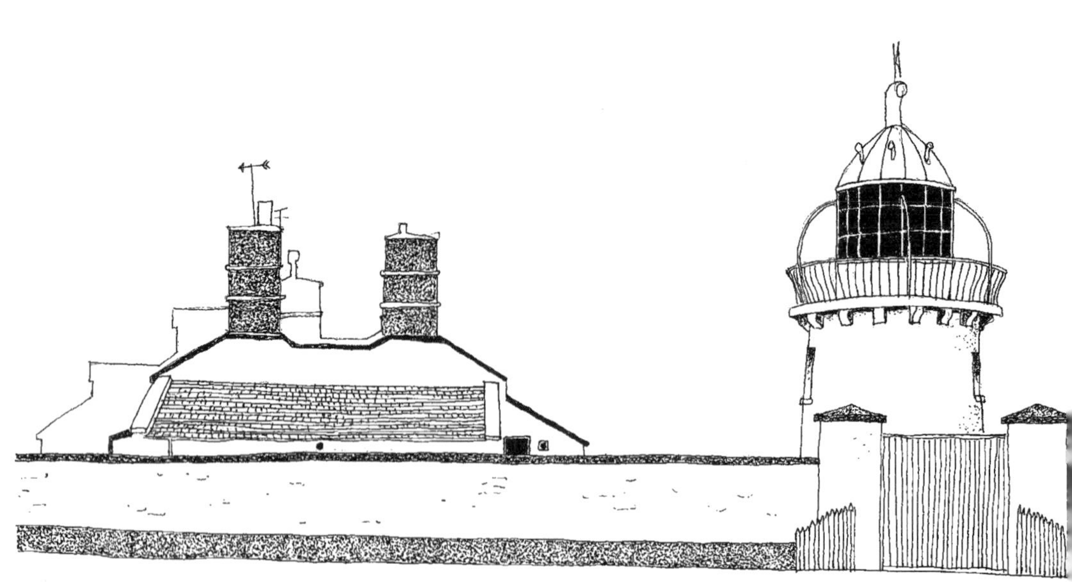

188

Automatic light
BLACK HEAD CO. CLARE 20TH C.

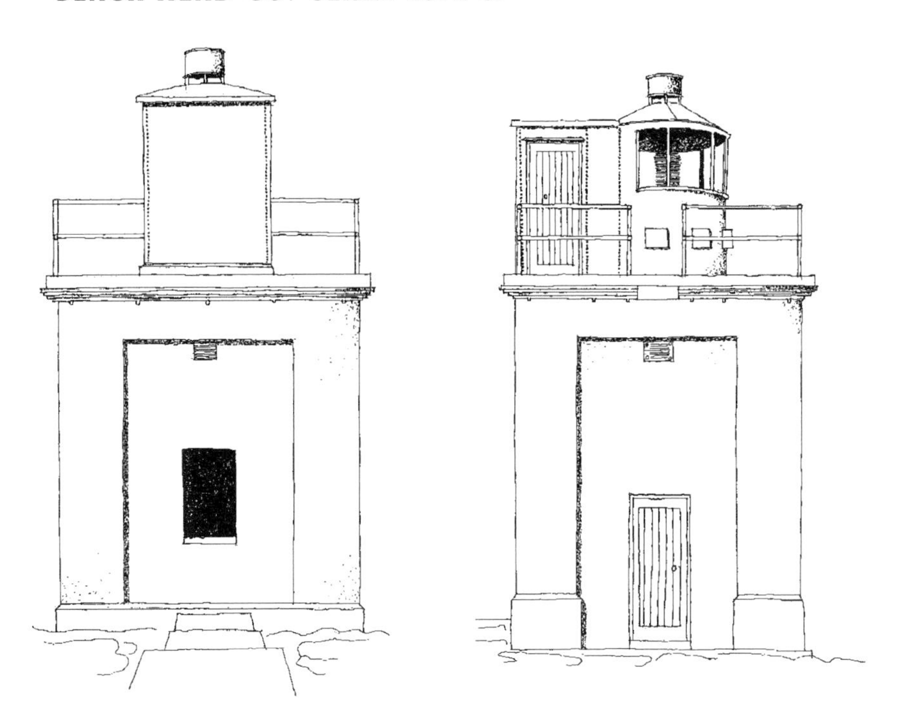

THIS SMALL square tower stands near Black Head on the south side of Galway bay, guarding the rocky limestone coast of the famous Burren region of Co. Clare. The tower is constructed in concrete and the plastered surface is painted white. Even though this is a simple modernist structure, the plain proportions are enlivened by set-back panels and a basic cornice. The lantern structure is in iron, with metal panels bolted on.

UNLIT BEACONS

There are many unlit beacons or daytime navigation marks around the Irish coastline which are interesting architectural features, and some of these types are unique to Ireland. Tall, slim masonry towers mark the way into the curious sheltered harbour of Crookhaven on the south-west coast of Co. Cork. Nearby, at Baltimore, there is an elegant-shaped beacon for navigation. The strangest examples of Irish beacons are the metal men of Sligo and Waterford. These cast-iron figures, clad in sailor's uniform, date from 1819 and it is said that the metal man on Newtown Head, Waterford harbour, points out to sea chanting, "Keep off, good ship, keep off from me, for I am the rock of Misery."

189

CLARE ISLAND CO. MAYO *c.*1835

THIS LIGHTHOUSE stands high on a cliff on the northern point of Clare Island, far out in Clew bay and facing the open Atlantic. The low tower and the long spreading cottages, hugging the ground, respond to the fierce gales which sweep the remote island. The cast-iron railings around the lantern enclose a walkway which was used for the cleaning of the windows. This lighthouse is another of the many by the Halpins, father and son, who were the most prolific builders of lighthouses in Ireland.

George Halpin senior was appointed engineer for the port of Dublin in 1810 and made a report on Irish lighthouses. He and his son, George junior, were responsible for the design and construction of about fifty-five lighthouses all around the coasts of Ireland up to the middle of the nineteenth century. The first of Halpin's towers was on the island of Inishtrahull and this most northerly light, off Malin Head in Co. Donegal, was completed in 1812. The lighthouse on the summit of Bailey, marking the entrance to Dublin bay, was one of the oldest in Ireland and Halpin replaced the open firelight there which had existed since 1665. The first great tower to be built by Halpin senior on an isolated rock was Tuskar, off the coast of Wexford and this was completed in 1815.

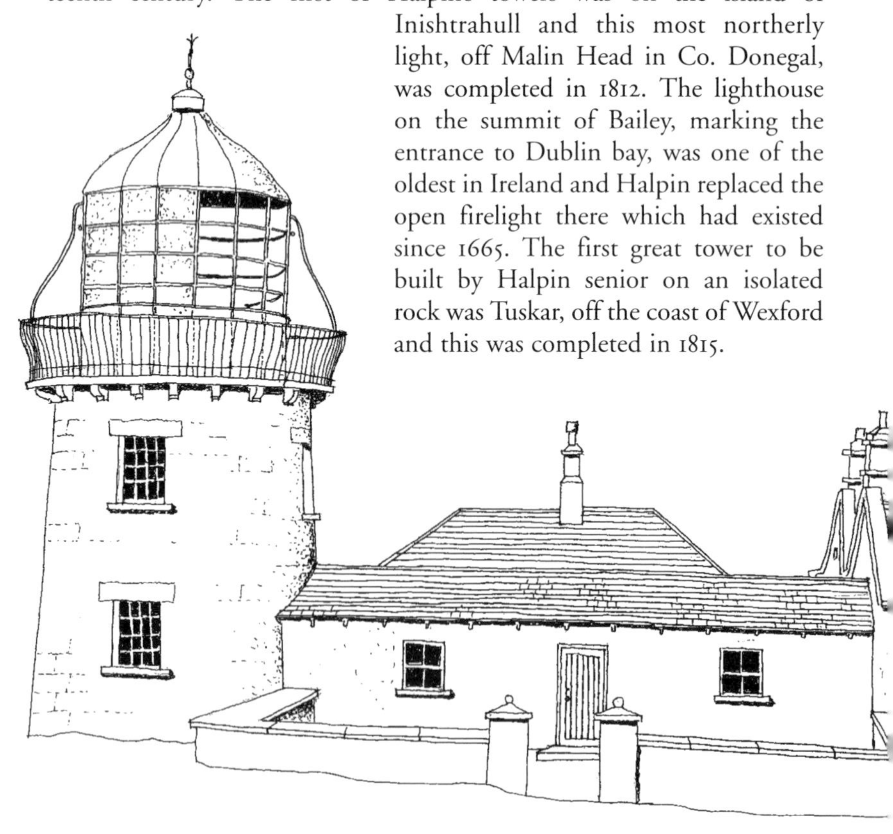

The two Halpins were responsible for the lights on the isolated rock Scelig Mhicíl, Co. Kerry, and for the Sligo towers on the Maidens Rocks, Eagle Island and the Black Rock. George Halpin senior died in 1854 and his son continued to build lighthouses, including the famous Fastnet Tower, off the south-west coast, which was completed in 1854. The nineteenth-century fascination with new materials led to this being constructed in cast-iron but in 1881 the experiment ended in disaster when the tower broke in two. The superb masonry tower which replaced it was the work of William Douglass. The younger Halpin also built two lighthouses on the Aran Islands, Eeragh and Inisheer. Sir John Rennie, son of the famous civil engineer, designed a beautifully tapered lighthouse tower at the entrance to the harbour at Donaghadee, Co. Down. Possibly the most architectural of all of the lighthouses of Ireland is the light at the end of the pier at Dunmore East, Co. Waterford, the work of Alexander Nimmo in 1826. The tower is shaped as a fat Doric column with the lantern perched on top of the cap.

Almost all of the lighthouses around Ireland are now automatic and unmanned but remain as the most visible evidence of a long maritime history. The towers and their clusters of small buildings are intimately related to the romantic landscape of headlands and cliffs.

190

Coastguard station

KILLYBEGS CO. DONEGAL *c.*1860

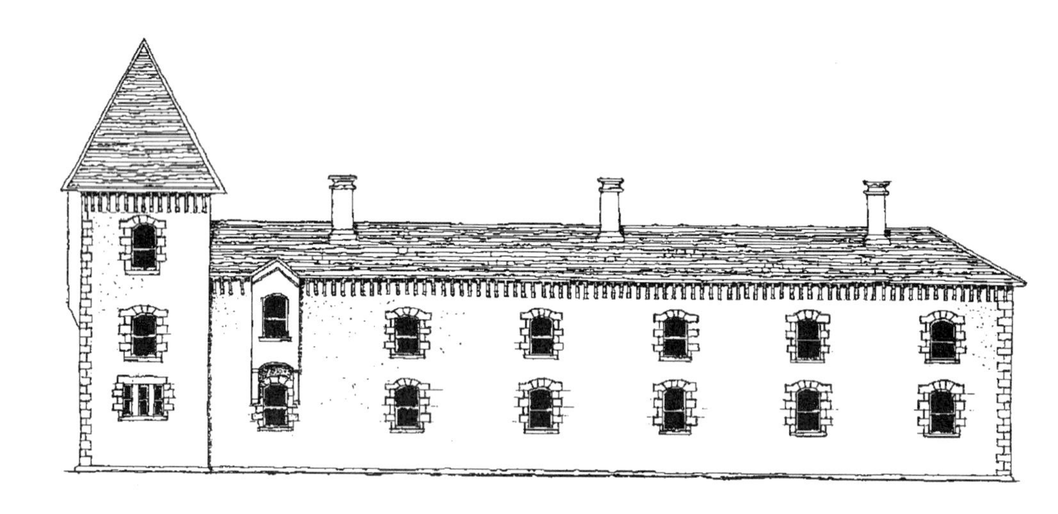

THE COASTGUARD SERVICE originated in the early nineteenth century and one of its most important first functions was to fight smuggling. From the eighteenth century there were high revenues to be collected from luxury goods such as tea, spirits and silks, and the enterprise of smuggling was widespread and attractive. The coastguard, a semi-naval force, had also the duties of giving assistance to vessels in distress and the enforcement of maritime laws. The coastguard service in Ireland originated in 1831 and was placed under the authority of the Admiralty in 1857. Over the next decade some 200 coastguard stations were built around the coasts and the designs had little variation. Most were long blocks of accommodation for the officers, and several had the characteristic square tower, shown here for the station at Killybegs, Co. Donegal, at one end. This had the dual purpose of providing a look-out post as well as a defensive feature to give flanking fire to the main walls. The Fenian Rising of 1867 made the authorities anxious to fortify the coastguard stations as these were seen as outposts of the establishment. The military character of the building at Killybegs is reinforced by the bartizans. While the earlier coastguard stations did not have any defensive features, many of the later buildings were provided with musket loops. Doors were sometimes stoutly made with slots on either side internally to take heavy beams for strengthening the entrance.

191

Lifeboat house
BALTIMORE CO. CORK

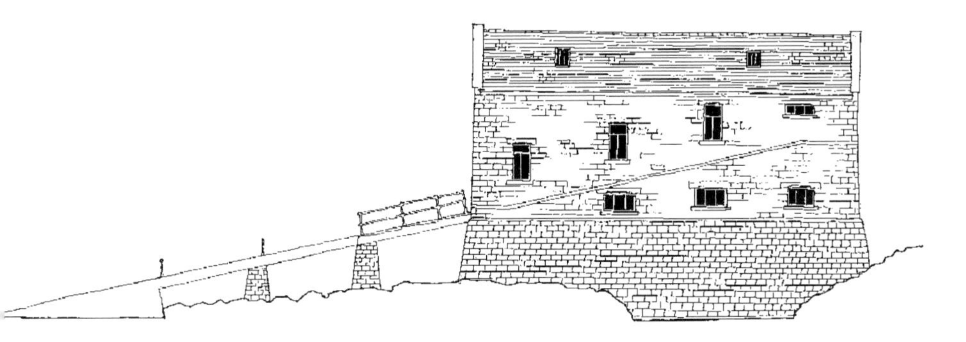

THE LIFEBOAT HOUSE at Baltimore, Co. Cork, is a relic from the times when lifeboats were made of wood and were housed on land when not in use. The modern lifeboat is a sophisticated sea-going vessel and is usually moored in the harbour for instant reaction to an emergency. The need for constant maintenance of a timber craft also demanded the facilities for dry-land docking. After returning from a rescue mission the boats were winched up a steep ramp into the lifeboat house. Metal rails were used to guide the trolleys and the steep ramp meant that the boat could be launched in a hurry. The big difference in the levels between high and low tides in this part of the world meant that the ramps were quite long and distinctive features at low water. The Baltimore lifeboat house has the line of the ramp expressed right through the side walls of the building – a piece of architectural indulgence unrelated to function.

Baltimore is a fishing port on the extreme south-west corner of the country and has a sheltered bay with a long history. The ruined mediæval castle of the O'Driscolls stands near the present pier. In the seventeenth century the town was attacked by pirates from Algiers who carried off 200 inhabitants to be sold as slaves!

192

Maritime houses

WEXFORD EARLY 19TH C.

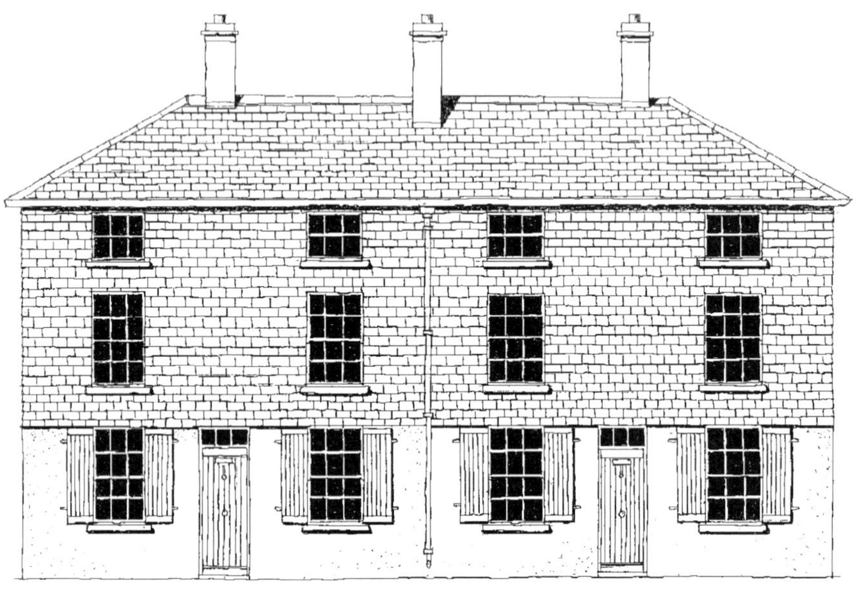

SLATE-HANGING to the fronts of houses is a characteristic feature of several of the older maritime towns. There are isolated examples of the practice in some inland places, Tralee, for instance, had a large three-storey detached house with vertical slates on the top two floors. The use of slate for wall cladding, however, is mainly confined to the south and in particular the maritime towns of the south-east to the south-west. The main purpose of covering walls in slate was protection from wind-driven rain on walls particularly exposed to the weather. There were two methods of hanging slates vertically. The most satisfactory method was to nail the slates to small wood battens which were fixed horizontally to the walls. The second method was to bed the individual slates in lime mortar. In maritime towns slate hanging was also considered to be an agreeable finish for the main house front and was used for aesthetic as well as practical reasons.

The pair of semi-detached houses shown are in the old town of Wexford, founded by Norse invaders in the early tenth century. The houses are on the quayside around the small harbour which was established in the early nineteenth century. The first settlement at Kinsale, Co. Cork, was about 1200 and the town, with its great natural harbour, developed a strategic importance by the seventeenth century. Vertical slate-hanging is one of the features which seems to give the town a special maritime flavour.

193

Port warehouse
RAMELTON CO. DONEGAL 1864

A GREAT BLOCK of gaunt abandoned warehouses stands by the quayside of the little town of Ramelton in the north of Co. Donegal. These are the remnants of a former busy sea port and also bear witness to a vanished industrial past. The town was founded in the seventeenth century by Sir William Stewart who built many houses and a church. By the early nineteenth century the river Leannan which flows through the town was lined with industrial buildings, including a brewery, corn mills and various linen works. Linen was a major industry of the northern half of the country for over 400 years, but industrialization from the end of the eighteenth century vastly increased the output and international importance of the export of the material. Bleach greens were another industrial enterprise which helped to finish the raw linen product and required buildings and bleach-fields or "greens" to spread out the material.

The warehouse shown is one of a group of four magnificent buildings which are now redundant. The lower windows and the entrance are given architectural importance with the Gibbsian surrounds. Ramelton is on the shores of Lough Swilly, an important naval anchorage in the eighteenth and nineteenth centuries. Massive forts, along with batteries, Martello towers and signal stations line both banks of the lough.

194

Yacht Club

COBH CO. CORK 1854

THE ROYAL CORK Yacht Club was founded in 1720 and is reputed to be the oldest yacht club in the world. The architect Anthony Salvin was commissioned to design a fine new clubhouse on the waterfront of the great port of Cobh in Cork harbour. The style chosen was an Italianate version of classical, which was considered appropriate for this waterside building. The centrepiece with the three arched windows, divided by pairs of small columns, is projected forward giving a viewing-deck on each side. The members here, drinks in hand, could see and criticize the boating skills of their friends on the waters below. The building has fine elevations on all four sides and is one of the most important works of architecture in this beautiful town which rises, in colourful tiers, up from the sea to the soaring spires of the Neo-Gothic cathedral. The building was allowed to fall into decay but has happily been rescued and well restored. It is now known as the Sirius Centre and used for various exhibitions.

There are three yacht clubs in Dun Laoghaire, Co. Dublin, which were erected in the nineteenth century. Two of these were designed by the architect J.S. Mulvany; the splendidly colonnaded Royal Irish Yacht Club was built in 1850 and the Royal St George in 1843. The third yacht club on the harbour front is the National, which was completed in 1870 and designed by William Stirling.

MAPS

Numbers denote illustrations in relation to County and Province

ULSTER

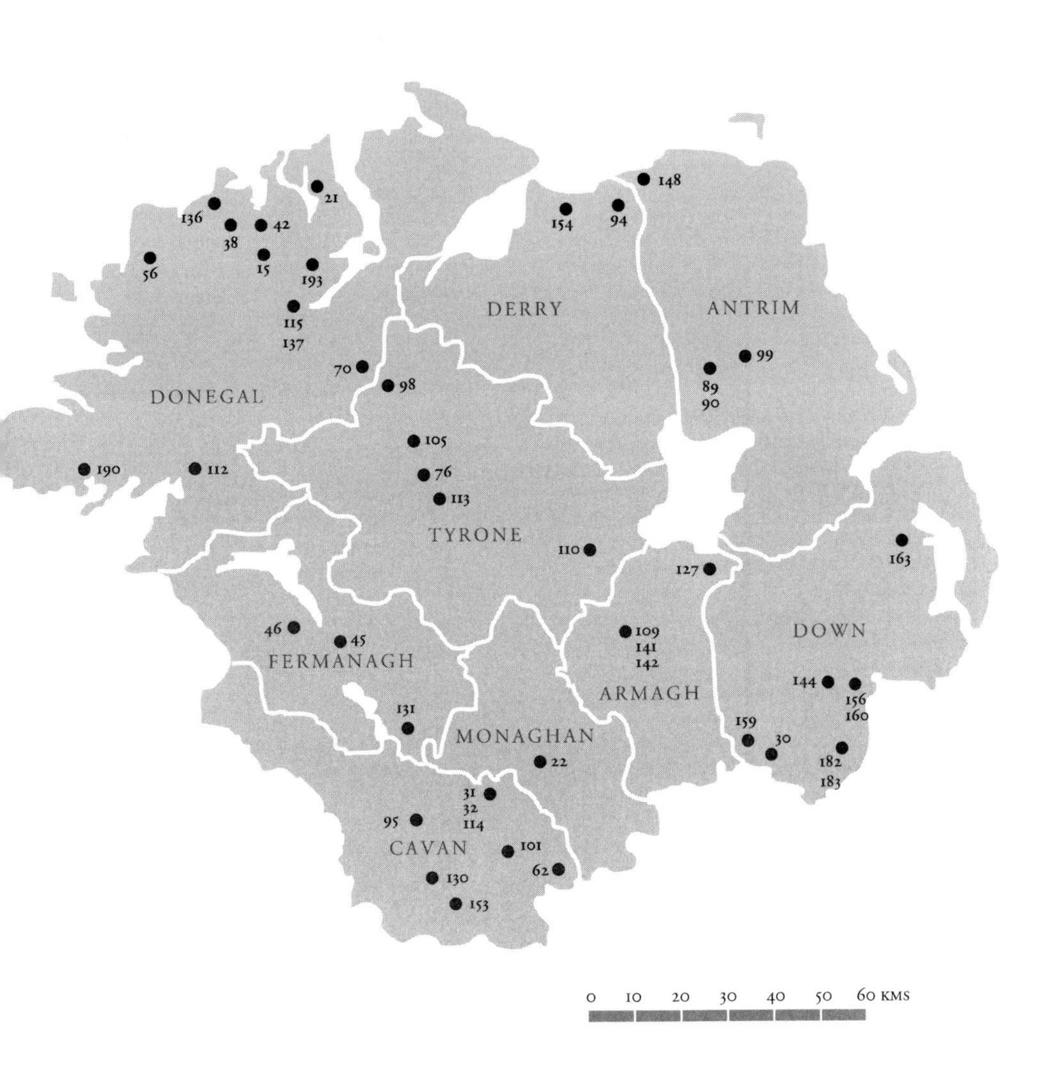
DONEGAL
DERRY
ANTRIM
TYRONE
FERMANAGH
ARMAGH
DOWN
MONAGHAN
CAVAN
21
136
38
42
56
15
193
115
137
70
98
148
154
94
99
89
90
105
190
112
76
113
110
127
163
46
45
109
141
142
144
156
160
131
159
30
182
183
22
31
32
114
95
101
62
130
153
0 10 20 30 40 50 60 KMS

MUNSTER

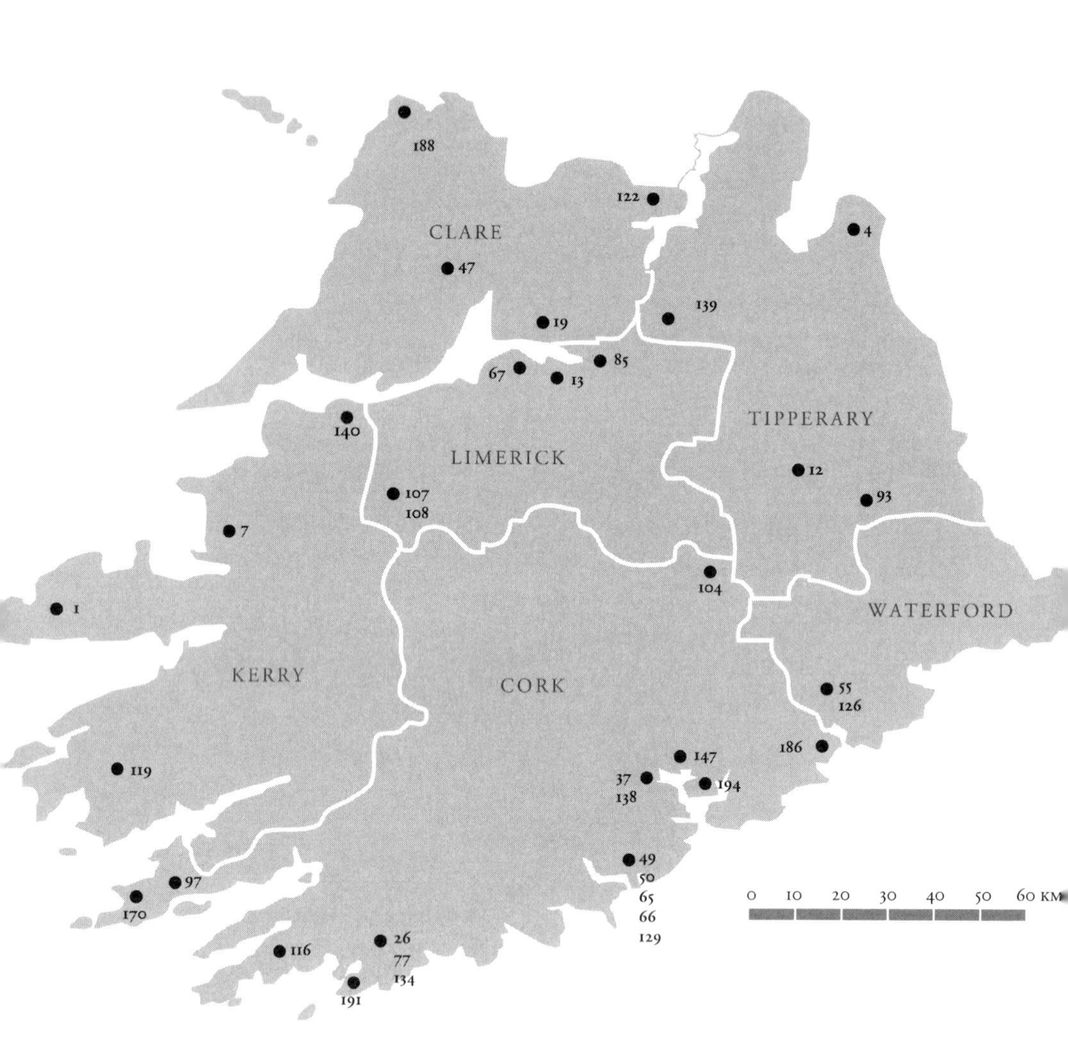

CLARE
LIMERICK
TIPPERARY
KERRY
CORK
WATERFORD
188
122
4
47
19
139
85
67
13
140
12
107
108
93
7
104
1
55
126
119
186
147
37
138
194
49
50
65
66
129
97
170
26
77
134
116
191
0 10 20 30 40 50 60 KM

LEINSTER

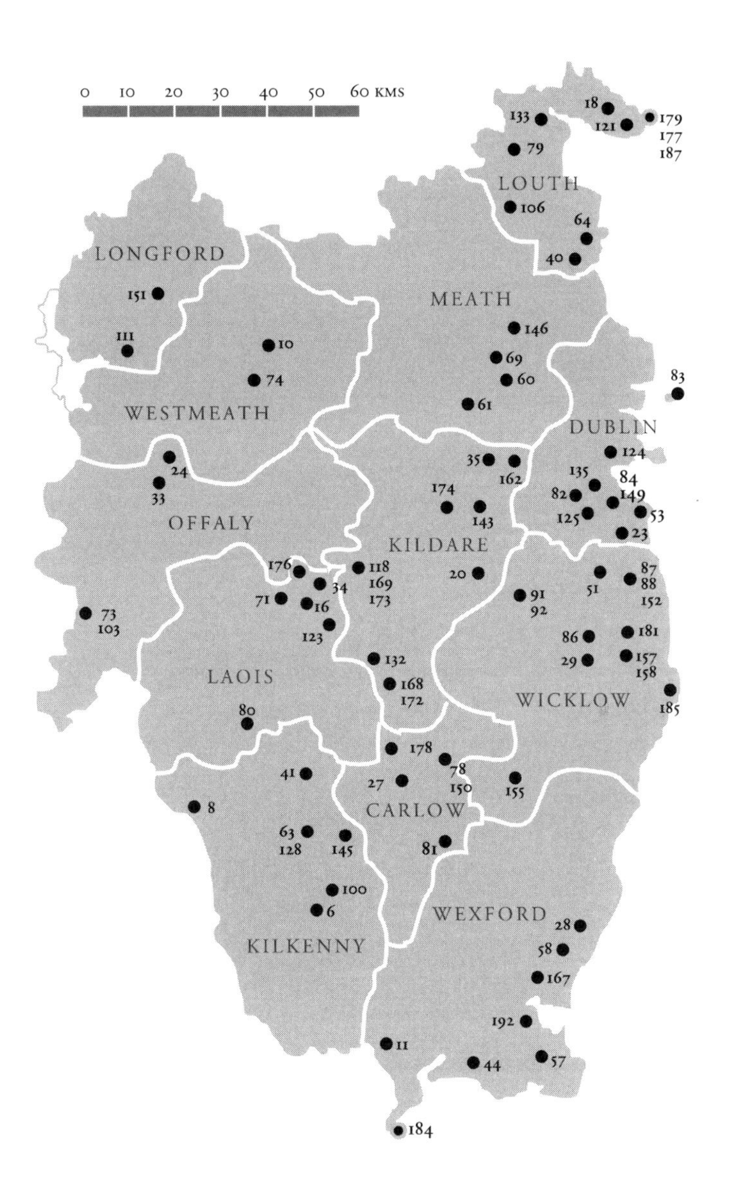

0 10 20 30 40 50 60 KMS
LOUTH
MEATH
LONGFORD
WESTMEATH
DUBLIN
OFFALY
KILDARE
LAOIS
WICKLOW
CARLOW
KILKENNY
WEXFORD

CONNACHT

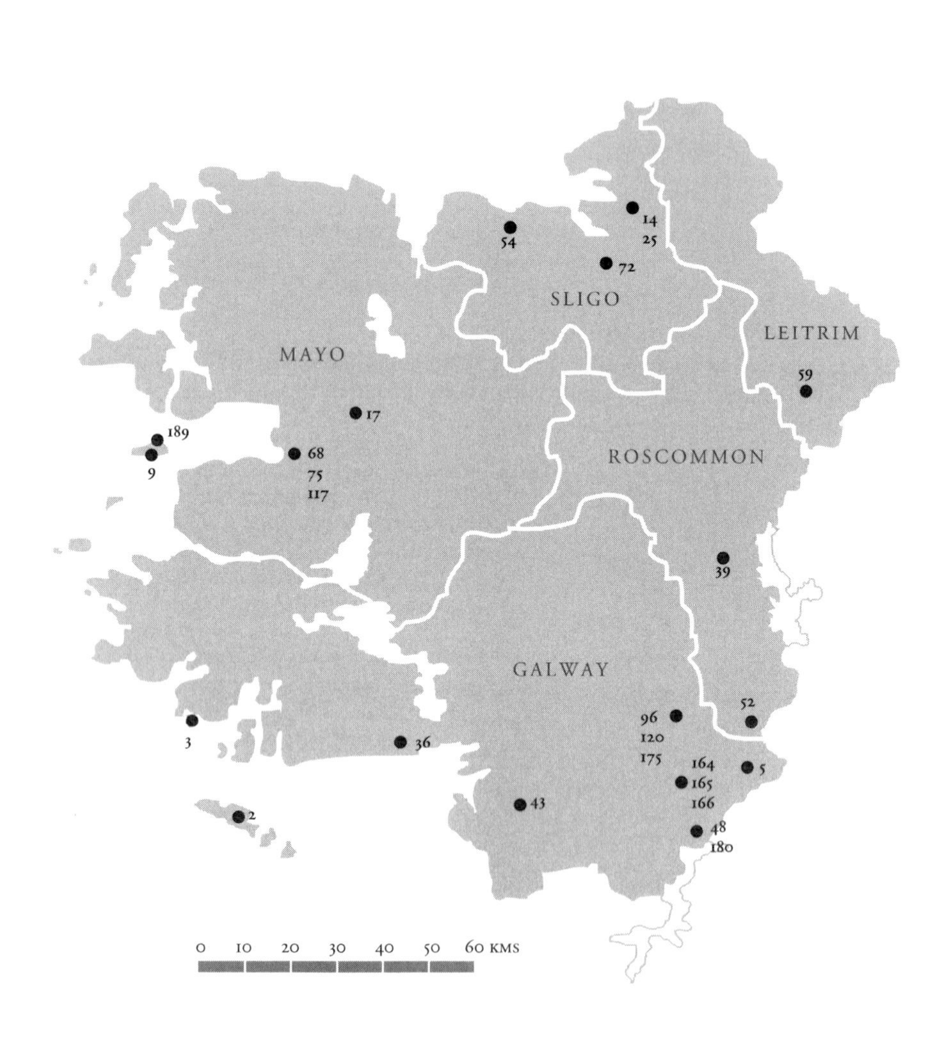

MAYO
SLIGO
LEITRIM
ROSCOMMON
GALWAY
54
14
25
72
59
17
189
9
68
75
117
39
52
96
120
175
164
165
166
5
3
36
43
2
48
180
0 10 20 30 40 50 60 KMS

SELECTED BOOKLIST FOR FURTHER READING

The following is a reading list of more detailed works for those who wish to learn more about the various types of buildings illustrated and described.

GENERAL

Casey, Christine and Rowan, Alistair, *The Buildings of Ireland: North Leinster: The Counties of Longford, Louth, Meath and Westmeath,* 1993.

Craig, Maurice, *The Architecture of Ireland* , 1982.

Harbison, Peter, *Guide National Monuments of Ireland*, 1970.

——, Potterton, Homan and Sheehy, Jeanne, *Irish Art and Architecture from Pre-History to the Present*, 1978.

McParland, Edward, "A Bibliography of Irish Architectural History", in *Irish Historical Studies,* xxvi, no. 102 (Nov. 1988).

Rowan, Alistair, *The Buildings of Ireland: North-West Ulster: The Counties of Londonderry, Donegal, Fermanagh and Tyrone*, 1979.

Ulster Architectural Heritage Society, *Lists and Surveys of Historic Buildings* etc., 1968–present.

THE CELTIC REVIVAL

Sheehy, Jeanne, *The Rediscovery of Ireland's Past: The Celtic Revival: 1830 –1930,* 1980.

THE NINETEENTH CENTURY

Williams, Jeremy, *A Companion Guide to Architecture in Ireland: 1837–1921*, 1994.

THE TWENTIETH CENTURY

Rothery, Sean, *Ireland and the New Architecture: 1900–1940*, 1991. Includes the work of Lutyens in Ireland.

CHURCHES

De Breffny, Brian and Mott, George, *The Churches and Abbeys of Ireland*, 1976.

Hurley, Richard and Cantwell, Wilfred, *Contemporary Irish Church Architecture*, 1985.

Leask, Harold, *Irish Churches and Monastic Buildings*, 3 vols, 1955, 1958, 1960.

MONASTERIES

Stalley, Roger, *The Cistercian Monasteries of Ireland*, 1987.

CASTLES
De Breffny, Brian, *Castles of Ireland*, 1977.
Leask, Harold, *Irish Castles and Castellated Houses*, 1941.

FORTIFICATIONS
Kerrigan, Paul M, *Castles and Fortifications in Ireland 1485–1945*, 1995.

MARTELLO TOWERS
Enoch, Victor, *The Martello Towers of Ireland*, 1975.

HOUSES
Bence-Jones, Mark, *Burke's Guide to Country Houses*, Vol. 1: Ireland, 1978.
Craig, Maurice, *Classic Irish Houses of the Middle Size*, 1976.
De Breffny, Brian and ffolliott, Rosemary, *The Houses of Ireland*, 1975.
Guinness, Desmond and Ryan, William, *Irish Houses and Castles*, 1971.

VERNACULAR HOUSES
Danaher, Kevin, *Ireland's Traditional Houses*, 1975.
Evans, Estyn E., *Irish Folk Ways*, 1957.
Gailey, Alan, *Rural Houses of the North of Ireland*, 1984.

PALLADIANISM
Guinness, Desmond and J.T. Sadler, *The Palladian Style in England, Ireland and America*, 1976.

ESTATE VILLAGES
Darley, Gillian, *Villages of Vision*, 1975.
Includes Irish estate villages.

DESERTED VILLAGES
Muir, Richard, *The Lost Villages of Britain*, 1982.
Includes Ireland.

TOWNS
Cullen, L.M., *Irish Towns and Villages*, 1979.
Garner, William, *Cobh: Architectural Heritage*, 1979.
——, *Bray: Architectural Heritage*, 1980.
——, *Carlow: Architectural Heritage*, 1980.
——, *Kinsale: Architectural Heritage*, 1980.
——, *Tullamore: Architectural Heritage*, 1980.
——, *Ennis: Architectural Heritage*, 1981.
——, *Galway: Architectural Heritage*, 1985.
——, *Drogheda: Architectural Heritage*, 1986.
Pearson, Peter, *Dún Laoghaire / Kingstown*, 1981.
Shaffrey, Patrick, *The Irish Town: An Approach to Survival*, 1975.

COURTHOUSES AND MARKET HOUSES
Brett, C.E.B, *Court Houses and Market Houses of Ulster*, 1973.

SHOPS

Rothery, Sean, *The Shops of Ireland,* 1978.

BANKS

Cullen, L.M., "Germination and Growth", in *Root and Branch: AIB,* 1979

PRISONS

Evans, Robin, *The Fabrication of Virtue: English Prison Architecture, 1750-1840,* 1982.
Includes discussion on Irish gaols and the penitentiary system.

WORKHOUSES

Gould, Michael, *The Workhouses of Ulster,* 1983.

THE ESTATE

Malins, Edward and The Knight of Glin, *Lost Demesnes,* 1976.

Malins, Edward, and Bowe, Patrick, *Irish Gardens and Demesnes from 1830,* 1980.

GATELODGES

Dean, J. A. K., *The Gate Lodges of Ulster,* 1994.

FOLLIES

Howley, James, *Follies and Garden Buildings of Ireland,* 1993.

BUILDINGS OF INDUSTRY

McCutcheon, W.A., *The Industrial Archaeology of Northern Ireland,* 1980.
Includes Railways of Northern Ireland.

CANALS

Delany, Ruth, *Canals of the South of Ireland,* 1966.

——, *The Grand Canal of Ireland,* 1995.

——, *Ireland's Inland Waterways,* 1988.

——, *Ireland's Royal Canal,* 1992.

Flanagan, Patrick, *The Ballinamore and Ballyconnell Canal,* 1972.

MINING

Williams, R.A., *The Berehaven Copper Mines,* 1991.

BRIDGES

O'Keeffe, Peter and Simington, Tom, *Irish Stone Bridges: History and Heritage,* 1991

LIGHTHOUSES

Hague, Douglas B. and Christie, Rosemary, *Lighthouses: Their Architecture, History and Archaeology,* 1977.
Includes Irish lighthouses and their builders.

RICHARD CASTLE

Fitzgerald, Desmond, Knight of Glin, "Richard Castle, architect, his biography and works", in *Irish Georgian Society Bulletin,* vii, no. 1 (Jan-Mar. 1964).

JAMES GANDON

McParland, Edward, *Vitruvius Hibernicus,* 1985.

FRANCIS JOHNSTON

McParland, Edward, "Francis Johnston, Architect, 1760–1829", in *Irish Georgian Society Bulletin,* xii, nos. 3, 4 (July-Dec. 1969).

J. J. MCARTHY

Sheehy, Jeanne, *J.J. McCarthy and the Gothic Revival in Ireland,* 1977.

A. W. N. PUGIN

Dixon, Roger and Muthesius, Stefan, *Victorian Architecture,* 1975. For A.W.N. Pugin's churches in Ireland.

BENJAMIN WOODWARD

Blau, Eve, *Ruskinian Gothic The Architecture of Deane and Woodward 1841-1861,* 1982.

Frederick O'Dwyer, *The Architecture of Deane and Woodward,* 1997.

GLOSSARY OF ARCHITECTURAL TERMS

Numbers in brackets refer to drawings where architectural terms are described and/or illustrated.

ANGLE BASTION *see* BASTION

ANTAE (3) The short projections of side walls on to gables. A typical feature of Early Irish Church architecture.

ARABESQUE (108) A surface decoration largely imitating intertwined foliage.

ARCADE (63) A series of arches supported on piers or columns. BLIND ARCADE (4) A series of arches applied to a wall surface to enliven the façade.

ARCH A structural device to span an opening. Blocks of stone or bricks are held together by mutual pressure and supported at the sides on piers, columns or walls. POINTED ARCH (6) Typical of Gothic architecture and consisting of two arcs drawn from centres on the line of springing or start of the curve. ROUND-HEADED ARCH The simplest form of arch, consisting of a semicircle. SEGMENTAL ARCH (94) An arch formed from a segment of a semicircle drawn from a centre below the line of springing of the arch. SOLDIER ARCH (177) A term to used describe a vertical course of bricks which spans a lintel over a door or window. FOUR-CENTRED TUDOR ARCH (145) A later development of the pointed arch with four arcs, each with a separate centre, the lower pair with centres drawn from the springing line and the upper pair drawn from centres below the springing line

ARCHITRAVE *see* ENTABLATURE.

ARRIS (113) The sharp edge or corner of a window or door opening.

ART DECO (37) A term used to describe a style movement of the 1920s and 1930s, strongly identified with cinema building and the jazz age.

ART NOUVEAU (104) Considered to be the earliest movement away from historical styles in the last two decades of the nineteenth century and the beginning of the twentieth. Characterized by the use of free flowing forms. Its greatest exponents were Charles Rennie Mackintosh in Glasgow, Louis Sullivan in Chicago, Victor Horta and van der Velde in Belgium.

ARTS AND CRAFTS (95) An art and architecture movement associated with William Morris in Britain in the last decades of the nineteenth century. The movement sought to restore creative craft work and fight the rise of mass production and the consequent lowering of standards.

ASHLAR (25) *see* MASONRY

BANDED RUSTICATION (94) *see* MASONRY

BARBICAN (39) Outer defensive work protecting the gateway to a castle.

BARGE. (22) Capping or coping to the edge of a roof at the gable to protect against entry of water.

BARGE-BOARDS (176) Timber boards placed along the edges of a gable to protect the roof timbers. Often elaborately carved.

BARN CHURCH (21) Vernacular Irish Roman Catholic church, characterized by a simple rectangular, "barn" plan.

BAROQUE (94) The style of architecture current in Italy in the seventeenth century. Characterized by a delight in complexity and a solid feeling of mass.

BARTIZAN (42) A small turret corbelled out, usually from the top of a castle wall, for defensive purposes. Often as a CORNER BARTIZAN (42), to protect the vulnerable corners of the wall.

BASTION A projection from the outer wall of a castle to enable the defenders to provide flanking fire to parts of the surrounding wall. The earliest bastion is known as a ROUND BASTION (46) A later development, with the invention of artillery, is the ANGLE or STAR-SHAPED BASTION (48) (49).

BATTER (5) The inward inclination of a wall or door frame, a characteristic of Early Irish Church architecture.

BATTLEMENTS The indented parapet of a castle to defend the outer wall. The openings are called EMBRASURES and the protective raised sections, MERLONS. IRISH BATTLEMENTS (44) are a type peculiar to Irish fortifications where the merlons are stepped.

BAUHAUS (85) The school of art and architecture, founded in 1906 at Weimar in Germany. When a new building was designed for the school at Dessau by its director Walter Gropius, the Bauhaus became highly influential in the development of Modern Architecture.

BAWN (46) The defensive wall around a tower-house.

BRACKET (77) A projection used as a support.

BELFRY (15) The section of a tower used to house a bell.

BELL CAST (71) An architectural device to make a roof appear to sit comfortably on top of the walls. This is achieved by nailing short pieces of timber to the ends of rafters to tilt roof angle slightly upwards.

BELL COTE (19) A small turret specially provided to hold a church bell.

BEVEL *see* CHAMFER.

BONDING (44) The method of building in brick or stone where alternative short and long sides of a block or brick are laid to interlock for structural strength.

BULLSEYE (79) A small round or oval-shaped window. *See also* OCULUS.

BUTTRESS (20) A vertical projection in masonry built against a structural wall to counteract the outward force of a pitched roof, vault or arch.

CASEMENT (42) In military architecture a strongly built, usually vaulted, chamber built within the castle bastions for storage or living quarters.

Also used as a strong defensive position when provided with gun loops or cannon embrasures.

CHEVRON (5) A moulding in a zig-zag shape. Associated with Irish Romanesque architecture.

CHAMFER (32) The oblique surface formed when a square angle or sharp arris is cut away.

CHANCEL The east end of a church where the altar is positioned.

CHOIR (12) Usually refers to the eastern end of a cruciform-shaped church. Where the services are sung.

CLASSICAL (15) A style derived from the architecture of ancient Greece and Rome.

CLERE-STOREY (6) The upper storey of the nave of a church, pierced by windows.

CLOISTER ARCADE (14) A covered walk around an open court. Usually associated with monasteries and used to provide a passage to and from the church to the refectory and other quarters.

COLLONETTE (99) A very small column.

CONSOLE (101) A carved bracket usually in the form of a scroll. Commonly used on traditional shopfronts to frame the nameboard.

CORBEL (1) An early structural technique where individual blocks of masonry are built out, each one above the other, to form a primitive stone vault. A term also used to describe projecting blocks or bricks used to support a turret, chimney stack, oriel window etc.

CORINTHIAN (108) *see* ORDER.

CORNER BARTIZAN *see* BARTIZAN

CORNICE (69) The top part of an entablature or a moulded projection at the top of a wall or an opening such as a door or window. Its main practical purpose is to throw off rainwater and to cast a shadow.

CROCKET (144) A small projection, in the form of a knob or a curved leaf, used to decorate a pinnacle or a gable. Associated with Gothic architecture.

CUPOLA (128) Small dome, usually on a roof.

CURTAIN WALL The outer defensive wall of a castle.

DENTIL (104) A small rectangular block, always arranged in a series and projecting from underneath a cornice. The purpose was to ensure a lively shadowed effect. Associated with classical orders, Doric, Ionic and Corinthian.

DIAMOND-POINTED RUSTICATION *see* MASONRY.

DIAPER PATTERN (67) A pattern of carved shapes, usually in lozenge form.

DIOCLETIAN WINDOW (70) Semicircular window divided into three. The centre space is usually wider than the outer spaces. Associated with Palladian architecture and, originally, with the Roman Baths of Diocletian.

DORMER (66) An attic window projecting from the slope of a roof.

DORIC *see* ORDER (133).

DUTCH GABLE (127) A gable with curves on each side and a pediment on top.

EAVES (21) The lower edge of a roof overhanging the wall.

EGG & DART (103) A carved pattern from classical architecture consisting of alternating oval and pointed motifs.

ELIZABETHAN (78) A style from the reign of Queen Elizabeth I which was a mixture of late mediæval details and ideas from the Renaissance.

EMBRASURE (24) *see* BATTLEMENTS

ENTABLATURE (107) The upper part of a classical order, consisting of three main parts: the ARCHITRAVE, immediately above the supporting column, the FRIEZE, in the centre, and the CORNICE, at the top.

EXPRESSIONIST (37) A short-lived architectural movement of the early decades of the twentieth century mainly associated with Germany and Holland. Characterized often by complex and bizarre forms.

FAÇADE Usually the principal front of a building or also the front elevation.

FLUTED COLUMN (101) A column carved with vertical grooves or flutes.

FINIAL (3) A small ornament used to finish off the top of a roof gable, a spire, pinnacle or pediment.

FOLIATED (115) Used to describe a carving in the form of plant leaves.

FRIEZE (113) The centre section of an entablature between the architrave and the cornice. Could also be used to describe a band of decoration.

GABLE (56) The triangular part of a wall at the end of a pitched roof.

GARDEROBE (41) A mediæval privy. Usually projecting from the upper part of a castle.

GARGOYLE (38) A prominent projecting spout from the end of a roof to throw off rainwater. In mediæval architecture often carved as a human or animal head.

GEORGIAN (147) A style of architecture from the reign of the Georges (1714–1830). Generally classical in spirit, following the ideas of Palladio.

GIBBS SURROUND *also* GIBBSIAN (15) A detail to doors and windows made popular by James Gibbs. Characterized by prominent keystones and projecting stone blocks in the jambs or sides.

GLACIS A term from military architecture. A long and gentle slope from the defensive parapet of an artillery fortification allowing sweeping fire from the defenders.

GOTHIC (7) The style of architecture of mediæval times characterized by the POINTED ARCH, RIBBED VAULT, flying buttress. GOTHIC REVIVAL (143) A recreation of Gothic architecture, largely in the nineteenth century. The mediæval revival in the eighteenth century is known as Gothick. Other names for the nineteenth-century Gothic are HIGH GOTHIC (115) and VICTORIAN GOTHIC (115).

GUÉRITE (49) A term from military architecture for a sentry box projecting from the top of a bastion or rampart.

GUTTAE (126) Tiny cone-shaped decorations projecting from under the TRIGLIPHS of a Doric entablature.

HIBERNO-ROMANESQUE (35) A term to describe the style of architecture in the late nineteenth and early twentieth centuries which sought to imitate the architecture of Early Irish Christian and Romanesque churches and art.

HIPPED ROOF (57) A pitched roof which slopes on all sides.

HOOD MOULDING (120) A projecting moulding over a window or door to throw off water. Associated with mediæval architecture.

ITALIAN STYLE (33) A term generally applied to an architectural revival style of the nineteenth century, influenced by the writings of John Ruskin (1819–1900). Characterized by the use of round-headed arches in the manner of the Italian Renaissance.

JACOBEAN (48) The style of architecture from the reign of James I. Generally characterized by the introduction of classical forms onto the earlier more informal Elizabethan style.

KEEP The main strong point of a castle, usually a tower well within the curtain walls. Another name for a keep is a Donjon.

KEYSTONE (71) The central wedge-shaped stone of an arch or lintel over a door or window.

LANCET WINDOW (7) A tall, narrow window, associated with early English architecture. In mediæval Irish churches the lancets are usually grouped in threes, or fives.

LINTEL (71) A horizontal beam or stone over a window or door opening.

LOOP. A term to describe a narrow vertical slot in the wall of a mediæval castle. ARROW LOOP (39) A narrow loop with a wide splay on the inside to allow a bowman to have freedom to aim and fire his weapon outwards and downwards. MUSKET LOOP (55) A later development of the arrow loop, often with a small round opening at the bottom to rest a musket for aiming.

MACHICOLATION (53) A horizontal projection built out from top of a castle wall on brackets and with openings to allow the dropping of boiling oil or heavy stones on attackers at the base of the wall.

MASONRY Stone walling built in various methods. RUSTICATED (73) Individual blocks emphasized by deeply recessed joints, often chamfered. BANDED RUSTICATED (94) Horizontal joints only are deeply emphasized. RUBBLE (69) Irregularly shaped stones fitted together in a random pattern. ASHLAR (68) Square or rectangular blocks of stone smoothly dressed and laid with fine joints in a regular pattern. SNECKED (82) A walling method where squared blocks of stone in random sizes are fitted together with very small squared blocks – the snecks – to close the pattern. DIAMOND-POINTED (61) Rusticated masonry where the blocks are hewn to create the effect of a shallow pyramid. In Irish vernacular architecture this effect was often created in paint of different shades to imitate shadows and an illusion of three dimensions.

MEDALLION (111) A round plaque.
MOAT A deep ditch, usually water filled, used for defence.
MODILLION (94) Small blocks set out at even spacing on the underside of a cornice.
MULLION The vertical member which divides the window into separate lights.
MURDERING HOLE (41) A small opening in the roof over the entrance porch to a castle or fortified house.
NAVE The main body of a church.
NICHE (69) A recess set into a wall, often designed to take a statue and usually with a semicircular top.
OCULUS (130) A small round window. *See also* BULLSEYE
OGEE ARCH (23) An arch formed by two concave arcs below and two convex arcs above, with a pointed centre.
ORDER The classical order consists of a column with its base, shaft and capital which supports the ENTABLATURE with its ARCHITRAVE, FRIEZE and CORNICE. CORINTHIAN (108) The Corinthian order is characterized by its foliated capital, often as acanthus leaves. DORIC (133) The column of the Greek order has no base but the shaft is fluted. The Roman Doric has a base and the shafts are sometimes plain. IONIC (99) The Ionic order is characterized by its distinctive capital in the shape of flowing volutes. TUSCAN The Tuscan order is a simple and plain version of the Doric.
ORIEL (63) A bay window which projects from an upper storey and which is usually supported on corbels or brackets.
PALLADIAN (69) Architecture influenced by Andrea Palladio (1508–80).
PANTILE (83) A curved roof tile, S-shaped.
PARAPET (69) The low wall above the cornice or top of the wall and which projects above the end of the roof rafters. On castles the parapet was usually battlemented for defensive purposes. On classical buildings the parapet gave an ordered appearance to the façade and hid the roof gutters.
PEDIMENT (5) A feature of classical architecture. A triangular gable, usually over an ENTABLATURE or above a door or window.
PICTURESQUE (72) The art movement known as picturesque dates from late eighteenth century and is mainly concerned with landscape. In architecture the ideal of the vernacular was evoked in small buildings such as the romantic cottage, characterized by informality and irregularity.
PIANO NOBILE (68) In classical or Renaissance architecture the principal floor containing formal reception rooms was raised above ground level.
PILASTER (26) A half column, of rectangular shape, built out a little from the main wall of a building.
PINNACLE (20) A small sharp spire, cone-shaped or pyramidal, used as a decoration on a roof gable or above a buttress. *See also* CROCKET and FINIAL.

PLINTH (22) The slightly projecting base of a wall or a column.
POLYCHROMY (149) A device of nineteenth-century architecture where bricks or stones of different colours are used on the same façade for decorative effect.
POLYGONAL (148) A complex stone-walling technique where the blocks are polygonal in shape and carefully laid against each other to create a highly informal pattern.
PORTICO (133) A covered porch to the entrance of a building.
QUATREFOIL (135) A group of four small arc openings in Gothic tracery.
QUOIN (15) The external angle or corner of a building, often rusticated. *See* MASONRY
REDOUBT (52) A small strongpoint in a castle or fortification.
RAMPART A defensive enclosure, of earth or stone, to a castle or fortification.
RENAISSANCE A term usually applied to the art and architecture of Italy from about 1420 to the sixteenth century.
REREDOS (24) An ornamental screen, usually behind the altar of a church.
RIDGE (58) The apex of a pitched roof.
ROMANESQUE (4) The style of architecture which was followed by Gothic. Usually characterized by the use of the round arch.
ROLL MOULDING (73) A plain moulding of semicircular shape.
ROOD SCREEN (14) A screen placed at the west end of the chancel of a church to separate the nave from the choir.
ROOF BARGE *see* BARGE
ROPE MOULDING (100) A moulding shaped like a rope.
ROUNDEL (94) A decorative small round medallion or panel.
RUBBLE *see* MASONRY
RUSKIN *see* ITALIAN STYLE
RUSTICATED *see* MASONRY
SASH WINDOW (79) A window, usually of wood, which slides up and down.
SANCTUARY (20) The part of a church around the altar.
SCALLOPED (149) A type of ornament consisting of a series of small curves.
SEGMENTAL ARCH *see* ARCH
SNECKED *see* MASONRY
SOLDIER ARCH (182) *see* ARCH
SPANDRIL (129) The triangular area on each side of an arch, above the curve and below the horizontal line or cornice above the arches.
SPLAY (7) The surface formed by the chamfering or cutting away of a sharp corner.
STRING COURSE (69) A moulding or square band running in a horizontal line across the façade of a building.
SWAG (106) A decorative device in the form of a garland of flowers or fruit.
TÊTE-DE-PONT (52) A fortification for the approach to a bridge.

TRACERY (8) Usually applied to later Gothic windows where the stone mullions in the upper part of the window are branched out to give an ornamental effect.

TRANSEPT (11) The arms of a church where the plan is cruciform in shape.

TRANSOM (65) The horizontal dividing member of a window.

TREFOIL A group of three small arc openings in Gothic tracery.

TRIGLYPH One of the rectangular blocks, with three grooves, in a Doric frieze.

TUDOR (78) The style of architecture from the culmination of Gothic to the end of the reign of Queen Elizabeth I.

TURRET (46) A small tower, usually attached to a building.

TUSCAN *see* ORDER

VAULT. An arched roof over a space. BARREL VAULT A vault of semicircular section. RIBBED VAULT System of cross vaulting in which thin ribs span over the sides and diagonals as a structural framework and where the spaces between are filled in with light-weight or thin material.

VENETIAN WINDOW (15) A tripartite window where the centre section is usually wider and arched and the side openings have flat lintels.

VERNACULAR (18) A term usually applied to the traditional style or building method of a particular region.

VICTORIAN GOTHIC (115) *see* GOTHIC

VOUSSOIR (82) A wedge-shaped stone used in a series to form an arch.

WAINSCOT Wood panelling. The term is usually applied to panelling which is built up to dado level (the lower part of the interior of a wall) only.

INDEX

Numbers in italic denote illustrations

Abbeyfeale, Co. Limerick, shops, *127-8*
Achill Island, Co. Mayo, Protestant settlement, 109
Adare, Co. Limerick; Augustinian friary, 21; castle, 21; Franciscan friary, *21*; St Nicholas Church, 21; White, "Trinitarian", monastery, 21
Aghavannagh, Co. Wicklow, barracks, 64, 68
Aherlow, Co. Tipperary, Franciscan friary, 21
Allihies, Co. Cork, copper mines, 116; engine house, *198*
Almshouses, Kinsale, Co. Cork, *80-1*
Antrim, Co. Antrim, workhouse, 159
Aran Islands; Teampull Benin, *8*
Ardagh, Co. Longford, cottage, *175;* estate village, 175
Ardee, Co. Louth, shop, *126*
Ardfert, Co. Kerry; Cathedral, *13*; Franciscan friary, 13
Ardrahan, Co. Galway, castle, *56*
Arklow, Co. Wicklow, Methodist church, 41
Armagh, Bank of Ireland, *129*; Cathedral, 39; Observatory, 129, *163-4*
Ashlin, George, 38, 135
Athassel Priory, Co. Tipperary, Augustinian monastery, *20*
Athenry, Co. Galway, Dominican monastery, 22; town walls, 52
Athlone, Co. Westmeath, railway station, 43, 204
Athy, market hall, *152;* Model School, 152; bridge, 200
Avoca, Co. Wicklow, mining buildings, 198

Bailieborough, Co. Cavan, shops, *120-1*
Ballinasloe, Co. Galway, Garbally House, 140; school, *140;* station, *204-5;* street, *115*
Ballinderry, Co. Antrim, Middle Church, 23
Ballinderry Lower, Co. Antrim, Moravian church, 26
Ballindoon, Co. Sligo, Dominican monastery, 22
Ballintubber, Co. Mayo, Augustinian monastery, 20
Ballitore, Co. Kildare, Quaker village, 43, 109
Ballybeg, Buttevant, Co. Cork, dovecot, 186
Ballyboden, Co. Dublin, County Council cottages, *98-9*
Ballybrittas, Co. Laois, Rathdaire Church, *44*
Ballycanew, Co. Wexford, vernacular house, *73*
Ballycorus, mining building, 198
Ballyduff, Co. Waterford, police barracks, *68;* library, *146*
Ballyfin, Mountrath, Co. Laois, 171
Ballyjamesduff, Co. Cavan, market house, *150*
Ballyknockan, Co. Wicklow, 29, barn, *111*; cottage, *110*; Quarry Manager's house, *110*
Ballylough, Bushmills, Co. Antrim, gate-lodge, *172*
Ballymahon, Co. Longford, National Bank, *131*
Ballymena, Co. Antrim, shop and house, *118*
Ballymore, Co. Donegal, St John's Church, *25*
Ballyshannon, Co. Donegal, bank, 132
Baltimore, Co. Cork, beacon, 221; castle, 225; lifeboat house, *225*
Baltinglass, Co. Wicklow, Cistercian monastery, 12, 19
Banagher, Co. Offaly, fortified bridgehead, 211
Banbridge, Co. Down, library, 147
Bangor, Co. Down, library, 147
Banks, Bank of Ireland, Armagh, *129;* Belfast Bank, Dungannon, Co. Tyrone, *130;* Hibernian Bank, Letterkenny, Co. Donegal, *135;* Munster and Leinster Bank, Schull, Co. Cork, *136;* National

Bank, Ballymahon, Co. Longford, *131;* Provincial Bank, Cootehill, Co. Cavan, *134;* Provincial Bank, Omagh, Co. Tyrone, *133;* Royal Bank, Donegal, *132*
Bantry, Co. Cork, courthouse, 154; Methodist church, 41
Bantry bay, defence works, 65; Martello tower, 66
Barnacullia, Co. Dublin, stonecutters' village, 145
Barrow Navigation, 200
Beardiville, Bushmills, Co. Antrim, gatelodge, *172*
Beaulieu, Co. Louth, *79*
Belfast City and District Water Commissioners, 213
Bellinter, Co. Meath, *84*
Bellvue, Lawrencetown , Co. Galway, 190-2
Belvedere, Mullingar, Co. Westmeath, 190
Benburb, Co. Tyrone, Castle, 59
Birr, Co. Offaly, Castle, 89; Oxmantown Mall, 89; town house,*89;* watchmaker's shop, *123*
Black Head, Co. Clare, automatic light, *221*
Blackwater, Co. Wexford, vernacular houses, 73
Board of First Fruits, 33, 90
Bowden, John, 153
Boyle, Co. Roscommon, Cistercian monastery, 19
Bray, Co. Wicklow, seaside resort, 216
Brocagh, Co. Wicklow, deserted village, *105*
Brownsbarn, Thomastown, Co. Kilkenny, *174*
Bryansford, Co. Down, Tollymore Park, 168
Bunclody (Newtownbarry), Co. Wexford, house, *97*
Burgh, Thomas, 23
Burke, Edmund, 109
Burn, William, 181
Burntcourt, Co. Tipperary, fortified house, 61
Burrishoole, Co. Mayo, Dominican monastry, 22
Burt, Co. Donegal, Catholic church 48,
Bush, Co. Louth, school, *141*
Bushmills, Co. Antrim, distillery, 197; gatelodge, Beardiville, *172*
Butler, W.D., 151
Byrne, Barry, 47
Byrne, T.J., 99
Caldbeck, William, 131
Canals, Barrow Navigation, 200; Grand Canal, 196, *199,* 200, 202; Lagan Navigation, 199; Lough Neagh-Newry, 199; Royal Canal, 144, 199, 202-3
Carlingford, Co. Louth, town walls, 52
Carlow, railway station, 94, *209;* courthouse, 153
Carna, Co. Galway, 8
Carnegie, Andrew, 146
Carnegie Library, Ballyduff, Co. Waterford, *146;* Banbridge, Co. Down, 147; Bangor, Co. Down, 147; Downpatrick, Co. Down, 147; Kilkenny, *148;* Lurgan, Co. Armagh, *147* Newry, Co Down, 147; Newtownards, Co. Down, 147; Portadown, Co. Armagh, 147
Carrigfergus, Co. Antrim, Castle, 51
Carroll, J. Rawson, 175
Carton , Maynooth, Co. Kildare, 85; shell house, 189
Cashel, Co. Tipperary; Cormac's Chapel, 10; Dominican monastery, 22
Cassels or Castle, Richard, 25, 76, 83, 84-5
Castlebar. Co. Mayo, Methodist church, 26
Castleblayney, Co. Monaghan, Catholic church, 46
Castlebridge, Co. Wexford, mill and waterwheel, *195*
Castle Browne, Clane, Co. Kildare, 167
Castleisland, Co. Kerry, shop, *122*
Castlelyons, Co. Cork, Dominican monastery, 22
Castletownbere, Co. Cork, street, *116;* Dunboy Castle, 198
Castletown Geoghegan, Co. Westmeath, Quaker village, 43
Castletown House, Co. Kildare, 82, 85; Wonderful Barn, 187
Castletroy, Limerick, modern house, *102*
Castlewellan, Co. Down, Castle, 181; dovecot, 181, *186;* estate farm, *180-1;* gatelodge, 181
Cavan, Co. Cavan, Cathedral, 47; Town Hall, *114*
Cavangarden, Ballyshannon, Co. Donegal, barn, *187*
Chambers, Sir William, 30
Charles Fort, Kinsale, Co. Cork, *62 -3*
Charleville Forest, Co. Offaly, 88
Church of Christ the King, Turner's Cross, Cork, *47*
Clane, Co. Kildare, Church of Ireland

church, 45; gateway, *167*
Clara, Co. Offaly, Quaker Meeting House, *43*
Clara Castle, Co. Kilkenny, *53*
Claregalway, Co. Galway, Franciscan friary, 21
Clare Island, Co. Mayo, Cistercian cell, *15;* lighthouse, *222*
Clifford, Smith and Newenham, 102
Clonfert Cathedral, Co. Galway, *11*
Clongowes Wood College, Clane, Co. Kildare, gateway, *167*
Clonmacnoise, Co. Offaly; Early Christian site, 9; Nuns' Church, 10
Clonmel, Co. Tipperary, courthouse, 112; Mainguard, 112; West Gate, *112;*
Clonmines, Co. Wexford, fortified church, 16
Clonsilla, Co. Dublin, school, *144*
Clontra, Shankill, Co. Dublin, 174
Coleraine, Co. Derry, Town Hall, *113*
Coastguard station, Killybegs, Co Donegal, *224*
Cobh, Co. Cork, Cathedral, 228; yacht club, *228*
Collooney, Co. Sligo, Markree Castle, *88*
Coolattin Park, Shillelagh, Co. Wicklow, farm steward's house, *179*
Coolbanagher, Co. Laois, church, *30*
Coolbawn, Enniscorthy, Co. Wexford, 94
Coolhull Castle, Duncormick, Co. Wexford, *57*
Cootehill, Co. Cavan, Methodist church, *41*; Presbyterian church, *42;* Provincial Bank, *134*
Corboy Presbyterian church, Edgeworthstown, Co. Longford, 26
Cork, Church of Christ the King, *47;* City Gaol, *160;* Gaol, 160; Honan Chapel, 45; Lee Maltings, 197; St Ann's, Shandon, 25; Skiddy's almhouses, 81
Cork harbour, defence works, 65; Martello tower, 66
Cormac's Chapel, Cashel, Co. Tipperary, 10
Corofin, Co. Clare, castle, *60*
Courthouse, Bantry, Co. Cork, 154; Carlow, 153; Clonmel, Co. Tipperary, 112; Dundalk, Co. Louth, *153;* Dundrum, Co. Dublin, *155;* Kinsale, Co. Cork, *149* Midleton, Co. Cork, 154; Newtownbutler, Co. Fermanagh, 151; Skibbereen, Co. Cork, 154; Tralee, Co. Kerry, 153
Cratloe, Co. Clare, Catholic church, *28 - 9*
Creeslough, Co. Donegal, Catholic church, *48;* Doe Castle, *54-5*
Cromwell's Island, river Shannon, Martello tower, 65
Crookhaven, Co. Cork, navigation tower, 221
Curle, John, 79

Damer House, Roscrea, Co. Tipperary, 82
Dance, George the Elder, 113
Darley, Frederick, 94, 152
Deane and Woodward, 155
Derry, town walls, 52
Deserted village, Blaskets, Co Kerry, 105; Brocagh, Co. Wicklow, *105*; Gola, Co. Donegal, 105; Inishkea, Co. Mayo, 105; Slievemore, Achill, Co. Mayo, 105
Desertigney, Co. Donegal, Catholic church, 48
Devenish, Co. Fermanagh, Early Christian site, 9
Doe Castle, Creeslough, Co. Donegal, *54-5*
Donaghadee, Co. Down, lighthouse, 223
Donegal, Co. Donegal, Royal Bank, *132*
Doneraile Court, Co. Cork, 82
Douglass, William, 223
Dovecot, Castlewellan, Co. Down, *186*; Ballybeg, Co. Cork, 186
Downhill, Co. Derry, 178, Bishop's Gate, 178; gamekeeper's lodge, *178;* Lion Gate, 178; mausoleum, 178; Mussenden Temple, 178
Downpatrick, Co. Down, almhouses, 81; library, 147
Dingle, Co. Kerry, 7
Drew, Sir Thomas, 90
Drogheda, Co. Louth, St. Laurence's Gate, *52;* town walls, 52; Townley Hall, 163-4
Dromoland Castle, Co. Clare, 60
Dromore West, Co. Sligo, signal tower, *67*
Drumgoff, Co. Wicklow, barracks, 64
Drumharsna Castle, Ardrahan, Co. Galway, *56*
Drumquin, Co. Tyrone, rectory, 92
Dublin, Bank of Ireland, 164; Black Church, 33; Blue Coat School, 138; Broadstone Station 43; hotel, 203; Chapel Royal, Dublin Castle, 164; Custom House 30; Dr Steevens' Hospital, 207; Four Courts, 30; General Post Office, 164; Guinness Brewery, 197; Harcourt Street station, 204; House of Lords 30; Irish National War Memorial, 100; John's Lane distillery, 197; Leinster House, 85; Loreto Convent,38; Market

Street Store House, 197; Merrion Road church, 45; Monkstown church, 33; Museum, Trinity College, 155; Portobello, canal hotel, 203; Robert Street House, 197; St Francis Xavier, 36; St George's Church; 85 St Stephen's Green, 85; Shaw's Bank, 132; St Werburgh's, 23; Sunday School, School St, 138; Tyrone House, 85;
Dunboy Castle, Castletownbere, Co. Cork, 198
Dunbrody Abbey, Co. Wexford, Cistercian monastery, *19*
Dundalk, Co. Louth, bank, 131; courthouse, *153*
Dundalk Newry and Greenore Railway, 208
Duncormick, Co. Wexford, castle, *57*
Dundrum, Co. Dublin, courthouse, *155*
Dundrum, Co. Tipperary, station, 207
Dunfanaghy, Co. Donegal, workhouse, *156-7*
Dungannon, Co. Tyrone, Belfast Bank, *130;* police barracks, 68
Dun Laoghaire, 205, 216, 228
Dunlewy, Co. Donegal, Catholic church, 45
Dunmore East, Co. Waterford, lighthouse, 223
Dunmurry, Co. Antrim, Presbyterian church, 26
Dunsink, Co. Dublin, observatory, 163
Durrow, Co. Offaly, Catholic church, *34*
Durrow Abbey, Durrow, Co. Offaly, 34
Durrow, Co. Laois, house, *96*

Eadestown, Co. Kildare, Catholic church, *28-9*
Edenderry, Co. Offaly, Catholic church, 46
Edgeworthstown, Co. Longford, Corboy Presbyterian church, 26
Emo Court, Co. Laois, 30
Ennis Co. Clare, Franciscan friary, 13
Enniscorthy, Co. Wexford, Catholic church, 38
Enniskerry, Co. Wicklow, blacksmith's house, *106;* forge, *107;* Powerscourt House, 85, 106, 176
Enniskillen, Co. Fermanagh, Castle and Watergate, *58*
Erganagh rectory, Mountjoy Forest, Co. Tyrone, *92*
Estate farm, Carriglas, Co. Longford, 185; Castlewellan, Co. Down, *180-1;* Kilcarty, Kilmessan, Co. Meath, 185; Narrow Water, Co. Down, *184-5*; Tiglin, Ashford, Co. Wicklow, *182-3*
Estate village, Abbeyleix, Co. Laois, 107; Adare, Co. Limerick, 107; Ardagh, Co. Longford, 175; Bagenalstown, Co. Carlow, 107; Blessington, Co. Wicklow, 107; Enniskerry, Co. Wicklow, 105-6, 176; Virginia, Co. Cavan, 177; Tyrrellspass, Co. Westmeath, 107
Eyrecourt, Co. Galway, 79

Farrell, William, 92
Fethard, Co. Tipperary, town walls, 52
Folly, Belvedere, Co. Westmeath, 'Jealous Wall', 190;
Lawrencetown, Co. Galway, eyecatcher, *190;* Gothic cottage, *191*; Volunteer's Arch, *192;* Rubane, Kircubbin, Co. Down, Pebble House, *189*; Carton, Maynooth, Co. Kildare, shell house, 189
Fore, Co. Westmeath, Benedictine Abbey, 18
Fuller, James, 45

Galilei, Alessandro, 85
Gallagher, Thaddeus, 27
Gallarus Oratory, Dingle, Co. Kerry,*7*
Galway, town walls, 52; Lynch's Castle, 78; St Mary's College, 114
Galway bay, defence works, 65
Gandon, James, 30, 185
Gardiner, Luke, 92
Garrison, Co. Fermanagh, Catholic church, 48
Gatelodge, Ballylough, Bushmills, Co. Antrim, 172; Beardiville, Bushmills, Co. Antrim, *172;* Fota Island, Co. Cork, *171*; Goatstown, Co. Dublin, *173;* Slane, Co. Meath, *170;* Tullow, Co. Carlow, *174*
Gateway, Ballyfin, Mountrath, Co. Laois, 171; Clane, Co. Kildare, *167*; Fota Island, Co. Cork, *171;* Kilruddery, Co. Wicklow, 171; Paulstown, Co. Kilkenny, *169*; Tollymore, Co. Down, *168;*
Gazebo, Leixlip, Co. Kildare, *188*
Geoghegan, Charles, 143
Giant's Causeway, Co. Antrim, 172
Gibbs, James, 25, 113
Glandore, Monkstown, Co. Dublin, 174
Glanmore Castle, Ashford, Co. Wicklow, 182
Glencree, Co. Wicklow, barracks, *64*, 68
Glendalough, Co. Wicklow; St Kevin's stone-roofed church, 9; Round Tower, 9; St Saviour's Priory, 10; St Kevin's

Catholic church, *39;* mining buildings, 198
Glenties, Co Donegal, Catholic church, 48
Glinsk Castle, Co. Galway, 61
Goatstown, Co. Dublin, gatelodge, *173*
Gorey, Co. Wexford, Catholic church, *38*
Gothic cottage, Lawrencetown, Co. Galway, *191*
Gracehill, Co. Antrim, Moravian village, *108-9*
Grand Canal, 196, 200, 202, lock-keeper's house, *199;* hotel, *202-3*
Grange, Co. Louth, Catholic church
Great Southern and Western Railway, 206, 209
Greenore, Co. Louth, lighthouse, 220; railway housing, *208;* water tank, *210*
Grey Abbey, Ards Peninsula, Co. Down, Cistercian monastery, 13
Grianán of Ailach, Co. Donegal, 48
Gweedore, Co. Donegal, vernacular house, *71*

Halpin, George snr and jnr, 220, 222-3
Heavey, Timothy, 45, 135
Hendy, Arnold, 145
Heywood House, Ballinakill, Co. Laois, 100
Hobart, Henry, 147
Holycross, Co. Tipperary, Cistercian abbey, 14, 19
Hook Head, Co. Wexford, lighthouse, 215,*217*
Howard, Ebenezer, 101
Howth Castle, Co. Dublin, 100

Inch, Inishowen, Co. Donegal, Presbyterian church, 26
Industrial village, Ballyknockan, Co. Wicklow, *110-11*; Bessbrook, Co. Armagh, 111; Portlaw, Co. Waterford, 111; Prosperous, Co. Kildare, 111; Sion Mills, Co. Tyrone, 111
Inishmurray, Co. Sligo, Early Christian site, 9
Irish National War Memorial, Islandbridge, Dublin, 100

Jacob, J.H. & E.T., 68
Jekyll, Gertrude, 100
Jerpoint Abbey, Co. Kilkenny, Cistercian monastery, *12,* 19
Johnston, Francis, 88, 129, 163-4, 170, 182
Johnstown Castle, Co. Wexford, 169
Jones and Kelly, 101
Jordanstown, Co. Armagh, St Patrick's Church, 45

Kanturk, Co. Cork, fortified house, 61
Keelogue, river Shannon, battery, 65
Kells, Co. Meath, bank, 131; St Columb's stone-roofed church, 9
Kilbeggan, Co. Westmeath, distillery, 197
Kilconnell, Co. Galway, Franciscan friary, 21
Kilcooley Abbey, Urlingford, Co. Kilkenny, *14*
Kilcrea, Co. Cork, Franciscan friary, 21
Kilkenny, Castle, 160; Dominican monastery, 22; library, *148;* Rothe House, *78;* Shee Almhouses, 78; town walls, 52
Killarney, Co. Kerry, Cathedral, 38
Killeshin, Co. Laois, Romanesque doorway, 10
Killone, Co. Clare, Augustinian convent, 20
Killybegs, Co. Donegal, coastguard station, *224*
Kilruddery, Bray, Co. Wicklow, 171
Kilmalkedar, Co. Kerry, 7
Kilmallock, Co. Limerick, Dominican friary, 22
Kilmore, Co. Cavan, Romanesque doorway, 10
Kilternan, Co. Dublin, Church of Ireland, *33*
Kingscourt, Co. Cavan, shop-pub, *77*
Kingstown (Dun Laoghaire), Co. Dublin, station, 205
Kinsale, Co. Cork, Charles Fort, *62-3;* courthouse, *149*; lighthouse, 215; slate-hung houses, 226; Southwell Gift Houses, *80*

Lagan Navigation, 199
Lambay Castle, Rush, Co. Dublin, *100*
Lanyon Lynn and Lanyon, 130
Laragh, Co. Wicklow, barracks, 64
Lawrencetown, Co. Galway, Bellvue estate, 190-2; eyecatcher, *190;* Gothic cottage, *191;* Volunteer Arch, *192*
Leamaneh Castle, Corofin, Co. Clare, *60*
Le Corbusier, 48, 102
Leitrim, Glen of Imaal, Co. Wicklow, barracks, 64
Leixlip Castle, Leixlip, Co. Kildare, gazebo, *188*

Letterkenny, Co. Donegal, Hibernian Bank, *135;* workhouse, *158-9*
Levitstown, Co. Kildare, castellated mill, *196;* lock-keeper's house, *200*
Lifeboat house, Baltimore, Co. Cork, *225*
Lifford, Co. Donegal, Catholic church, 48; courthouse, 25; Port Hall, *86*
Lighthouse, Bailey, 222; Barry Oge's Castle; Black Head, *221*; Black Rock, 223; Clare Island, 222; Donaghadee, 223; Dunmore East, 223; Eagle Island, 223; Eeragh, 223; Greenore, *220;* Fastnet, 223; Haulbowline Rock, 220; Hook Head, 215, *217;* Howth, 215; Inisheer, 223; Inishtrahull, 222; Isle of Magee, 215; Larne harbour, 220; Loop Head; Maidens Rocks, 223; Old Head of Kinsale; Scelig Mhicíl, 223; Tuskar, 222; Wicklow Head, *218;* Youghal, *219*
Limerick, town walls, 52
Lisnaskea, Co. Fermanagh, market house, 151
Lisreaghan, Lawrencetown, Co. Galway, estate, 191
Listowel, Co. Kerry, Pat McAuliffe plasterwork, 127-8
Locke's Distillery, Kilbeggan, Co. Westmeath, 197
Longford, Co. Longford, bank, 131
Lorrha, Co. Tipperary, Dominican monastery, 22
Loughrea, Co. Galway, Carmelite priory, 18; Catholic cathedral, 46
Lough Neagh to Newry canal, 199
Lough Swilly, defence works, 65, 227
Louth, Co. Louth, house, *95*
Lurgan, Co. Armagh, library, *147*
Lutyens, Sir Edwin, 100
Lowrey, E. Stewart & Son, 148
Lynch's Castle, Galway, 78
Lynn, W.H., 45, 130

McAuliffe, Pat, 127-8
McCarthy, J.J., 39
McCormick, Liam and Partners, 48
McCullough, E.W., 213
MacNeill, Sir John, 207, 209
Manisternagalliaghduff Abbey, mediæval nunnery, 18
Market house, Athy, Co. Kildare, *152;* Ballyjamesduff, Co. Cavan, *150;* Lisnaskea, Co. Fermanagh, 151 Newtownbutler, Co. Fermanagh, *151*
Markree Castle, Collooney, Co. Sligo, *88*
Martello tower, Sandycove, Co. Dublin, *66*
Massmount Church, Rosnakill, Co. Donegal, *31*
Mastergeehey, Co. Kerry, school, *139*
Maynooth, Co. Kildare, College, 38; O'Growney tomb, *45;* Carton, 85
Mellifont, Co. Louth, Cistercian monastery, 19
Midland Great Western railway, 205
Midleton, Co. Cork, courthouse, 154
Milford, Co. Carlow, castellated mill, 196
Milford, Co. Donegal, Catholic church, 48
Mill, Levitstown, Co. Kildare, *196*; Milford, Co. Carlow, 196; mill and waterwheel, Castlebridge, Co. Wexford, *195;* Newhaggard, Trim, Co. Meath, 196; Slane, Co. Meath, 196
Mining buildings, Allihies, Co. Cork, engine house, *198;* Avoca, Co. Wicklow, 198; Carrickmines, Co. Dublin, chimney, 198; Glendalough, Co. Wicklow, 198
Mitchelstown, Co. Cork, almhouses, 81; chemist's shop, *124*
Moate, Co. Westmeath, bank, 131
Mohill, Co. Leitrim, vernacular house, *74*
Moira, Co. Down, church, 25
Monasterevan, Co. Kildare, aqueduct; distillery building, *197;* school, *138;* station, 207; warehouse, *201*
Monea, Co. Fermanagh, Catholic church, 46; Castle, *59*
Moore, Co. Roscommon, Catholic church, 46
Moravian village, Gracehill, Co. Antrim, church, *108;* houses, *109*
Morrison, Sir Richard, 112, 171
Morrison, William Vitruvius, 153
Mount Ievers, Sixmilebridge, Co. Clare, 82
Mountjoy Forest, Co. Tyrone, 92
Mountmellick, Co. Laois, Summergrove, *87*
Mount Merrion, Co. Dublin, suburban house, *101*
Mountshannon, Co. Clare, school, *142*
Moyne, Co. Mayo, Franciscan friary, 21
Moyvalley, Co. Kildare, canal hotel, 203
Mullingar, Co. Westmeath, bank, 131; Catholic Cathedral 47; Church of all Saints, 90; railway station 43; rectory, *90*;
Mulvany, J.S., 43, 228

New Geneva, Passage West, Co. Waterford, 107

Newhaggard, Trim, Co. Meath, flour mill, 196
Newport, Co. Tipperary, gaol, *161*
New Ross, Co. Wexford, town walls, 52
Newry, Co. Down, library, 147
Newtownards, Co. Down, library, 147
Newtownbreda, Co. Down, church, 25
Newtownbutler, Co. Fermanagh, courthouse, 151; market house, *151*
Newtownstewart, Co. Tyrone, draper's shop, *125*
Nimmo, Alexander, 223
Nurney, Co. Carlow, Church of Ireland, *37*

Observatory, Armagh, *163-4*
O'Conor Sligo monument, Sligo, 22
O'Flynn, B., 136
O'Growney Tomb, Maynooth, Co. Kildare, *45*
O'Kelly, E.W., 107
Omagh, Co. Tyrone, Provincial Bank, *133*
Omer, Thomas, 199

Pain brothers, 160
Pain, George, 154
Pain, William, 122
Palladio, Andrea, 84, 127
Parke, Edward, 153
Passage West, Co Waterford, settlement, 107
Paulstown, Co. Kilkenny, Shankill Castle, 169
Pearce, Sir Edward Lovett, 76, 81, 85
Pentland, Howard, 137
Picturesque barn, Cavangarden, Ballyshannon, Co. Donegal, *187;* Wonderful Barn, Castletown, Co. Kildare, 187
Police barracks, Ballyduff, Co. Waterford, *68*
Portadown, Co. Armagh, library, *147*
Portarlington, Co. Laois, Huguenot settlement, 87; station, *206-7*
Port Hall, Lifford, Co. Donegal, *86*
Portrush, Co. Antrim, 216
Portumna, Co. Galway, bridge, 211; bridge operator's cottage, *211;* Castle, *61;* Dominican monastery, 22
Port warehouse, Ramelton, Co. Donegal, *227*
Post Office, Tara, Co. Meath, *75*
Powerscourt, Enniskerry, Co. Wicklow, House, 85, 106; estate houses, *176*
Priestly, Michael, 25, 86
Prisons, Cork City Gaol, *160;* Cork Gaol, 160; Newport, Co. Tipperary, *161*; Tarbert, Co. Kerry, *162*
Pugin, Augustus Welby, 24, 38
Pugin E.W., 38, 135

Quaker Meeting House, Clara, Co. Offaly, *43*
Quin, Co. Clare, Franciscan friary, 21

Rahan, Co. Offaly, Romanesque doorway, 10
Railway station, Athlone, Co. Westmeath, 204; Ballinasloe, Co. Galway, *204-5;* Carlow, *209;* Dundrum, Co. Tipperary, 207; Harcourt St. Dublin, 204; Kingsbridge, Dublin, 207; Kingstown (Dun Laoghaire), Co. Dublin, 205; Monasterevan, Co. Kildare, 207; Portarlington, Co. Laois, *206-7*; Thurles, Co. Tipperary, 207
Ramelton, Co. Donegal, port warehouse, *227*
Raphoe, Co. Donegal, Bishop's Palace, 61
Rathdaire Church of Ireland, Ballybrittas, Co. Laois, *44*, 46
Rathdrum, Co. Wicklow, Catholic church, 39
Rathfran, Co. Mayo, Dominican monastery, 22
Rathfarnam Castle, Co. Dublin, 49, 61
Rathmachnee Castle, Co. Wexford, 57
Rathmolyon, Co. Meath, pub, *76*
Rathmullan, Co. Donegal, Carmelite priory, 18
Reading, Sir Robert, 217
Rennie, Sir John, 223
Richhill Castle, Co. Armagh, 79
Riddlestown, Co. Limerick, 82
Robertson, Daniel, 169
Robertson, William, 160, 169
Robertstown, Co. Kildare, hotel, 202-3
Robinson, William, 62
Roche Castle, Co. Louth, 49, 51
Rockcorry, Co. Monaghan, Catholic church, *32*
Ronchamp, *Notre-Dame-du-Haut,* 48
Roscommon, Co. Roscommon, Dominican friary, 22; Castle, *51*
Rosnakill, Co. Donegal, Catholic church, *31*
Roscrea, Co. Tipperary, Damer House, 82; St Cronan's, *10*
Rosserk, Co. Mayo, Franciscan friary, 21
Rothe House, Kilkenny, *78*
Rothery family, 82

Roundwood, Co. Wicklow, reservoir, 212
Royal Canal, 144, 199, 202-3
Rubane, Kircubbin, Co. Down, Pebble House, *189*
Ruskin, John, 43, 130
Russborough, Blessington, Co. Wicklow, 85

St Austin's Abbey, Tullow, Co. Carlow, 174
St Colmcille's Church, Durrow, Co. Offaly, *34*
St Columb's House, Kells, Co. Meath, 9
St Cronan's Church, Roscrea, Co. Tipperary, *10*, 45
St Flannan's Oratory, Killaloe, Co. Clare, 9
St George's, Dublin, 164
St James Catholic church, Grange, Co. Louth, *26-7*
St John's Church, Ballymore, Co. Donegal, *25*
St Kevin's Catholic church, Glendalough, Co. Wicklow, *39*
St Laurence's Gate, Drogheda, Co. Louth, *52*
St McDara's Island, Carna, Co. Galway, *9*
St Michael's, Creeslough, Co. Donegal, *48*
St Munna, Co. Westmeath, *16*
St Peter's College Chapel, Wexford,
St Patrick's Church, Jordanstown, Co. Armagh, 45
St Patrick's Church, Waterford
Sandycove, Co. Dublin, Martello tower, 66
Sandyford, Co. Dublin, school, 145
Semple, John, 33
Scelig Mhicíl, 7, 223
Schools, Ballinasloe, Co. Galway, *140*; Bush, Co. Louth, 141; Clonsilla, Co. Dublin, *144*; Mastergeehey, Co. Kerry, *139;* Monasterevan, Co. Kildare, *138;* Mountshannon, Co. Clare, *142;* Sandyford, Co. Dublin, *145;* Vicarstown, Co. Laois, *143*
Schull, Co. Cork, Munster and Leinster Bank, *136*
Scott, William Anthony, 24, 45, 46, 114
Screen, Co. Wexford, vernacular houses, 73
Shackleton, Abraham, 109
Shanagolden, Co. Limerick, Manisternagalliagduff Abbey, 18
Shankill Castle, Paulstown, Co. Kilkenny, gate and gatelodge, *169*
Shannonbridge, Co. Roscommon - Co. Offaly, barracks, *65*, 211; seventeen-arch bridge, 211
Shannon estuary, defence works, *65*
Shannongrove, Co. Limerick, *82*
Shannon Harbour, hotel, 202
Shannon waterway, 211
Shaw, Norman, 147
Shee Almhouses, Kilkenny, 78
Sheridan, George P., 146
Shops, Abbeyfeale, Co. Limerick, *127-8;* Ardee, Co. Louth, *126;* Bailieborough, Co. Cavan, *120-1*; Ballymena, shop and house, *118;* Birr, Co. Offaly, watchmaker jeweller, *123;* Castleisland, Co. Kerry, *122;* Mitchelstown, Co. Cork, chemist, *124;* Newtownstewart, Co. Tyrone, draper, *125;* Strabane, Co Tyrone, printer, *117;* Thomastown, Co. Kilkenny, bootmaker, *119*
Shortall, Michael, 46
Signal tower, Dromore West, Co. Sligo, *67*
Silent Valley, Kilkeel, Co. Down, waterworks, *213;* Water Commissioner's gatelodge, *214*
Sixmilebridge, Co. Limerick, Mount Ievers, 82
Skibbereen, Co. Cork, courthouse, *154*; presbytery, *93;* Pro-Cathedral, *36*
Skiddy's Almhouses, Cork, 81
Slane, Co. Meath, gatelodge, *170;* mill, 196
Slane Castle, Co. Meath, 88, 170
Sligo, Co. Sligo, bank, 132; Dominican friary, *22;* metal man, 221; shipping office, 215; Wesley chapel, *35*
South Dublin Rural Council, 99
Southwell Charity, 80 - 1
Southwell Gift Houses, Kinsale, Co. Cork, 80 - 1
Spiddal, Co. Galway, Catholic church *46;* 114; Spiddal House, 46
Steelstown, Co. Derry, Catholic church, 48
Stirling, William, 228
Stonecutters' village, Ballyknockan, Co. Wicklow, *110-1*
Storrs, John, 47
Strabane, Co. Tyrone, printer's shop, 117
Strade, Co. Mayo, Friary, 14
Summergrove, Mountmellick, Co. Laois, *87*
Summerhill, Co. Meath, 76

Taghmon church, St Munna, Co. Westmeath, *16*, 26
Tagoat, Co. Wexford, vernacular house, *72*
Tara, Co. Meath, Post Office, *75*
Tarbert, Co. Kerry, bridewell, *162*
Teampull Benin, Inismore, Aran Islands, *8*

Telford, Thomas, 209
Thomastown, Co. Kilkenny, bootmaker's shop, *119*
Thurles, Co. Tipperary, station, 207
Tiglin, Ashford, Co. Wicklow, farm, *182-3*
Timoleague, Co. Cork, Franciscan friary, 21
Toll house, Blessington, Co. Wicklow, 193; Leixlip, Co. Kildare, 193
Tollymore Park, Co. Down, Barbican Gate, 168; Bryansford Gate, *168*; Clanbrassil Barn, 168; Foley's Bridge, 168; Horn Bridge, 168; Ivy Bridge, 168; Old Bridge, 168; Lord Limerick's Follies, 168
Town Hall, Cavan, *114;* Coleraine, *113*
Townley Hall, Drogheda, Co. Louth, 163-4
Tracey, Joe, 48
Trail, John, 218
Tralee, Co. Kerry, courthouse, 153
Trim, Co. Meath, Castle, 51
Triumphal Arch, Ballymurray, Co. Roscommon, 192; Bantry House, Co. Cork, 192; Lawrencetown, Co. Galway, *192*
Tullamore, Co. Offaly, maltings, 197; harbour and hotel, 203
Tullow, Co. Carlow, Ballykealy House, 94; sexton's house, *94*
Turner, Thomas, 113
Tyars and Jago, 148

Ulster Railway, 205
Ulysses, 22

Valentia Island, Co. Kerry, 7
Valleymount, Co. Wicklow, Catholic church, 29
Vartry Reservoir, Roundwood, Co. Wicklow, 212; draw-off tower, *212*
Venice, 130
Vernacular church, Castlebar, Co. Mayo, *26-7;* Cratloe, Co. Clare, *28-9;* Eadestown, Co. Kildare, *28-9;* Grange, Co. Louth, *26-7;* Massmount, Co. Donegal *31;* Rockcorrig, Co. Monaghan, *32*
Vernacular house, Ballycanew, Co. Wexford, *73*; Gweedore, Co. Donegal, *71*; Mohill, Co. Leitrim, *74;* Tagoat, Co. Wexford, *72*
Vernacular pub, Rathmolyon, Co. Meath, *76*
Vernacular shop pub, Kingscourt, Co. Cavan, *77*
Vicarstown, Co. Laois, school, *143;* bridge, 200
Virginia, Co. Cavan, estate houses, *177*; estate village, 177

Warrenpoint, Co. Down, Presbyterian church, *40;*
seaside resort houses, 216
Waterford. Co. Waterford, metal man, 221; Reginald's Tower, 52; St Patrick's Church, 36; town walls, 52
Waterford harbour, defence works, 65
Watergate, Enniskillen Castle, Co. Fermanagh, *58*
Welland and Gillespie, 90
Wesley Chapel, Sligo, *35*
Westport, Co. Mayo, House, *83*, 91; rectory, *91;* post office, *137*
Wexford, maritime houses, *226*; St Peter's College Chapel, 38; town walls, 52
Wicklow Head, Co. Wicklow, lighthouse, *218*
Wilkinson, George, 156-8, 204
Wood, Sancton, 206-7
Woodword, Benjamin, 155, 174
Workhouse, Antrim, Co. Antrim, 159; Dunfanaghy, Co Donegal, *156-7;* Letterkenny, Co. Donegal, *158-9*
Wright, Frank Lloyd, 47
Wyatt, James, 83, 88, 91, 170

Yacht Club, Cobh, Co. Cork, *228;* Dun Laoghaire, Co. Dublin, National, Royal Irish, Royal St George, 228
Youghal, Co. Cork, almhouses, 80; Dominican monastery, 22; lighthouse, *219;* town walls, 52

A FIELD GUIDE TO THE

BUILDINGS OF IRELAND

A Field Guide to th

ILLUSTRATI